Symbol and Myth
in Modern Literature

HAYDEN HUMANITIES SERIES

F. PARVIN SHARPLESS, *Series Editor*
Headmaster, The Park School of Baltimore

Symbol and Myth
in Modern Literature

F. PARVIN SHARPLESS

HAYDEN BOOK COMPANY, INC.
Rochelle Park, New Jersey

Library of Congress Cataloging in Publication Data

Main entry under title:

Symbol and myth in modern literature.

   (Hayden humanities series)
   Bibliography: p.
   1. Symbolism — Literary collections. I. Sharpless,
F. Parvin.
PN6071.S96S9   820'.8'15   75-45154
ISBN 0-8104-5071-2

2   3   4   5   6   7   8   9   PRINTING

77 78 79 80 81 82 83 84   YEAR

Preface

The Hayden Humanities Series uses the term "humanities" in both a narrower and broader sense than in many examples of current curriculum structuring. We see humanities texts neither as conglomerations of stuff from literature, art, music, history, and philosophy purporting to express the spirit of a given time or place, nor as collections of readings supposedly illuminating vaguely suggested themes or subjects. Rather, we see them as focusing on the abiding ideas and values that men have wrestled with and lived by, as reflected through literature (broadly defined) and as informed by a variety of man-centered disciplines: psychology, sociology, anthropology, religion, philosophy, history.

The texts in this series deal with the significant human concerns upon which all human actions, great or small, social or individual, are based, whether we know it and admit it or not. These concerns are the stuff of all literature, yesterday and today; and they provide a background for recognizing, understanding, and defining the issues of the moment that claim our attention and wonder.

The approach in these texts is thematic, since such a structure has proved useful in traditional teaching units and in newer elective programs. But again there is a difference. The weakness of the thematic approach has been its tendency to yield units which are impossibly vague or impossibly broad, or both. What we have tried to do is declare and define an idea or issue thoughtfully and deeply so that others may test that declaration and definition through what they read and know, and find dealing with it a cumulative, organic experience, allowing growth and change.

In contrast to most thematically arranged anthologies, these texts do not pretend a faceless editor or the illusion of authorial objectivity or distance. The compiler has a voice and a point of view, and a conviction that he knows what he is talking about. The introductory essay both introduces and interprets; it defines an idea or issue—in this case *Symbol and Myth in Modern Literature*—and then tries to see it in the round by explaining its past, asserting its continuing vitality and viability, and suggesting some of the things that can be done with it.

This approach takes us far beyond the usual "knowing about" or "talking about" to which literature is too often reduced. We believe the themes have lasting value as organizing constructs for making sense out of our world and for comprehending how the literary artist makes sense out of it. The themes also have a coherence that such thematic structures as, say, "Man and Society" or "Man and the Environment" or "War and Peace" cannot possibly have. One import of both these observations is that the question of "modern" literature vs. "classical" or "traditional" makes little real sense. Literature, by our lights, is always new and renewable. Forever is now. The idiom and the cultural demands and expectations may be different, but the underlying human concerns that the artist is examining are timeless and universal—and that's what counts.

The reader is not expected to agree with everything in the introduction, but is urged to consider it carefully; a casual reading won't do. The argument needs to be understood, and then questions must be raised about validity, emphasis, application, ramification, relevance to experience, and ultimate usefulness in ordering ideas, feelings, beliefs and values. The defining essay should be a point of departure and a point of return. Along with the headnotes and questions for each group of selections, it serves as a guide for analysis and discussion, not as a gospel to be ingested, remembered, and regurgitated.

There is no attempt in these texts at coverage of literary periods or schools of writing, but there is a variety of genres, modes, backgrounds, times, and writers. Certain long works have been excerpted; enough has been included from any work to feed the thematic demands and yet not misrepresent the total piece. The aim throughout has been to show how widely diffused in our literature the central concern of each text has been and still is. In the final section, suggestions are made for reading full novels and plays that could not be included in a text of this size.

Symbol and Myth in Modern Literature is a generalist's book, which attempts to simplify and put into more common use a few complex and significant ideas. It is intended therefore for generalists—both students and teachers—who find education more useful when it offers large ideas with some evidence and context than when it offers small ideas with copious documentation.

There are, of course, more specialized approaches to these topics through anthropology, linguistics, psychology, religion, and history, as well as traditional literary study. But some ideas are too central to liberal and humane learning to be left exclusively to the scholars, and if we wait until we are fully wise enough, it might be too late.

F. PARVIN SHARPLESS
Series Editor

Contents

The cultivation of those sciences which have enlarged the limits of the empire of man over the external world, has, for want of the poetical faculty, proportionally circumscribed those of the internal world; and man, having enslaved the elements, remains himself a slave. . . . The cultivation of poetry is never more to be desired than at periods when, from an excess of the selfish and calculating principle, the accumulation of the materials of external life exceeds the quantity of the power of assimilating them to the internal laws of human nature.

—*Percy Bysshe Shelley (1821)*

Literalism makes a universe of stone, and men astonished, petrified. Literalism is the ministration of death, written and engraven in stones; tables of stone and stony heart. The incarnation of symbols gives us a new heart, a heart for the first time human, a heart for the first time, or is it the second time, made of flesh.

—*Norman O. Brown (1966)*

By symbols, accordingly, is man guided and commanded, made happy or made wretched.

—*Thomas Carlyle (1833)*

Symbol and Myth
in Modern Literature

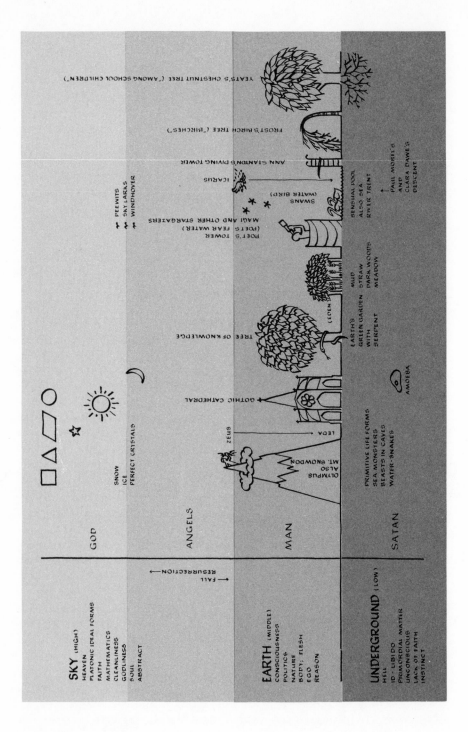

SKY (HIGH)
HEAVEN
PLATONIC IDEAL FORMS
FAITH
MATHEMATICS
CLEANLINESS
GODLINESS
SOUL
ABSTRACT

GOD

← FALL
RESURRECTION →

ANGELS

EARTH (MIDDLE)
CONSCIOUSNESS
POLITICS
NATURE
BODY, FLESH
EGO
REASON

MAN

UNDERGROUND (LOW)
HELL
ID - LIBIDO
PRIMORDIAL MATTER
UNCONSCIOUS
LACK OF FAITH
INSTINCT

SATAN

SNOW
ICE
PERFECT CRYSTALS

PEEWITS
SKY LARKS
WINDHOVER

YEATS'S CHESTNUT TREE ("AMONG SCHOOL CHILDREN")

FROST'S BIRCH TREE ("BIRCHES")

ANN STANTON'S DIVING TOWER

ICARUS

SWANS (WATER BIRD)

MAGI AND OTHER STARGAZERS
POET'S TOWER
(POET'S FEAR WATER)

SENSUAL POOL
ALSO SEA
RIVER TRENT

PAUL MOREL'S
AND
CLARA DAWES
DESCENT

TREE OF KNOWLEDGE

EARTH'S
GREEN GARDEN
WITH
SERPENT

MUD
STRAW
DARK WOODS
MEADOW

(EDEN)

GOTHIC CATHEDRAL

ZEUS

LEDA

OLYMPUS
ALSO
MT. SNOWDON

PRIMITIVE LIFE FORMS
SEA MONSTERS
BEASTS IN CAVES
WATER-SNAKES

AMOEBA

Introduction

The first questions we must face are very basic ones. What makes myth and symbol necessary? What causes a form of expression to exist where things mean something other than what they say, in which an object is not an object but something else, in which we must deal with double meanings, with indirection, with hints and allusions? If the poet or the novelist wishes to say something about the Soul, about the Powers of Darkness, about the Journey through Life, about Divine Revelation or Christian Grace, about Sexual Desire, why doesn't he talk about these matters in a straightforward way, as a reasonable man? Why indulge these complicated means, means which confuse or even antagonize readers?

Though history is a harmless pursuit, as practical people, with practical affairs on our minds, we find it hard to understand why we should bother with Adam and Eve and Evictions from Gardens, with Odysseus and his fantastic travels, with the whole collection of Greek, Roman, Teutonic, and Celtic stories of people and gods and events of the most unlikely sort. Nor does it help to discover patterns, "archetypal patterns," to defend the study of myth by complicated classifications of Descent Stories, of Quest Motifs, of Fertility Tales, or to dwell on their imagery: their snakes, beasts, birds, rivers, towers, caves, mountains, moons, suns, and crossroads; nor even less reason to consider the rounded, receptive, uterine shapes, the elongated, phallic shapes.

The topic is vexing and difficult, hard to speak of clearly without losing oneself in theoretical speculation, producing definitions but not understanding. Yet, skeptical as we may be, the frequency of appearance of these modes in modern literature—though they have a long and honorable history—and the new interest which connects literature with psychology require that we address ourselves to these questions and attempt to answer them. We may do so with the hope that by studying basic questions, by emphasizing theory before dealing with practice, the *why* as well as the *how*, we can understand that there are compelling reasons —historical, cultural, as well as psychological—which *cause* these figurative devices to occur so often in modern literature. An understanding of these connections may make us not only better informed, but more sympathetic to the literature which employs myth and symbol and to the human experience which literature ultimately reflects and interprets.

The Life of the Spirit

Perhaps the simplest explanation of myth and symbol lies in an obvious aspect of human nature. For most people, at least some of the time, emotional, nonrational (affective) states of mind—in short, feelings —comprise the substance of their reality, and provide central values around which their rational decisions and acts form. Whatever the "content" of the feelings—love of God, of other human beings, of children, of money or hatred of evil, of the neighbors, of foreigners, of minorities or passion for power, sexual gratification, success, or any other goal of behavior and life style—it is emotional energy, things we believe and love, not just know, which provides the primary ground and basis for action and choice. Our reason explains, devises techniques by which we may reach our ends, but the movements of the psyche, of the spirit, provide the motive. As the tradition has it, the spirit giveth life. And symbolism and mythology are the natural life of the spirit.

The other half of that statement, that the letter kills, is also important. Scientific and analytic modes concentrate on the letter of the thing, on its mechanism—not on how its heart feels but on how its heart works —and therefore tend to destroy simpler emotional responses. Under analytic habits of mind, feelings are changed from direct, unselfconscious expressions to cooler and more detached "knowledge about." The dangers in this are apparent, and contemporary culture has a keen sense of both the appeal of analysis and its cost. For only as we recognize ideas or people as more than mechanisms and abstractions can we "relate" to people and to values as significantly more than objects and things.

Such a doctrine is hardly new; it is, in one way or another, basic to most religions. It is, of course, one of the central ideas of the Judeo-Christian tradition, and it looms large in the attitude of mind associated with the Romantic movement in art and philosophy. But the contrary impulse, the need to name and locate, to discover and understand, to bring as much as possible of experience out of the realm of feeling and its associated mystical and religious circumstances into the realm of reason, is also a large part of the tradition of Western Civilization. Nor is there any point arguing the superiority of one over the other, or to lament, as it has become the fashion in some quarters, the emphasis given to rationalist thought and the technological and materialist ways of life which it supports. What should concern us is to see that the conflict between the necessary "openness" of symbolic forms and the necessary restraints of literal and scientific modes of perception is a basic antithesis of human psychology, and embodies one of the essential dualities of our cultural history. It is also, essentially, what this book is about.

Science itself has suggested that symbolizing behavior derives from a fundamental aspect of psychological activity which Freud called "primary process." Simply defined, primary process refers to the ways in which the unconscious part of the mind reorders the images and objects received from the outside world into new patterns by converting literal things into figurative meanings. Such a process apparently satisfies crucial needs of the unconscious. As Freud's accounts of dreams illustrate, these constructions by the unconscious contain symbolic transformations in which illogical and bizarre sequences of cause and effect are allowed. In effect, the scientific view of the world is discarded, and replaced by a radically different sense of things. Symbolism is, therefore, the *natural* language of the unconscious, and part of everyone's thinking is done in it.

Techniques and Transformations

We need not accept Freudian theory to find reasons for the uses of symbolism in literature. From the writer's point of view, there are other advantages. One is economy, the shorthand of expression which symbolism offers. By creating a relationship between an image in a work and broader philosophical or psychological meanings, the poet can achieve a concision offering a depth and density which literal, denotative accounts lack. This shorthand is similar to the efficiency of language itself, in which words are signs for objects they name; any noun becoming a substitute (a synecdoche) for any thing. A simple object may represent important feelings and ideas, as when the Cross or the Flag or the *V* sign, or in a literary context a river, or a road, or a tree, or a scarlet letter, may summarize with simple means complex meanings and their associated emotions and traditions of usage. Primary process employs images and objects of everyday life to translate the abstractions, the ideas, the worn-out metaphors of the past into a language of things. Indeed, this transmutation of ideas and feelings into a language of things is one of the special "holy" or "priestly" functions of the artist, common objects (bread and wine, for instance) being translated into thing of great power and authority.

There are other advantages, too. The substitution of concrete objects for abstractions may make the latter easier to understand and respond to. By giving them a substance, an objectivity, they can be arranged in a narrative. It is easier to tell a story about a guilty woman than about Guilt, easier to respond to a human being journeying down a road or river than to the abstraction Time, more interesting to consider blessing water snakes than Blessingness. This story-making aspect of symbolism gives rise to that frequently vexing "doubleness" which occurs when the same narrative offers acceptable literal and figurative meanings at the same time. Some of the problems of interpretation which this creates will be discussed below. But there need exist no conflict between the two. A literal narrative may not need symbolic elaboration to be worth our attention. There are realities which if documented with denotative detail suffice as a basis for interesting fiction. Other writers may happily balance literal and symbolic, as in the best poems of Robert

Frost or James Dickey, where the two modes are almost indistinguishable, the literal sliding or blending imperceptibly into the figurative, the fact taking on extended meaning as we consider it more carefully.

Finally, symbolism offers the writer a way to mediate between traditional, sanctioned ideas and values, and his personal and perhaps idiosyncratic vision of reality. By modifying older materials, or by using common images or objects (air, water, earth) in a new way, he may keep in the reader's mind the ways these objects have been understood in the past. He may thus avoid constructing a too personal and subjective world obscure to anyone else, yet preserve an individual, personal sense of things. This is a difficult task, and modern writers, accused of obscurity, may indeed be guilty of failing to adapt their personal view sufficiently to traditional forms of expression. On the other hand, where traditional usage is known, obscurity may be diminished.

The Artist: Poeta Nascitur, Non Fit°

The view of literature taken here asks the reader to consider seriously two ideas. The first is the one outlined above: that there is some spiritual or emotional quality to a work of art beyond the reach of literal, scientific analysis. The second follows from the first: that there are people with a special talent, or genius, or aptitude, which enables them to understand and use nonrational modes of expression more easily than the rest of us. Such people are poets or, in the broader term, artists, whether they write primarily poems or novels. The question, therefore, what is poetry? really asks, what is a poet?

This is a complicated question, but the special capabilities of the poet are important to a study of myth and symbolism. One of these is the poet's ability to see through the letter or objects of life to larger symbolic meaning. He has a "natural" perception of analogies, parallels, and relationships; he is quick to notice connections between things, similarities and differences, contrasts and congruities. Instead of being interested in narrower definitions of objects and experiences, his mind goes in the opposite direction, away from the particular toward the general, from detail to the whole, from the letter to the spirit.

Similarly, the poet is quicker to notice how people feel, quicker to recognize emotions, both conscious and unconscious, which behavior reveals. He is subtler in perceiving motives, more aware of ambiguities and paradoxes in human actions. Either because of a special kind of self-consciousness, or because he himself feels more deeply and strongly than others, he recognizes similar feelings in others. He thus comes to be more

---

°*Poeta . . . Fit:* Poets are born, not made.

familiar than the rest of us with the basic psychological currents of human life, and capable thereby of creating fictions, either dramatic or narrative, in which voices of people who are emotionally real speak to us. Such talent or sensibility is not learned, not even, in some cases, dependent upon any particular upbringing or environment, but can arise almost spontaneously and unaccountably: a Shakespeare, a Keats, a Whitman, a Dickens.

Or the poet's particular talent may arise from a special sense of patterns of order, from a personality which finds in itself a need for coherences in the world, a nagging oppressive dissatisfaction with the randomness of nature, with the undifferentiated and unvalued events of life. To such a person, art is a means of ordering, an imposition of patterns of value. Symbolic forms are a particularly effective way to provide that value, to see events as having greater meanings.

This poetic or symbolic sense of the emotional meaning of experience probably exists in everyone to a degree, but it is hard put to stand against the weight given to objective and scientific modes of thinking in our educational systems and against the necessary, practical concerns of life. Because most of us practice science, or at least a modest form of rationality a good bit of the time for simple mundane purposes such as paying the bills and staying out of various kinds of trouble, we have some difficulty understanding the poet or admitting that his vision of the world, his different sense of what things mean, may be of value to us.

But it can be argued that it is just this primacy of the common daily workaday world which indicates our need for imaginative richness, for the balancing of literality with emotion, and which suggests that we should approach the poet's language and vision with open-mindedness and without hostility. The more radically the poet's sense of experience differs from our ordinary one, the greater is our need to understand these modes of expression. Without them we are forced, when we do consider nonliteral questions, to consider them in abstract terms which stale the intelligence and dry up the emotions; we will find our emotions and spiritual lives reduced to mechanism and discover ourselves to be out of touch with the deeper aspects of our inner lives.

Modern Mythology

Myth is so useful a term that it has acquired too great currency, being freely used by historians, classicists, anthropologists, psychologists, and literary critics. The discussion which follows attempts to concentrate on the literary uses of mythology. Thus it defines myth as a narrative model (story, plot) by which a culture, a community, a tribe, a nation—any social grouping—understands, articulates, and organizes its spiritual, psychological, and emotional life. Myth symbolizes, or contains images which symbolize (convert from cognitive, scientific terms to affective, emotional ones), vital philosophic, social, and moral ideas, ideas affecting how people live together, the sense of man's relation to nature, to God, or to gods. Thus, its subject will not be the literal events of the narrative model (the fantastic nature of many mythic materials indicates the myth-maker's lack of interest in fact) but larger questions: national honor, tribal honor, heritage, and identity; love, marriage, sexuality; natural forces, the nonhuman powers of the universe; the essential psychological questions of life: Aggression, Eros, Guilt, Power, and Property. The person who makes or tells these stories is exercising a poetic function, whether he is artlessly rehearsing given materials or self-consciously making an "original" myth out of his own imagination.

One of the most important inquirers into the relationship between myth and literature and culture, Northrop Frye, has defined the social usefulness of myth by calling such beliefs "myths of concern."

> The myth of concern exists to hold society together, so far as words can help to do this. For it, truth and reality are not directly connected with reasoning or evidence, but are socially established. What is true, for concern, is what society does and believes in response to authority, and a belief, so far as a belief is verbalized, is a statement of willingness to participate in a myth of concern.[a]

The most important such myth for European and American culture is the Judeo-Christian myth deriving from the Bible and from the interpretations and elaborations of those stories.

Two qualifications may make this definition easier to understand. First, mythology is often fragmented by the variety of "concerns" which use it. "Society," especially in contemporary America, is pluralistic, or open; that is, it consists of many people believing many different things. A particular writer can reflect only a part of this society, and his vision may be understood and set up as myth for only a few. This situation accounts for the sense of alienation felt by many modern artists, as well as for the low repute in which serious art is held by many. By contrast, broader forms of "popular" mythology, encouraged by mass media, from folklore to television situation comedy, appeal to broader audiences. But whether serious or superficial, myth represents a given body of shared belief, an agreement which is necessary for any sense of community to exist.

Second, since myth contains the "beliefs" of a culture, its content changes as the strength and credibility of various social and moral ideas

---

[a] *The Critical Path: An Essay on the Social Context of Literary Criticism*, Indiana University Press, 1971, pp. 36-37.

change. Such alterations decisively affect the poet's situation. In a homogenous society whose members share most ideas and beliefs and a commonly accepted mythology, the poet will work within these beliefs and the forms in which they are contained. For example, in Western Europe during the Middle Ages, Christian mythology dominated cultural and aesthetic forms, and virtually everyone recognized and responded to Biblical texts and stories and to literary representations of them, even though these responses ranged from sophisticated and elitist to simple and popular. The art of such a period will emphasize neither innovation nor independence, and the very names of artists may be unknown, their individuality submerged in the general cultural vision or belief. Under these circumstances, individuality expresses itself by means of a refinement of detail in the basic pattern, like the illuminations done by unknown monks on manuscripts, or in some monumental summary of an entire mythology, bringing together in a collective work most of its attitudes and values, as in Chartres cathedral.

But as the power and universality of that myth has declined, the artist has been released (or cast adrift) and has—for good or ill—become more aware of his own imaginative power and of the possibilities for individualized expression. At the same time, within the social community there has arisen the need for a new myth to replace the faded outlines of the old. The slow development of this consciousness in Western Culture, beginning in the Renaissance and accelerated since 1800, marks the rise of Modern Mythology.

The major force in this long evolution is the rise of rationalist science, which began in the late Middle Ages, and by the middle of the 18th century, reached the dominant position it still holds in Western Culture. A major result of this movement is the increasing opposition already spoken of between the letter and the spirit. By the middle of the 18th century, rational modes of thought were being applied not only to the physical universe in physics, astronomy, and chemistry but to social phenomena and to human behavior. Rationalist social and political theories had wide currency, influencing revolutionary movements in France and America. Rationalist religions such as Deism specifically denied aspects of supernatural phenomena in traditional beliefs. By the 19th century, scientific discoveries in anthropology, geology, and biology made literalist interpretations of the book of Genesis difficult to sustain. At the same time, improved methods of scientific historiography gave rise to new, nonmythical accounts of the life of Jesus. In the world at large, rationalist and scientific attitudes were verified by the industrial and technological society based upon them, by growth in population and improvements in the standard of living; but, to those concerned with the life of the spirit, the consequences of these "advances" were catastrophic, and for poets, theologians, philosophers, and ordinary sensitive people, the 19th century is a time of doubt, of loss of faith, of religious crisis, of many dark nights of the soul.

As poets became conscious of these problems, modern mythology began. This consciousness may be individual or social, arising from the poet's concern to help himself or from his wish to help his society as well. In either case the poet's work is to make or remake myths, and his art, whether poem, story, novel, or drama, becomes a new poetic mythology, replacing, modifying, "remythologizing" the old.

Basically this is what myth and poetry have always been and what great poets have always done. What is different about "modern" mythology is only that the poet is more conscious of the process in which he is involved, and feels more on his own, less supported by traditional materials of the Judeo-Christian myth. There are, of course, differences in this regard. It is possible, as in the work of T. S. Eliot, to use traditional materials sympathetically, nostalgically, looking at the contrast between the present and times when they had greater mythic power. (The Church itself has carried out its own remythologizing, as it has redefined doctrine, changed liturgical meanings and practices. Protestantism may be seen as a remythologizing, as it shifted emphasis from the Roman Catholic myth.)

Other poets (William Butler Yeats is a good example) are more individual, using radical redefinitions of the older materials which turn them upsidedown. The structure of modern mythology is the work of a number of important 19th and 20th century poets, but the three most important mythmakers are William Blake, Percy Bysshe Shelley, and Yeats. Whether the changes are produced by individual artists or by institutional forces, they have similar purposes: the strengthening of the spiritual bonds of the community through the attempt to make a better, more attractive verbal statement of the common ground of belief and concern against the analytic encroachments of reason and science.

One final distinction may be helpful. This book deals with the theory and practice of both myth and symbol, and it defines them as two often overlapping parts of the same function. Both are literary modes which extend meaning beyond literality and denotation, conveying value and encouraging response in affective terms. They differ only in that a symbol has a narrower focus—a thing, an event, an image, a part of a story capable of being considered by itself or of being transplanted from one context to another. It is often derived from a common event or experience, a well-known historical person, or a daily routine. A myth is simply the larger context, the story or stories in which the symbols occur. As we use the terms, *The Rime of the Ancient Mariner* is a myth; the sea, the wind, the albatross, indeed the Mariner himself are symbols. Obviously they go together, and to look at one is to imply the other.

PART I

Theory: The Fact Does Not Exist

Theory: The Fact Does Not Exist

The first thing to understand about modern mythology is that for literary purposes the "fact," in any literal, historical sense, does not exist: No story, character, or situation from traditional sources has or ever had a fixed and absolute meaning. This means that we must not confuse myth with history in the modern "scientific" sense (the notion that it reports things as they *really* happened) nor with anthropological studies of ancient or remote cultures. For the poet as mythmaker, the characters, plots, situations, settings of traditional materials offer a pattern from which and on which his imagination and talent may work. It may—as in medieval cathedrals—work happily within traditional outlines, or—as in modern mythology—it may attempt self-conscious revaluations of that tradition. In either case, we must recognize as clearly as possible the distinction between fact and fiction. Even the "matter of Troy," perhaps the best-known literary mythology, though stemming from historical events, is not, even in Homer's account, a report from the front, and subsequent considerations of it by other mythographers, even those who claimed an interest in objectivity, inevitably reflect other "modern" patterns of perception, other values, other subjectivities than Homer's. In older myths, such as the "prehistorical" accounts of the Fall of Man, the creation myths of Greece and Rome, or primitive stories about the forces of nature, we see even more clearly that the matter of myth is not science but art.

But as readers of modern mythologies, we must also remember that no writer who takes his art seriously can fail to take its history seriously. This means that he will always have in mind the history of the themes with which he is working in their most important appearances. One pattern, therefore, that we may recognize in modern mythology is what George Steiner has called "the long legacy of echo," and this pattern plays a crucial role in the work of the major writers of the 20th century: Yeats, Joyce, Eliot, and Pound.

A second source of pattern in modern mythology, one which has been argued for most strongly by anthropologists and students of psychoanalysis, is found in the "archetypal patterns" which literature contains and reveals. An archetype is, as one definition has it, "the type brought to the highest level of generalization," that is, it is the reference to basic and permanent patterns of behavior and psychological structure. Sources of these patterns, it is argued, lie either in the given physiological "stuff" of men's minds or in the similarity of all human psychological environments, all men undergoing similar stages of growth, these stages in turn producing poetic and mythic materials common to all men. For example, since acceptance of a relationship to family or social unit is common to almost all child development, myth which refers to this process of psychological growth will find response in all men. Taken further, this argument holds that individual cultural differences—local customs, habits, and even language itself—are merely the dress of the permanent psychic organization of the mind. Literature based upon myth is therefore merely the archetype dressed in the particular style, or as Leslie Fiedler would say, the "signature" of the writer, containing the particular kind and form of consciousness of his particular age and temperament. Because the reader possesses the same sense of the meaning of the archetype, its presence in the work will offer a special intensity, a more than literal force, and will give poetry and mythology their special psychological and cultural importance.

The question of the existence of archetypal patterns not only divides literary critics, but reflects a division in the ranks of anthropologists and psychologists as well, some arguing for the existence of universal cultural patterns derived from psychological events, others taking the view that behavior is to be explained functionally, that is, as a result of its use in a particular culture or environment. Those who argue for universal patterns point to common occurrences of certain themes in cultures from different locations in time and geography. Creation stories, for example, occur in almost all folklores, as do stories of heroic quests, stories referring to tribal ancestry and lineage, as well as to subtler philosophic questions: the meaning of evil, control of aggressive and erotic energies, and so forth. Cultural anthropology and psychology have made decisive contributions to literary study by showing the relation between mythologies of the past and the present.

A third source of pattern in modern mythology comes from the obvious commonality of objects in the ordinary environment: sea, sky, air, trees, animals, plants, earth, water, fire, and so forth. Since such objects belong to the experience of all but the most urbanized of men, they offer a way in which common experience, neither literary nor cultivated, may form a bond between writer and reader and between past and present, serving, in short, as a way of establishing and using "tradition." For example, the simple association between the moon and the idea of the female or between water and fertility are so elementary and universal as to offer a wide range of uses in mythology; to be, in short, "natural" symbols, having their basis in nature. As is typical of such symbols, the idea is simple, yet capable of complex extension, which gives rise to some of the difficulties of interpretation that will concern us below.

The three essays that follow offer statements about the basic sources of symbolic behavior, one from a psychologist, one from a poet, and one from a literary critic. While they do not resolve all questions in this complex matter, they offer the beginnings of a theory upon which our reading of mythologies may be based, a way of understanding how to go about problems of literary study and analysis.

The Psychologist

A basic question raised by the study of symbolic behavior refers to reasons for its very existence. If we look at the evolution of human behavior from lower, less complex organic forms, we notice that a primary principle of the process of evolution has been that changes in form of a species must be functional, must adapt it better to its environment, must be called into existence by the interplay between external forces and the capacities of the organism itself. Put another way, all behavior should satisfy some environmentally created *need*. This is as true of mental or psychological developments as it is of the grosser aspects of bodily form: it affects as much the number and quality of brain cells as the number and quality of limbs and muscles.

The correctness of this view of things—called genetic psychology—is challenged by the discussion which follows. Essentially Susanne Langer argues that the existence of a great deal of human symbolic behavior cannot be accounted for by citing any adaptive need. Some behavior, indeed, is nonadaptive, producing errors and faulty apprehensions of reality. Yet, men take certain forms of symbolic behavior—art and religion—very seriously. She concludes that the need to "symbolify" is not an externally created function, but the result of an interior need, dependent upon some given (innate?) quality of the particular kind of mind we call human. Such a view makes a study of symbolism crucial to any psychological theory and basic to philosophic questions about the nature of man.

SYMBOLIC TRANSFORMATION
Susanne K. Langer (1895–   )

> *The vitality and energies of the imagination do not operate at will; they are fountains, not machinery.*
>
> D. G. James, *Skepticism and Poetry*

A changed approach to the theory of knowledge naturally has its effect upon psychology, too. As long as sense was supposed to be the chief factor in knowledge, psychologists took a prime interest in the organs that were the windows of the mind, and in the details of their functioning; other things were accorded a sketchier and sometimes vaguer treatment. If scientists demanded, and philosophers dutifully admitted, that all true belief must be based on sense-evidence, then the activity of the mind had to be conceived purely as a matter of recording and combining; then intelligence had to be a product of impression, memory, and association. But now, an epistemological° insight has uncovered a more potent, howbeit more difficult, factor in scientific procedure—the use of symbols to attain, as well as to organize, belief. Of course, this alters our conception of intelligence at a stroke. Not higher sensitivity, not longer memory or even quicker association sets man so far above other animals that he can regard them as denizens of a lower world: no, it is the power of using symbols—the power of *speech*—that makes him lord of the earth. So our interest in the mind has shifted more and more from the acquisition of experience, the domain of sense, to the *uses* of sense-data, the realm of conception and expression.

The importance of symbol-using, once admitted, soon becomes paramount in the study of intelligence. It has lent a new orientation especially to genetic psychology, which traces the growth of the mind; for this growth is paralleled, in large measure, by the observable uses of language, from the first words in infancy to the complete self-expression of maturity, and perhaps the relapse into meaningless verbiage that accompanies senile decline. Such researches have even been extended from the development of individuals to the evolution of mental traits in nations and races. There is an increasing *rapprochement* between philology and psychology—between the science of language and the science of what we do with language. The recent literature of psychogenetics bears ample witness to the central position which symbol-using, or language in its most general sense, holds in our conception of human mentality. Frank Lorimer's *The Growth of Reason* bears the sub-title: "A Study of the Role of Verbal Activity in the Growth and Structure of the Human Mind." Grace De Laguna's *Speech: its Function and Development* treats the acquisition of language as not only indicative of the growth of concepts, but as the principal agent in this evolution. Much the same view is held by Professor A. D. Ritchie, who remarks, in *The Natural History of the Mind*: "As far as thought is concerned, and at all levels of thought, it [mental life] is a symbolic process. It is mental not because the symbols are immaterial, for they are often material, perhaps always material, but because they are symbols. . . . The essential act of thought is symbolization." There is, I think, more depth in this statement than its author realized; had he been aware of it, the proposition would have occurred earlier in the book, and given the whole work a somewhat novel turn.

°*epistemological:* concerned with the nature and limits of knowledge

As it is, he goes on to an excellent account of sign-using and sign-making, which stand forth clearly as the essential means of intellection.

Quotations could be multiplied almost indefinitely, from an imposing list of sources—from John Dewey and Bertrand Russell, from Brunschwicg and Piaget and Head, Köhler and Koffka, Carnap, Delacroix, Ribot, Cassirer, Whitehead—from philosophers, psychologists, neurologists, and anthropologists—to substantiate the claim that symbolism is the recognized key to that mental life which is characteristically human and above the level of sheer animality. Symbol and meaning make man's world, far more than sensation; Miss Helen Keller, bereft of sight and hearing, or even a person like the late Laura Bridgman, with the single sense of touch, is capable of living in a wider and richer world than a dog or an ape with all his senses alert.

Genetic psychology grew out of the study of animals, children, and savages, both from a physiological and from a behavioristic angle. Its fundamental standpoint is that the responses of an organism to the environment are adaptive, and are dictated by that organism's *needs*. Such needs may be variously conceived; one school reduces them all to one basic requirement, such as keeping the metabolic balance, persisting in an ideal status; others distinguish as elementary more specific aims—e.g., nutrition, parturition,° defense—or even such differentiated cravings as physical comfort, companionship, self-assertion, security, play. The tenor of these primary concepts is suggested largely by the investigator's starting point. A biologist tends to postulate only the obvious needs of a clam or even an infusorian;° an animal-psychologist generalizes somewhat less, for he makes distinctions that are relevant, say, to a white rat, but hardly to a clam. An observer of childhood conceives the cardinal interests on a still higher level. But through the whole hierarchy of genetic studies there runs a feeling of continuity, a tendency to identify the "real" or "ultimate" motive conditions of human action with the needs of primitive life, to trace all wants and aims of mankind to some initial protoplasmic response. This dominant principle is the most important thing that the evolutionist school has bestowed upon psychology—the assumption, sometimes avowed, more often tacit, that *"Nihil est in homine quod non prius in amoeba erat."*°

When students of mental evolution discovered how great a role in science is played by symbols, they were not slow to exploit that valuable insight. The acquisition of so decisive a tool must certainly be regarded as one of the great landmarks in human progress, probably the starting point of all genuinely intellectual growth. Since symbol-using appears at a late stage, it is presumably a highly integrated form of simpler animal

---

°*parturition:* childbirth   °*infusorian:* a type of protozoa   °*"Nihil . . . erat":* Nothing is found in a man which was not first found in an amoeba.

activities. It must spring from biological needs, and justify itself as a practical asset. Man's conquest of the world undoubtedly rests on the supreme development of his brain, which allows him to synthesize, delay, and modify his reactions by the interpolation of *symbols* in the gaps and confusions of direct experience, and by means of "verbal signs" to add the experiences of other people to his own.

There is a profound difference between using symbols and merely using signs. The use of signs is the very first manifestation of mind. It arises as early in biological history as the famous "conditioned reflex," by which a concomitant of a stimulus takes over the stimulus-function. The concomitant becomes a *sign* of the condition to which the reaction is really appropriate. This is the real beginning of mentality, for here is the birthplace of *error*, and therewith of truth. If truth and error are to be attributed only to belief, then we must recognize in the earliest misuse of signs, in the inappropriate conditioned reflex, not error, but some prototype of error. We might call it *mistake*. Every piano player, every typist, knows that the hand can make mistakes where consciousness entertains no error. However, whether we speak of truth and error, or of their respective prototypes, whether we regard the creature liable to them as conscious or preconscious, or dispense with such terms altogether, the use of signs is certainly a *mental* function. It is the beginning of intelligence. As soon as sensations function as signs of conditions in the surrounding world, the animal receiving them is moved to exploit or avoid those conditions. The sound of a gong or a whistle, itself entirely unrelated to the process of eating, causes a dog to expect food, if in past experience this sound has always preceded dinner; it is a sign, not a part, of his food. Or, the smell of a cigarette, in itself not necessarily displeasing, tells a wild animal that there is danger, and drives it into hiding. The growth of this sign-language runs parallel with the physical development of sense organs and synaptic nerve-structure.° It consists in the transmission of *sense messages* to muscles and glands—to the organs of eating, mating, flight and defense—and obviously functions in the interest of the elementary biological requirements: self-preservation, growth, procreation, the preservation of the species.

Even animal mentality, therefore, is built up on a primitive semantic;° it is the power of learning, by trial and error, that certain phenomena in the world are signs of certain others, existing or about to exist; adaptation to an environment is its purpose, and hence the measure of its success. The environment may be very narrow, as it is for the mole, whose world is a back yard, or it may be as wide as an eagle's range and as complicated as a monkey's jungle preserve. That depends on the vari-

---

°*synaptic nerve-structure:* that part of the nervous system tissue by which impulses are transmitted from one neuron to another   °*semantic:* a pattern of sign-meaning

ety of *signals* a creature can receive, the variety of combinations of them to which he can react, and the fixity or adjustability of his responses. Obviously, if he has very fixed reactions, he cannot adapt himself to a varied or transient environment; if he cannot easily combine and integrate several activities, then the occurrence of more than one stimulus at a time will throw him into confusion; if he be poor in sensory organs—deaf, or blind, hard-shelled, or otherwise limited—he cannot receive many signals to begin with.

Man's superiority in the race for self-preservation was first ascribed to his wider range of signals, his greater power of integrating reflexes, his quicker learning by trial and error; but a little reflection brought a much more fundamental trait to light, namely his peculiar use of "signs." Man, unlike all other animals, uses "signs" not only to *indicate* things, but also to *represent* them. To a clever dog, the name of a person is a signal that the person is present; you say the name, he pricks up his ears and looks for its object. If you say "dinner," he becomes restive, expecting food. You canot make any communication to him that is not taken as a signal of something immediately forthcoming. His mind is a simple and direct *transmitter* of messages from the world to his motor centers. With man it is different. We use certain "signs" among ourselves that do not point to anything in our actual surroundings. Most of our words are not signs in the sense of signals. They are used to talk *about* things, not to direct our eyes and ears and noses toward them. Instead of announcers of things, they are reminders. They have been called "substitute signs," for in our present experience they take the place of things that we have perceived in the past, or even things that we can merely imagine by combining memories, things that *might* be in past or future experience. Of course such "signs" do not usually serve as vicarious stimuli to actions that would be appropriate to their meanings; where the objects are quite normally not present, that would result in a complete chaos of behavior. They serve, rather, to let us develop a characteristic attitude toward objects *in absentia*, which is called "thinking of" or "referring to" what is not here. "Signs" used in this capacity are not *symptoms* of things, but *symbols*.

The development of language is the history of the gradual accumulation and elaboration of verbal symbols. By means of this phenomenon, man's whole behavior-pattern has undergone an immense change from the simple biological scheme, and his mentality has expanded to such a degree that it is no longer comparable to the minds of animals. Instead of a direct transmitter of coded signals, we have a system that has sometimes been likened to a telephone-exchange, wherein messages may be relayed, stored up if a line is busy, answered by proxy, perhaps sent over a line that did not exist when they were first given, *noted down and kept* if the desired number gives no answer. Words are the plugs in this super-switchboard; they connect impressions and let them function together; sometimes they cause lines to become crossed in funny or disastrous ways.

This view of mentality, of its growth through trial and error, its apparently complicated but essentially simple aims—namely, to advance the persistence, growth, and procreation of the organism, and to produce, and provide for, its progeny—brings the troublesome concept of Mind into line with other basic ideas of biology. Man is doing in his elaborate way just what the mouse in his simplicity is doing, and what the unconscious or semiconscious jellyfish is performing after its own chemical fashion. The ideal of *"Nihil est in homine . . ."* is supported by living example. The speech line between man and beast is minimized by the recognition that speech is primarily an instrument of social control, just like the cries of animals, but has acquired a representative function, allowing a much greater degree of cooperation among individuals, and the focussing of personal attention on absent objects. The passage from the sign-function of a word to its symbolic function is gradual, a result of social organization, an instrument that proves indispensable once it is discovered, and develops through successful use.

If the theoretic position here attributed to students of genetic psychology requires any affidavit, we can find it in the words of a psychologist, in Frank Lorimer's *The Growth of Reason*:

"The apes described by Köhler," he says, "certainly have quite elaborate 'ape-ways' into which a newcomer is gradually acculturated, including among other patterns ways of using available instruments for reaching and climbing, a sort of rhythmic play or dance, and types of murmurs, wails and rejoicings. . . .

"It is not surprising that still more intelligent animals should have developed much more definite and elaborate 'animal ways,' including techniques of tool-uses and specific mechanisms of vocal social control, which gradually developed into the 'folk-ways' of the modern anthropologist. . . .

"Vocal acts are originally involved in the intellectual correlation of behaviour just as other physiological processes are. During the whole course of meaningless vocal chatter, vocal processes gradually accumulate intensity and dominance in behaviour. . . . Specific vocables become dominant *foci* of fixed reactions to various situations and the instruments of specific social adjustments. . . . The gradual differentiation and expansion of the social functions of vocal activity, among a race of animals characterized by increasingly complex nervous systems, is the fundamental principle of the historic trend of *vocal* activity to *verbal* activity, and the emergence of language."

An interpretation of observed facts that adjusts them to a general scientific outlook, a theory that bridges what used to appear as a *saltus naturae,*° a logical explanation displacing a shamefaced resort to miracle, has so much to recommend it that one hates to challenge it on any count. But the best ideas are also the ones most worth reflecting on. At first glance it seems as though the genetic conception of language, which regards the power of symbol-using as the latest and highest device of practical intelligence, an added instrument for gaining animal ends, must be the key to all essential features of human mentality. It makes rationality plausible, and shows at once the relationship of man and brute, and the gulf between them as a fairly simple phenomenon.

The difficulty of the theory arises when we consider how people with synaptic switchboards between their sense organs and their muscles should use their verbal symbols to make the telephone-exchange work most efficiently. Obviously the only proper use of the words which "plug in" the many complicated wires is the denotation of *facts*. Such facts may be concrete and personal, or they may be highly general and universal; but they should be chosen for the sake of orientation in the world for better living, for more advantageous practice. It is easy to see how *errors* might arise, just as they occur in overt action; the white rat in a maze makes mistakes, and so does the trout who bites at a feather-and-silk fly. In so complicated an organ as the human cortex, a confusion of messages or of responses would be even more likely than in the reflex arcs of rodents or fish. But of course the mistakes should be subject to quick correction by the world's punishments; behavior should, on the whole, be rational and realistic. Any other response must be chalked up as failure, as a miscarriage of biological purposes.

There are, indeed, philosophical and scientific thinkers who have accepted the biogenetic theory of mind on its great merits, and drawn just the conclusions indicated above. They have looked at the way men really use their power of symbolic thinking, the responses they actually make, and have been forced to admit that the cortical telephone-exchange does business in most extraordinary ways. The results of their candid observations are such books as W. B. Pitkin's *Short Introduction to the History of Human Stupidity*, Charles Richet's *L'homme Stupide* (which deals not with men generally regarded as stupid, but with the impractical customs and beliefs of aliens, and the folly of religious convictions), and Stuart Chase's *The Tyranny of Words*. To contemplate the unbelievable folly of which symbol-using animals are capable is very disgusting or very amusing, according to our mood; but philosophically it is, above all, confounding. How can an instrument develop in the interests of better practice, and survive, if it harbors so many dangers for the creature possessed of it? How can language increase a man's efficiency if it puts him at a biological disadvantage beside his cat?

°*saltus naturae:* a gap or jump in nature

Mr. Chase, watching his cat Hobie Baker, reflects:

"Hobie can never learn to talk. He can learn to respond to my talk, as he responds to other signs. . . . He can utter cries indicating pain, pleasure, excitement. He can announce that he wants to go out of doors. . . . But he cannot master words and language. This in some respects is fortunate for Hobie, for he will not suffer from hallucinations provoked by bad language. He will remain a realist all his life. . . . He is certainly able to think after a fashion, interpreting signs in the light of past experience, deliberately deciding his course of action, the survival value of which is high.

"Instead of words, Hobie sometimes uses a crude gesture language. We know that he has a nervous system corresponding to that of man, with messages coming in to the receptors in skin, ear and eye and going over the wires to the cortex, where memories are duly filed for reference. There are fewer switchboards in his cortex than in mine, which may be one of the reasons why he cannot learn to talk. . . .

"Meaning comes to Hobie as it comes to me, through past experience. . . .

"Generally speaking, animals tend to learn cumulatively through experience. The old elephant is the wisest of the herd. This selective process does not always operate in the case of human beings. The old are sometimes wise, but more often they are stuffed above the average with superstitions, misconceptions, and irrational dogmas. One may hazard the guess that erroneous identifications in human beings are pickled and preserved in words, and so not subject to the constant check of the environment, as in the case of cats and elephants. . . .

"I find Hobie a useful exhibit along this difficult trail of semantics. What 'meaning' connotes to him is often so clear and simple that I have no trouble in following it. I come from a like evolutionary matrix. 'Meaning' to me has like roots, and a like mechanism of apprehension. I have a six-cylinder brain and he has a one-lunger, but they operate on like principles.

". . . Most children do not long maintain Hobie Baker's realistic appraisal of the environment. Verbal identifications and confused abstractions begin at a tender age. . . . Language is no more than crudely acquired before children begin to suffer from it, and to misinterpret the world by reason of it."

A cat with a "stalking-instinct," or other special equipment, who could never learn to use that asset properly, but was forever stalking chairs or elephants, would scarcely rise in animal estate by virtue of his talent. Men who can use symbols to facilitate their practical responses, but use them constantly to confuse and inhibit, warp and misadapt their actions, *and gain no other end by their symbolic devices,* have no prospect of inheriting the earth. Such an "instinct" would have no chance to develop by any process of successful exercise. The error-quotient is too great. The commonly recognized biological needs—food and shelter, security, sexual satisfaction, and the safety of young ones—are probably better assuaged by the realistic activities, the meows and gestures, of Hobie Baker than by the verbal imagination and reflection of his master. The cat's world is not falsified by the beliefs and poetic figments that language creates, nor his behavior unbalanced by the bootless rites and sacrifices that characterize religion, art, and other vagaries of a word-mongering mind. In fact, his vital purposes are so well served without the intervention of these vast mental constructions, these flourishes and embellishments of the cerebral switchboard, that it is hard to see why such an overcomplication of the central exchange was ever permitted, in man's "higher centers," to block the routes from sensory to motor organs and garble all the messages.

The dilemma for philosophy is bad enough to make one reconsider the genetic hypothesis that underlies it. If our basic needs were really just those of lower creatures much refined, we should have evolved a more realistic language than in fact we have. If the mind were essentially a recorder and transmitter, typified by the simile of the telephone-exchange, we should act very differently from the way we actually do. Certainly no "learning-process" has caused man to believe in magic; yet "word-magic" is a common practice among primitive peoples, and so is vicarious treatment—burning in effigy, etc.—where the proxy is plainly a mere symbol of the desired victim. Another strange, universal phenomenon is ritual. It is obviously symbolic, except where it is aimed at concrete results, and then it may be regarded as a communal form of magic. Now, all magical and ritual practices are hopelessly inappropriate to the preservation and increase of life. My cat would turn up his nose and his tail at them. To regard them as mistaken attempts to control nature, as a result of wrong synapses, or "crossed wires," in the brain, seems to me to leave the most rational of animals too deep in the slough of error. If a savage in his ignorance of physics tries to make a mountain open its caverns by dancing round it, we must admit with shame that no rat in a psychologist's maze would try such patently ineffectual methods of opening a door. Nor should such experiments be carried on, in the face of failure, for thousands of years; even morons should learn more quickly than that.

Another item in human behavior is our serious attitude toward art. Genetic psychology usually regards art as a form of play, a luxury product of the mind. This is not only a scientific theory, it is a common-sense view; we *play an instrument*, we *act a play*. Yet like many common-sense doctrines, it is probably false. Great artists are rarely recruited from the leisure class, and it is only in careless speech that we denote music or tragedy as our "hobby"; we do not really class them with tennis or bridge. We condemn as barbarous people who destroy works of art, even under the stress of war—blame them for ruining the Parthenon, when only a recent, sentimental generation has learned to blame them for ruining the homes that surrounded the sanctuary of Beauty! Why should the world wail over the loss of a play product, and look with its old callousness on the destruction of so much that dire labor has produced? It seems a poor economy of nature that men will suffer and starve for the sake of play, when play is supposed to be the abundance of their strength after their needs are satisfied. Yet artists as a class are so ready to sacrifice wealth and comfort and even health to their trade, that a lean and hollow look has become an indispensable feature in the popular conception of genius.

There is a third factor in human life that challenges the utilitarian doctrine of symbolism. That is the constant, ineffectual process of *dreaming* during sleep. The activity of the mind seems to go on all the time, like that of the heart and lungs and viscera; but during sleep it serves no practical purpose. That dream-material is symbolic is a fairly established fact. And symbols are supposed to have evolved from the advantageous use of *signs*. They are representative signs, that help to retain things for later reference, for comparing, planning, and generally for purposive thinking. Yet the symbolism of dreams performs no such acquired function. At best it presents us with the things we do *not* want to think about, the things which stand in the way of practical living. Why should the mind produce symbols that do not direct the dreamer's activities, that only mix up the present with unsuitable past experiences?

There are several theories of dream, notably, of course, the Freudian interpretation. But those which—like Freud's—regard it as more than excess mental energy or visceral disturbance do not fit the scientific picture of the mind's growth and function at all. A mind whose semantic powers are evolved from the functioning of the motor arc should *only* *think*; any vagaries of association are "mistakes." If our viscera made as many mistakes in sleep as the brain, we should all die of indigestion after our first nursing. It may be replied that the mistakes of dream are harmless, since they have no motor terminals, though they enter into waking life as memories, and we have to learn to discount them. But why does the central switchboard not rest when there is no need of making connections? Why should the plugs be popped in and out, and set the whole system wildly ringing, only to end with a universal "Excuse it, please"?

The love of magic, the high development of ritual, the seriousness of art, and the characteristic activity of dreams, are rather large factors to leave out of account in constructing a theory of mind. Obviously the mind is doing something else, or at least something more, than just connecting experiential items. It is not functioning simply in the interest of those biological needs which genetic psychology recognizes. Yet it is a natural organ, and presumably does nothing that is not relevant to the total behavior, the response to nature that constitutes human life. The moral of this long critique is, therefore, *to reconsider the inventory of human needs*, which scientists have established on a basis of animal psychology, and somewhat hastily set up as the measure of a man. An unrecorded motive might well account for many an unexplained action. I propose, therefore, to try a new general principle: to conceive the mind, still as an organ in the service of primary needs, but of *characteristically human needs*; instead of assuming that the human mind tries to do the same things as a cat's mind, but by the use of a special talent which miscarries four times out of five, I shall assume that the human mind is *trying to do something else*; and that the cat does not act humanly *because he does not need to*. This difference in fundamental needs, I believe, determines the difference of function which sets man so far apart from all his zoölogical brethren; and the recognition of it is the key to those paradoxes in the philosophy of mind which our too consistently zoölogical model of human intelligence has engendered.

It is generally conceded that men have certain "higher" aims and desires than animals; but what these are, and in what sense they are "higher," may still be mooted° without any universal agreement. There are essentially two schools of opinion: one which considers man the highest animal, and his supreme desires as products of his supreme mind; and another which regards him as the lowest spirit, and his unique longings as a manifestation of his otherworldly admixture. To the naturalists, the difference between physical and mental interests, between organismic will and moral will, between hungry meows and harvest prayers, or between faith in the mother cat and faith in a heavenly father, is a difference of complexity, abstractness, articulateness, in short: a difference of degree. To the religious interpreters it seems a radical distinction, a difference, in each case, of kind and cause. The moral sentiments especially are deemed a sign of the ultimate godhead in man; likewise the power of prayer, which is regarded as a gift, not a native and natural power like laughter, tears, language, and song. The Ancient Mariner, when suddenly he could pray, had not merely found his speech; he had received grace, he was given back the divine status from which he had fallen. According to the religious conception, man is at most half-brother to the beast. No matter how many of his traits may be identified as simian° features, there is that in him yet which springs from a different source and is forever unzoölogical. This view is the antithesis of the naturalistic; it breaks the structure of genetic psychology in principle. For, the study of psychogenesis has grown up on exactly the opposite creed—that man is a true-blooded, full-franchised denizen of the animal kingdom, without any

---

°*mooted:* debated   °*simian:* apelike

alien ancestors, *and therefore has no features or functions which animals do not share in some degree.*

That man is an animal I certainly believe; and also that he has no supernatural essence, "soul" or "entelechy°" or "mind-stuff," enclosed in his skin. He is an organism, his substance is chemical, and what he does, suffers, or knows, is just what this sort of chemical structure may do, suffer, or know. When the structure goes to pieces, it never does, suffers, or knows anything again. If we ask how physical objects, chemically analyzable, can be conscious, how ideas can occur to them, we are talking ambiguously; for the conception of "physical object" is a conception of chemical substance *not* biologically organized. What causes this tremendous organization of substances is one of the things the tremendous organisms do not know; but with their organization, suffering and impulse and awareness arise. It is really no harder to imagine that a chemically active body wills, knows, thinks, and feels, than that an invisible, intangible something does so, "animates" the body without physical agency, and "inhabits" it without being in any *place.*

Now this is a mere declaration of faith, preliminary to a confession of heresy. The heresy is this: that I believe there is a primary need in man, which other creatures probably do not have, and which actuates all his apparently unzoölogical aims, his wistful fancies, his consciousness of value, his utterly impractical enthusiasms, and his awareness of a "Beyond" filled with holiness. Despite the fact that this need gives rise to almost everything that we commonly assign to the "higher" life, it is not itself a "higher" form of some "lower" need; it is quite essential, imperious, and general, and may be called "high" only in the sense that it belongs exclusively (I think) to a very complex and perhaps recent genus. It may be satisfied in crude, primitive ways or in conscious and refined ways, so it has its own hierarchy of "higher" and "lower," elementary and derivative forms.

This basic need, which certainly is obvious only in man, is the *need of symbolization.* The symbol-making function is one of man's primary activities, like eating, looking, or moving about. It is the fundamental process of his mind, and goes on all the time. Sometimes we are aware of it, sometimes we merely find its results, and realize that certain experiences have passed through our brains and have been digested there.

Hark back, now, to a passage already quoted above, from Ritchie's *The Natural History of the Mind*: "As far as thought is concerned, and at all levels of thought, it is a symbolic process. . . . The essential act of thought is symbolization." The significance of this statement strikes us more forcibly now. For if the material of thought is symbolism, then the thinking organism must be forever furnishing symbolic versions of its

---

°*entelechy:* roughly, "built-in purpose"

experiences, in order to let thinking proceed. As a matter of fact, it is not the essential act of thought that is symbolization, but an act *essential to thought*, and prior to it. Symbolization is the essential act of mind; and mind takes in more than what is commonly called thought. Only certain products of the symbol-making brain can be used according to the canons of discursive reasoning. In every mind there is an enormous store of other symbolic material, which is put to different uses or perhaps even to no use at all—a mere result of spontaneous brain activity, a reserve fund of conceptions, a surplus of mental wealth.

The brain works as naturally as the kidneys and the blood-vessels. It is not dormant just because there is no conscious purpose to be served at the moment. If it were, indeed, a vast and intricate telephone-exchange, then it should be quiescent when the rest of the organism sleeps, or at most transmit experiences of digestion, of wanted oxygen or itching toes, of after-images on the retina or little throbbings in pressed arteries. Instead of that, it goes right on manufacturing ideas—streams and deluges of ideas, that the sleeper is not using to *think* with about anything. But the brain is following its own law; it is actively translating experiences into symbols, in fulfilment of a basic need to do so. It carries on a constant process of ideation.

Ideas are undoubtedly made out of impressions—out of sense messages from the special organs of perception, and vague visceral reports of feeling. The law by which they are made, however, is not a law of direct combination. Any attempt to use such principles as association by contiguity or similarity soon runs into sheer unintelligible complication and artifice. Ideation proceeds by a more potent principle, which seems to be best described as a principle of symbolization. The material furnished by the senses is constantly wrought into *symbols*, which are our elementary ideas. Some of these ideas can be combined and manipulated in the manner we call "reasoning." Others do not lend themselves to this use, but are naturally telescoped into dreams, or vapor off in conscious fantasy; and a vast number of them build the most typical and fundamental edifice of the human mind—religion.

Symbolization is pre-rationative, but not pre-rational. It is the starting point of all intellection in the human sense, and is more general than thinking, fancying, or taking action. For the brain is not merely a great transmitter, a super-switchboard; it is better likened to a great transformer. The current of experience that passes through it undergoes a change of character, not through the agency of the sense by which the perception entered, but by virtue of a primary use which is made of it immediately: it is sucked into the stream of symbols which constitutes a human mind.

Our overt acts are governed by representations whose counterparts can nowhere be pointed out, whose objects are "percepts" only in a Pickwickian sense. The representations on which we act are symbols of various kinds. This fact is recognized in a vague and general way by most epistemologists; but what has not received their due recognition is the enormous importance of the *kinds*. So long as we regard sensations as *signs* of the things which are supposed to give rise to them, and perhaps endow such signs with further reference to past sensations that were similar signs, we have not even scratched the surface of the symbol-mongering human mind. It is only when we penetrate into the varieties of symbolific activity—as Cassirer, for instance, has done—that we begin to see why human beings do not act as super-intelligent cats, dogs, or apes would act. Because our brain is only a fairly good transmitter, but a tremendously powerful transformer, we do things that Mr. Chase's cat would reject as too impractical, if he were able to conceive them. So they would be, for him; so are they for the psychologist who deems himself a cat of the nth degree.

The fact that the human brain is constantly carrying on a process of symbolic transformation of the experiential data that come to it causes it to be a veritable fountain of more or less spontaneous ideas. As all registered experience tends to terminate in action, it is only natural that a typically human function should require a typically human form of overt activity; and that is just what we find in *the sheer expression of ideas*. This is the activity of which beasts appear to have no need. And it accounts for just those traits in man which he does not hold in common with the other animals—ritual, art, laughter, weeping, speech, superstition, and scientific genius.

Only a part—howbeit a very important part—of our behavior is practical. Only some of our expressions are *signs*, indicative or mnemonic, and belong to the heightened animal wisdom called common sense; and only a small and relatively unimportant part are immediate *signs of feeling*. The remainder serve simply to express ideas that the organism yearns to express, i.e. to act upon, without practical purpose, without any view to satisfying other needs than the need of completing in overt action the brain's symbolic process.

How else shall we account for man's love of talk? From the first dawning recognition that words can *express* something, talk is a dominant interest, an irresistible desire. As soon as this avenue of action opens, a whole stream of symbolic process is set free in the jumbled outpouring of words—often repeated, disconnected, random words—that we observe in the "chattering" stage of early childhood. Psychologists generally, and perhaps correctly, regard such babble as *verbal play*, and explain it through its obvious utilitarian function of developing the lines of *communication* that will be needed later in life. But an explanation by final causes does not really account for the occurrence of an act. What gives a child the present stimulus to talk? Surely not the prospect of acquiring a useful tool toward his future social relations! The impulse must be motivated by a present need, not a prospective one. Mr. Chase, who sees no use in words except their practical effect on other people, admits the puzzling fact that "children practice them with as much gusto as Hobie stalks a mouse." But we can hardly believe that they do so for the sake of practice. There must be immediate satisfaction in this strange exercise, as there is in running and kicking. The effect of words on other people is only a secondary consideration. Mrs. De Laguna has pointed this out in her book on the general nature of speech: "The little child," she says there, "spends many hours and much energy in vocal *play*. It is far more agreeable to carry on this play with others . . . but the little child indulges in language-play even when he is alone. . . . Internal speech, fragmentary or continuous, becomes the habitual accompaniment of his active behaviour and the occupation of his idle hours." Speech is, in fact, the readiest active termination of that basic process in the human brain which may be called *symbolic transformation of experiences*. The fact that it makes elaborate communication with others possible becomes important at a somewhat later stage. Piaget has observed that children of kindergarten age pay little attention to the response of others; they talk just as blithely to a companion who does not understand them as to one who gives correct answers. Of course they have long learned to use language practically; but the typically infantile, or "egocentric," function persists side by side with the progressively social development of communication. The sheer *symbolific* use of sounds is the more primitive, the easier use, which can be made before conventional forms are really mastered, just as soon as any *meaning*-experience has occurred to the vociferous little human animal. The practical use, though early, is more difficult, for it is not the direct fulfilment of a craving; it is an adaptation of language for the satisfaction of *other* needs.

Words are certainly our most important instruments of expression, our most characteristic, universal, and enviable tools in the conduct of life. Speech is the mark of humanity. It is the normal terminus of thought. We are apt to be so impressed with its symbolistic mission that we regard it as the only important expressive act, and assume that all other activity must be practical in an animalian way, or else irrational—playful, or atavistic (residual) past recognition, or mistaken, i.e., unsuccessful. But in fact, speech is the natural outcome of only one *kind* of symbolic process. There are transformations of experience in the human mind that have quite different overt endings. They end in acts that are neither practical nor communicative, though they may be both effective and communal; I mean the actions we call *ritual*.

Human life is shot through and through with ritual, as it is also with animalian practices. It is an intricate fabric of reason and rite, of knowledge and religion, prose and poetry, fact and dream. Just as the results of that primitive process of mental digestion, verbal symbolism, may be used for the satisfaction of other needs than symbolization, so all other instinctive acts may serve the expressive function. Eating, traveling, asking or answering questions, construction, destruction, prostitution—any or all such activities may enter into *rites*; yet rites in themselves are not practical, but expressive. Ritual, like art, is essentially the active termination of a symbolic transformation of experience. It is born in the cortex, not in the "old brain"; but it is born of an *elementary need* of that organ, once the organ has grown to human estate.

If the "impractical" use of language has mystified philosophers and psychologists who measured it by standards it is not really designed to meet, the apparent perversity of ritual from the same point of view has simply overcome them. They have had to invent excuses for its existence, to save the psychogenetic theory of mind. They have sought its explanation in social purposes, in ulterior motivations of the most unlikely sort, in "mistakes" of sense and reason that verge on complete imbecility; they have wondered at the incorrigibility of religious follies, at the docility of the poor dupes who let themselves be misled, and at the disproportionate cost of the supposed social advantages; but they have not been led to the assumption of a peculiarly human *need* which is fed, as every need must be, at the expense of other interests.

The ethnologists who were the first white men to interest themselves in the ritual of primitive races for any other purpose than to suppress or correct it were mystified by the high seriousness of actions that looked purely clownish and farcical to the European beholder; just as the Christian missionaries had long reported the difficulty of making the gospels plausible to men who were able to believe stories far more mysterious and fantastic in their own idiom. Andrew Lang, for instance, discussing the belief in magic, makes the following observation:

"The theory requires for its existence an almost boundless credulity. This credulity appears to Europeans to prevail in full force among savages. . . . But it is a curious fact that while savages are, as a rule, so credulous, they often 'laugh consumedly' at the religious doctrines taught them by missionaries. Savages and civilized men have different standards of credulity. Dr. Moffat remarks, 'To speak of the Creation, the Fall, and the Resurrection, seemed more fabulous, extravagant, and ludicrous to them than their own vain stories of lions and hyaenas.' . . . It is, apparently, in regard to imported and novel opinions about religion and science alone that savages imitate the conduct of the adder which, according to St. Augustine, is voluntarily deaf. . . ."

Frobenius, also a pioneer in the study of primitive society, describes an initiation ceremony in New South Wales, in the course of which the older men performed a dog-dance, on all fours, for the benefit of the young acolytes who watched these rites, preliminary to the painful honor of having a tooth knocked out. Frobenius refers to the ritual as a "comedy," a "farce," and is amazed at the solemnity with which the boys sat through the "ridiculous canine display." "They acted as if they never caught sight of the comical procession of men." A little later he describes a funeral among the Bougala, in the Southern Congo; again, each step in the performance seems to him a circus act, until at last "there now followed, if possible, a still more clownish farce. The deceased had now himself to declare what was the cause of his death." The professor is at a loss to understand how even the least intelligent of men can reach such depths of folly. Perhaps the savages who "laughed consumedly" at a tonsured father's sacraments with Holy Water, his God-eating and his scriptural explanations, were having a similar difficulty!

Later scholars gradually realized that the irrationality of customs and rites was so great that they could not possibly be "mistakes" of practice, or rest on "erroneous" theories of nature. Obviously they serve some natural purpose to which their practical justification or lack of justification is entirely irrelevant. Mrs. De Laguna seeks this purpose in the social solidarity which a prescribed ritual imparts: "Those elaborate and monstrous systems of belief," she says, "cannot possibly be accounted for by any simple theory that beliefs are determined by their successful 'working' in practice. . . . The truth is . . . that some more or less organized system of beliefs and sentiments is an absolute necessity for the carrying on of social life. So long as group solidarity is secured by some such system, the particular beliefs which enter into it may to an indefinite degree lead to behavior ill-adapted to the objective order of nature." But why should this social purpose not be served by a sensible dogma which the members of the society could reasonably be called on to believe, instead of "elaborate and monstrous" creeds issuing in all sorts of cruel rites, mutilations, and even human sacrifices, such as Baal or the Aztec gods demanded? Why did the Cults of Reason set up in post-Revolutionary France and in early Soviet Russia not serve the purpose of social solidarity every bit as well as the "Christian hocus-pocus" they displaced, and much better than the dog-dances and interrogation of the dead that disturbed Frobenius by their incredibility? Why should a priesthood primarily interested in accomplishing a social end demand that its laity should believe in immoral and unreasonable gods? Plato, who treated religion in just this sociological spirit, found himself confronted with this question. The established religion of Greece was not only irrational, but the social unity that might be achieved by participating in one form of worship and following one divine example was off-set by the fact that this worship was often degrading and the example bad. How could any wise ruler or rulers prescribe such ritual, or indorse such a mythology?

The answer is, of course, that ritual is not prescribed for a practical purpose, not even that of social solidarity. Such solidarity may be one of its effects, and sophisticated warlords may realize this fact and capitalize on it by emphasizing national religion or holding compulsory prayers before battle; but neither myth nor ritual arose originally for this purpose. Even the pioneers in anthropology, to whom the practices of savage society must have been more surprising than to us who are initiated through their reports, realized that the "farces" and "antics" of primitive men were profoundly serious, and that their wizards could not be accused of bad faith. "Magic has not its origin in fraud, and seems seldom practiced as an utter imposture," observed Tylor, seventy years ago. "It is, in fact, a sincere but fallacious system of philosophy, evolved by the human intellect by processes still in great measure intelligible to our minds, and it had thus an original standing-ground in the world." Its roots lie much deeper than any conscious purpose, any trickery, policy, or practical design; they lie in that substratum of the mind, the realm of fundamental ideas, and bear their strange if not poisonous fruits, by virtue of the human need for *expressing* such ideas. Whatever purpose magical practice may serve, its direct motivation is the desire to symbolize great conceptions. It is the overt action in which a rich and savage imagination automatically ends. Its origin is probably not practical at all, but ritualistic; its central aim is to symbolize a Presence, to aid in the formulation of a religious universe. "Except ye see signs and wonders, ye will not believe." Magic is never employed in a commonplace mood, like ordinary causal agency; this fact belies the widely accepted belief that the "method of magic" rests on a mistaken view of causality. After all, a savage who beats a tom-tom to drive off his brother's malaria would never make such a practical mistake as to shoot his arrow blunt end forward or bait his fishline with flowers. It is not ignorance of causal relations, but the supervention of an interest stronger than his practical interest, that holds him to magical rites. This stronger interest concerns the *expressive* value of such mystic acts.

Magic, then, is not a method, but a language; it is part and parcel of that greater phenomenon, *ritual*, which is the language of religion. Ritual is a symbolic transformation of experiences that no other medium can adequately express. Because it springs from a primary human need, it is a spontaneous activity—that is to say, it arises without intention, without adaptation to a conscious purpose; its growth is undesigned, its pattern purely natural, however intricate it may be. It was never "imposed" on people; they acted thus quite of themselves, exactly as bees swarmed and birds built nests, squirrels hoarded food, and cats washed their faces. No one made up ritual, any more than anyone made up Hebrew or Sanskrit or Latin. The forms of expressive acts—speech and gesture, song and sacrifice—are the symbolic transformations which minds of certain species, at certain stages of their development and communion, naturally produce.

Franz Boas remarked, even in one of his early works, that ritual resembled language in the unconscious development of its forms; and furthermore he saw, though less clearly, that it had certain symbolistic functions. After a discussion of the role played by language in the actual division and arrangement of sense experience, he says: "The behavior of primitive man makes it perfectly clear that all these linguistic classes have never risen to consciousness, and that consequently their origin must be sought, not in rational, but in entirely unconscious, processes of the mind. . . . It seems very plausible . . . that the fundamental religious notions . . . are in their origin just as little conscious as the fundamental ideas of language." And a few pages later he touches, howbeit only tentatively and vaguely, upon the expressive nature of those practices which seem "impractical" to us:

"Primitive man views each action not only as adapted to its main object, each thought related to its main end, as we should perceive them, but . . . he associates them with other ideas, often of a religious or at least a symbolic nature. Thus he gives them a higher significance than they seem to us to deserve. Every taboo is an example of such associations of apparently trifling actions with ideas that are so sacred that a deviation from the customary mode of performance creates the strongest emotions of abhorrence. The interpretation of ornaments as charms, the symbolism of decorative art, are other examples of association of ideas that, on the whole, are foreign to our mode of thought."

A year after Boas' book, there appeared the articles by Sigmund Freud which are now collected under the title of *Totem and Taboo*. It was Freud who recognized that ritual acts are not genuine instrumental acts, but are motivated primarily *a tergo*°, and carry with them, consequently, a feeling not of purpose, but of compulsion. They *must* be performed, not to any visible end, but from a sheer inward need; and he is familiar enough with such compulsive acts in other settings to suspect at once that in the religious sphere, too, they are best interpreted as *expressive* behavior. Empirically senseless, they are none the less important and justified when we regard them as symbolic presentations rather than practical measures. They are spontaneous transformations of experience, and the form they take is normal for the primitive mind. In civilized society, the same phenomena are apt to be pathological; there is a good reason for this, but that must be postponed to a later chapter.

The great contribution of Freud to the philosophy of mind has been the realization that human behavior is not only a food-getting strategy,

---

°*a tergo:* from the rear or from the inside

but is also a language; that every *move* is at the same time a *gesture*. Symbolization is both an end and an instrument. So far, epistemology has treated it only in the latter capacity; and philosophers have ample reason to wonder why this purely utilitarian trait of man's mind so frequently plays him false, why nature permitted it to grow beyond the limits of usefulness, to assume a tyrant role and lure him into patently impractical ventures. The fact is, I believe, that it did not originate purely in the service of other activities. It is a primary interest, and may require a sacrifice of other ends, just as the imperative demand for food or sex-life may necessitate sacrifices under difficult conditions. This fundamentally—not adventitiously—symbolific function of the mind was suggested to Freud by his psychiatric studies, but in later works he has given it a very general development, notably in the book already cited, *Totem and Taboo*. Certainly he has carried his theories far enough to make a philosophical study of "impractical" actions—rites, formalities, dramatizations, and above all, the unapplied arts—relevant and promising in the light of them. Yet few epistemologists have seriously taken advantage of the new ideas that fairly cry to be explored.

The reason is, probably, that traditional theory of mind is epistemology—theory of *knowledge*; and Freud's psychology is not directly applicable to the problems which compose this field. Symbolism, as it enters into the structure of knowledge, is better typified by mathematical "expressions" than by swastikas or genuflexions. Language, not ritual, is its main representative.

In order to relate these two distinct conceptions of symbolism, and exhibit the respective parts they play in that general human response we call a *life*, it is necessary to examine more accurately that which makes *symbols* out of anything—out of marks on paper, the little squeaks and grunts we interpret as "words," or bended knees—the quality of *meaning*, in its several aspects and forms. Meaning rests upon a condition which is, in the last analysis, logical; therefore the next chapter will have to concern itself mainly with logical structure, and cannot help being somewhat technical. But without such a grounding the whole argument would remain intangible, unfounded, and would probably appear more fantastic than cogent; so a short account of what constitutes meaning, what characterizes symbols, and also the different kinds of symbolism and their logical distinctions, will have to precede any further elaborations of the ideas so far suggested.

* * *

The Poet

No one has had greater influence on the actual uses of myth and symbol by modern poets than William Butler Yeats. Indeed, if any one man can be said to be the maker (or discoverer) of the outlines of modern mythology, it is he. (Examples of his own practice as mythmaker are found elsewhere in this book.) The essay which follows is perhaps exaggerated or even fanciful in its account of the importance of symbolic discourse, but because it is written by a poet who "saw" clearly many of the images out of which much of modern literature has been made, it is worth our careful attention.

Yeats felt very deeply the encroachment of "progress," in the form of science and rationalism, on the emotions, on the attachments of men's hearts. He sees the major poets of the 19th century (Tennyson, for example) stricken by self-consciousness, by an enervating concern for technical detail, and by reliance upon worn-out symbolic materials and used up myths. The evocative power of the symbol, Yeats feels, its power to reach beyond idea (though not to replace it) and to recall "ancient names and meanings," is the necessary restorative for the life of poetry.

To argue this seriously is, as Yeats knew, to go counter to much of the modern spirit. The reader may, therefore, find a number of statements in this essay difficult to accept or to understand, even if he takes into account the extravagance of Yeats's tone and rhetoric. He is, for example, anxious to assert the existence of the "divine life," which genuine poetry tries to embody and which science and journalism try to suppress. He asserts, for another example, that the poet evokes "certain disembodied powers" and that these powers gain force until they flow into daily life, affecting history and grand external events, and "make and unmake mankind."

How much and in what exact sense Yeats believed in these ideas is difficult to determine. Throughout his life he was always anxious to acknowledge spiritual and occult and extrasensory phenomena, yet he was also a man of great intelligence who knew that poetry's power depends as much upon hardness of conception and toughness of thought as upon ancient powers and symbolic evocation. It may be that the best way of viewing this question is to see Yeats as asserting nothing more (or less!) than the essentiality of the emotional life to the psychic health of an individual or a society and to the vitality of its poetic expression.

THE SYMBOLISM OF POETRY

William Butler Yeats (1865–1939)

I

Symbolism, as seen in the writers of our day, would have no value if it were not seen also, under one "disguise or another, in every great imaginative writer," writes Mr. Arthur Symons in *The Symbolist Movement in Literature*,° a subtle book which I cannot praise as I would, because it has been dedicated to me; and he goes on to show how many profound writers have in the last few years sought for a philosophy of poetry in the doctrine of symbolism, and how even in countries where it is almost scandalous to seek for any philosophy of poetry, new writers are following them in their search. We do not know what the writers of ancient times talked of among themselves, and one bull is all that remains of Shakespeare's talk, who was on the edge of modern times; and the journalist° is convinced, it seems, that they talked of wine and women and politics, but never about their art, or never quite seriously about their art. He is certain that no one who had a philosophy of his art, or a theory of how he should write, has ever made a work of art, that people have no imagination who do not write without forethought and afterthought as he writes his own articles. He says this with enthusiasm, because he has heard it at so many comfortable dinner-tables, where someone had mentioned through carelessness, or foolish zeal, a book whose difficulty had offended indolence, or a man who had not forgotten that beauty is an accusation. Those formulas and generalizations, in which a hidden sergeant has drilled the ideas of journalists and through them the ideas of all but all the modern world, have created in their turn a forgetfulness like that of soldiers in battle, so that journalists and their readers have forgotten, among many like events, that Wagner spent seven years arranging and explaining his ideas before he began his most characteristic music; that opera, and with it modern music, arose from certain talks at the house of one Giovanni Bardi° of Florence; and that the Pléiade° laid the foundations of modern French literature with a pamphlet. Goethe has said, "a poet needs all philosophy, but he must

---

°*The Symbolist Movement in Literature:* first published in 1899; Symons was a poet, critic, editor, and essayist. He called Yeats the "chief representative" of the symbolist movement.   °*journalist:* i.e., a popular writer, one who cannot think seriously about art   °*Bardi:* Italian scholar and music patron, 1534?-1612 °*Pléiade*: French poets of the late 16th century who tried to improve the quality of French verse of the time

keep it out of his work," though that is not always necessary; and almost certainly no great art, outside England, where journalists are more powerful and ideas less plentiful than elsewhere, has arisen without a great criticism, for its herald or its interpreter and protector, and it may be for this reason that great art, now that vulgarity has armed itself and multiplied itself, is perhaps dead in England.

All writers, all artists of any kind, in so far as they have had any philosophical or critical powers, perhaps just in so far as they have been deliberate artists at all, have had some philosophy, some criticism of their art; and it has often been this philosophy, or this criticism, that has evoked their most startling inspiration, calling into outer life some portion of the divine life, or of the buried reality, which could alone extinguish in the emotions what their philosophy or their criticism would extinguish in the intellect. They have sought for no new thing, it may be, but only to understand and to copy the pure inspiration of early times, but because the divine life wars upon our outer life, and must needs change its weapons and its movements as we change ours, inspiration has come to them in beautiful startling shapes. The scientific movement brought with it a literature which was always tending to lose itself in externalities of all kinds, in opinion, in declamation, in picturesque writing, in word-painting, or in what Mr. Symons has called an attempt "to build in brick and mortar inside the covers of a book"; and now writers have begun to dwell upon the element of evocation, of suggestion, upon what we call the symbolism in great writers.

II

In "Symbolism in Painting," I tried to describe the element of symbolism that is in pictures and sculpture, and described a little the symbolism in poetry, but did not describe at all the continuous indefinable symbolism which is the substance of all style.

There are no lines with more melancholy beauty than these by Burns:—

> The white moon is setting behind the white wave,
> And Time is setting with me, O!

and these lines are perfectly symbolical. Take from them the whiteness of the moon and of the wave, whose relation to the setting of Time is too subtle for the intellect, and you take from them their beauty. But, when all are together, moon and wave and whiteness and setting Time and the last melancholy cry, they evoke an emotion which cannot be evoked by any other arrangement of colours and sounds and forms. We may call this metaphorical writing, but it is better to call it symbolical writing, because metaphors are not profound enough to be moving, when they are not symbols, and when they are symbols they are the most perfect of all, because the most subtle, outside of pure sound, and through them one can best find out what symbols are. If one begins the reverie with any beautiful lines that one can remember, one finds they are like those by Burns. Begin with this line by Blake:—

The gay fishes on the wave when the moon sucks up the dew;

or these lines by Nash:°—

Brightness falls from the air,
Queens have died young and fair,
Dust hath closed Helen's eye;

or these lines by Shakespeare:—

Timon hath made his everlasting mansion
Upon the beached verge of the salt flood;
Who once a day with his embossed froth
The turbulent surge shall cover;

or take some line that is quite simple, that gets its beauty from its place in a story, and see how it flickers with the light of the many symbols that have given the story its beauty, as a sword-blade may flicker with the light of burning towers.

All sounds, all colours, all forms, either because of their preordained energies or because of long association, evoke indefinable and yet precise emotions, or, as I prefer to think, call down among us certain disembodied powers, whose footsteps over our hearts we call emotions; and when sound, and colour, and form are in a musical relation, a beautiful relation to one another, they become, as it were, one sound, one colour, one form, and evoke an emotion that is made out of their distinct evocations and yet is one emotion. The same relation exists between all portions of every work of art, whether it be an epic or a song, and the more perfect it is, and the more various and numerous the elements that have flowed into its perfection, the more powerful will be the emotion, the power, the god it calls among us. Because an emotion does not exist, or does not become perceptible and active among us, till it has found its expression, in colour or in sound or in form, or in all of these, and because no two modulations or arrangements of these evoke the same emotion, poets and painters and musicians, and in less degree because their effects are momentary, day and night and cloud and shadow, are continually

---

°*Nash:* Thomas Nash (1567-1601?), English dramatist

making and unmaking mankind. It is indeed only those things which seem useless or very feeble that have any power, and all those things that seem useful or strong, armies, moving wheels, modes of architecture, modes of government, speculations of the reason, would have been a little different if some mind long ago had not given itself to some emotion, as a woman gives herself to her lover, and shaped sounds or colours or forms, or all of these, into a musical relation, that their emotion might live in other minds. A little lyric evokes an emotion, and this emotion gathers others about it and melts into their being in the making of some great epic; and at last, needing an always less delicate body, or symbol, as it grows more powerful, it flows out, with all it has gathered, among the blind instincts of daily life, where it moves a power within powers, as one sees ring within ring in the stem of an old tree. This is maybe what Arthur O'Shaughnessy meant when he made his poets say they had built Nineveh with their sighing;° and I am certainly never sure, when I hear of some war, or of some religious excitement, or of some new manufacture, or of anything else that fills the ear of the world, that it has not all happened because of something that a boy piped in Thessaly. I remember once telling a seeress to ask one among the gods who, as she believed, were standing about her in their symbolic bodies, what would come of a charming but seeming trivial labour of a friend, and the form answering, "the devastation of peoples and the overwhelming of cities." I doubt indeed if the crude circumstance of the world, which seems to create all our emotions, does more than reflect, as in multiplying mirrors, the emotions that have come to solitary men in moments of poetical contemplation; or that love itself would be more than an animal hunger but for the poet and his shadow the priest, for unless we believe that outer things are the reality, we must believe that the gross is the shadow of the subtle, that things are wise before they become foolish, and secret before they cry out in the market-place. Solitary men in moments of contemplation receive, as I think, the creative impulse from the lowest of the Nine Hierarchies, and so make and unmake mankind, and even the world itself, for does not "the eye altering alter all"?

> Our towns are copied fragments from our breast;
> And all man's Babylons strive but to impart
> The grandeurs of his Babylonian heart.

°*Arthur O'Shaughnessy . . . sighing:* O'Shaughnessy was an Anglo-Irish poet (1844-1881). Nineveh was the greatest city of the Assyrian empire; thus Yeats's meaning is that great worldly things (Nineveh) have their beginnings in the emotions of poets.

III

The purpose of rhythm, it has always seemed to me, is to prolong the moment of contemplation, the moment when we are both asleep and awake, which is the one moment of creation, by hushing us with an alluring monotony, while it holds us waking by variety, to keep us in that state of perhaps real trance, in which the mind liberated from the pressure of the will is unfolded in symbols. If certain sensitive persons listen persistently to the ticking of a watch, or gaze persistently on the monotonous flashing of a light, they fall into the hypnotic trance; and rhythm is but the ticking of a watch made softer, that one must needs listen, and various, that one may not be swept beyond memory or grow weary of listening; while the patterns of the artist are but the monotonous flash woven to take the eyes in a subtler enchantment. I have heard in meditation voices that were forgotten the moment they had spoken; and I have been swept, when in more profound meditation, beyond all memory but of those things that came from beyond the threshold of waking life. I was writing once at a very symbolical and abstract poem, when my pen fell on the ground; and as I stooped to pick it up, I remembered some fantastic adventure that yet did not seem fantastic, and then another like adventure, and when I asked myself when these things had happened, I found that I was remembering my dreams for many nights. I tried to remember what I had done the day before, and then what I had done that morning; but all my waking life had perished from me, and it was only after a struggle that I came to remember it again, and as I did so that more powerful and startling life perished in its turn. Had my pen not fallen on the ground and so made me turn from the images that I was weaving into verse, I would never have known that meditation had become trance, for I would have been like one who does not know that he is passing through a wood because his eyes are on the pathway. So I think that in the making and in the understanding of a work of art, and the more easily if it is full of patterns and symbols and music, we are lured to the threshold of sleep, and it may be far beyond it, without knowing that we have ever set our feet upon the steps of horn or of ivory.

IV

Besides emotional symbols, symbols that evoke emotions alone,—and in this sense all alluring or hateful things are symbols, although their relations with one another are too subtle to delight us fully, away from rhythm and pattern,—there are intellectual symbols, symbols that evoke ideas alone, or ideas mingled with emotions; and outside the very definite traditions of mysticism and the less definite criticism of certain modern poets, these alone are called symbols. Most things belong to one or another kind, according to the way we speak of them and the companions we give them, for symbols, associated with ideas that are more than fragments of the shadows thrown upon the intellect by the emotions they evoke, are the playthings of the allegorist or the pedant, and soon pass away. If I say "white" or "purple" in an ordinary line of poetry, they evoke emotions so exclusively that I cannot say why they move me; but if I bring them into the same sentence with such obvious intellectual symbols as a cross or a crown of thorns, I think of purity and sovereignty. Furthermore, innumerable meanings, which are held to "white" or to "purple" by bonds of subtle suggestion, and alike in the emotions and in the intellect, move visibly through my mind, and move invisibly beyond the threshold of sleep, casting lights and shadows of an indefinable wisdom on what had seemed before, it may be, but sterility and noisy violence. It is the intellect that decides where the reader shall ponder over the procession of the symbols, and if the symbols are merely emotional, he gazes from amid the accidents and destinies of the world; but if the symbols are intellectual too, he becomes himself a part of pure intellect, and he is himself mingled with the procession. If I watch a rushy pool in the moonlight, my emotion at its beauty is mixed with memories of the man that I have seen ploughing by its margin, or of the lovers I saw there a night ago; but if I look at the moon herself and remember any of her ancient names and meanings, I move among divine people, and things that have shaken off our mortality, the tower of ivory, the queen of waters, the shining stag among enchanted woods, the white hare sitting upon the hilltop, the fool or Faery with his shining cup full of dreams, and it may be "make a friend of one of these images of wonder," and "meet the Lord in the air." So, too, if one is moved by Shakespeare, who is content with emotional symbols that he may come nearer to our sympathy, one is mixed with the whole spectacle of the world; while if one is moved by Dante, or by the myth of Demeter, one is mixed into the shadow of God or of a goddess. So, too, one is furthest from symbols when one is busy doing this or that, but the soul moves among symbols and unfolds in symbols when trance, or madness, or deep meditation has withdrawn it from every impulse but its own. "I then saw," wrote Gérard de Nerval° of his madness, "vaguely drifting into form, plastic images of antiquity, which outlined themselves, became definite, and seemed to represent symbols of which I only seized the idea with difficulty." In an earlier time he would have been of that multitude whose souls austerity withdrew, even more perfectly than madness could withdraw his soul, from hope and memory, from desire and regret, that they might reveal those processions of symbols that men bow to before

---

°*Gérard de Nerval:* symbolist writer discussed by Symons in *The Symbolist Movement in Literature*

altars, and woo with incense and offerings. But being of our time, he has been like Maeterlinck,° like Villiers de l'Isle-Adam° in *Axel*,° like all who are preoccupied with intellectual symbols in our time, a foreshadower of the new sacred book, of which all the arts, as somebody has said, are beginning to dream. How can the arts overcome the slow dying of men's hearts that we call the progress of the world, and lay their hands upon men's heartstrings again, without becoming the garment of religion as in old times?

V

If people were to accept the theory that poetry moves us because of its symbolism, what change should one look for in the manner of our poetry? A return to the way of our fathers, a casting out of descriptions of nature for the sake of nature, of the moral law for the sake of the moral law, a casting out of all anecdotes and of that brooding over scientific opinion that so often extinguished the central flame in Tennyson, and of that vehemence that would make us do or not do certain things; or, in other words, we should come to understand that the beryl stone was enchanted by our fathers that it might unfold the pictures in its heart, and not to mirror our own excited faces, or the boughs waving outside the window. With this change of substance, this return to imagination, this understanding that the laws of art, which are the hidden laws of the world, can alone bind the imagination, would come a change of style, and we would cast out of serious poetry those energetic rhythms, as of a man running, which are the invention of the will with its eyes always on something to be done or undone; and we would seek out those wavering, meditative, organic rhythms, which are the embodiment of the imagination, that neither desires nor hates, because it has done with time, and only wishes to gaze upon some reality, some beauty; nor would it be any longer possible for anybody to deny the importance of form, in all its kinds, for although you can expound an opinion, or describe a thing, when your words are not quite well chosen, you cannot give a body to something that moves beyond the senses, unless your words are as subtle, as complex, as full of mysterious life, as the body of a flower or of a woman. The form of sincere poetry, unlike the form of "popular poetry," may indeed be sometimes obscure, or ungrammatical as in some of the best of the *Songs of Innocence and Experience*,° but it must have the perfections that escape analysis, the subtleties that have a new meaning every day, and it must have all this whether it be but a little song

---

°*Maeterlinck . . . Villiers de l'Isle-Adam:* symbolist writers discussed by Symons in *The Symbolist Movement in Literature*   °*Axel:* a long dramatic poem published in 1890, which for a while had a large influence upon Yeats
°*Songs of Innocence and Experience:*   poems by William Blake

made out of a moment of dreamy indolence, or some great epic made out of the dreams of one poet and of a hundred generations whose hands were never weary of the sword.

*　　*　　*

The Critic

Leslie Fiedler is a novelist, teacher, and author of numerous essays on literary theory and the relation of literature to myth. In the passage which follows he supplies a number of useful ways of thinking about the relationship between the individuality of the particular writer and the permanent or archetypal elements which tradition and the universal aspects of human experience supply. His knowledge of the creative process in literature is broader and less abstract than Langer's and less subjective and esoteric than Yeats's.

ARCHETYPE AND SIGNATURE

Leslie Fiedler (1917–　　)

I

. . . . The word "Archetype" is the more familiar of my terms; I use it instead of the word "myth," which I have employed in the past but which becomes increasingly ambiguous, to mean any of the immemorial patterns of response to the human situation in its most permanent aspects; death, love, the biological family, the relationship with the Unknown, etc., whether these patterns be considered to reside in the Jungian Collective Unconscious or in the Platonic World of Ideas.° The archetypal belongs to the infra- or meta-personal, to what Freudians call the id or the unconscious; that is, it belongs to the Community at its deepest, pre-conscious levels of acceptance.

I use the word "Signature" to mean the sum total of individuating factors in a work, the sign of the Persona or Personality through which an Archetype is rendered, and which itself tends to become a subject as well as a means of the poem. Literature, properly speaking, can be said

---

°*Jungian . . . Ideas:* C. G. Jung's view that all men share certain unconscious responses, and Plato's view that Real Things are imitations of Ideal Things never seen in the physical world

to come into existence at the moment a Signature is imposed upon the Archetype. The purely archetypal without signature elements is the myth.

The theory of "realism" or "naturalism" denies both the Archetype and the Signature, advocating, in its extreme forms, that art merely "describes nature or reality" in a neutral style, based on the case report of the scientist. Art which really achieves such aims becomes, of course, something less than "poetry" as I have used the term here, becoming an "imitation" in the lowest Platonic sense, "thrice removed from the truth." Fortunately, the great "realists" consistently betray their principles, creating Archetypes and symbols willy-nilly, though setting them in a Signature distinguished by what James° called "solidity of specification." The chief value of "realism" as a theory is that it helps create in the more sophisticated writer a kind of blessed stupidity in regard to what he is really doing, so that the archetypal material can well up into his work uninhibited by his intent; and in a complementary way, it makes acceptance of that archetypal material possible for an audience which thinks of itself as "science-minded" and inimical to the demonic and mythic. It constantly startles and pleases me to come across references to such creators of grotesque Archetypes as Dostoevsky and Dickens and Faulkner as "realists."

A pair of caveats are necessary before we proceed. The distinction between Archetype and Signature, it should be noted, does not correspond to the ancient dichotomy of Content and Form. Such "forms" as the structures of Greek Tragedy, . . . New Comedy, and Pastoral Elegy are themselves *versunkene*° Archetypes, capable of being re-realized in the great work of art. . . .

Nor does the present distinction cut quite the same way as that between "impersonal" (or even "nonpersonal") and "personal." For the Signature, which is rooted in the ego and superego, belongs, as the two-fold Freudian division implies, to the social collectivity as well as to the individual writer. The Signature is the joint product of the "rules" and "conventions," of the expectations of a community, and the idiosyncratic responses of the individual poet, who adds a personal idiom or voice to a received style. The difference between the communal element in the Signature and that in the Archetype is that the former is *conscious*—that is, associated with the superego rather than the id. . . .

The intrinsicist° is completely unnerved by any reference to the role of the Archetype in literature, fearing such references as strategies

---

°*James:* Henry James (1843-1916), novelist and essayist   °*versunkene:* stagnant or decayed   °*intrinsicist:* one who holds that meaning is only intrinsic, that is, derived from the single poem itself, not from any outside (extrinsic) source or connection

to restore the criterion of the "marvelous" to respectable currency as a standard of literary excellence; for not only is the notion of the "marvelous" pre-scientific but it is annoyingly immune to "close analysis." Certainly, the contemplation of the Archetype pushes the critic beyond semantics, and beyond the kind of analysis that considers it has done all when it assures us (once again!) that the parts and whole of a poem cohere. The critic in pursuit of the Archetype finds himself involved in anthropology and depth psychology (not because these are New Gospels, but because they provide useful tools); and if he is not too embarrassed at finding himself in such company to look about him, he discovers that he has come upon a way of binding together our fractured world, of uniting literature and nonliterature *without the reduction of the poem.*°

It is sometimes objected that though the archetypal critic can move convincingly between worlds ordinarily cut off from each other, he sacrifices for this privilege the ability to distinguish the essential qualities of literary works, and especially that of evaluating them. Far from being irrelevant to evaluation, the consideration of the archetypal content of works of art is essential to it! One of the earlier critics of Dante says some place that poetry, as distinguished from rhetoric (which treats the credible as credible), treats of the "marvelous" as credible. Much contemporary criticism has cut itself off from this insight—that is, from the realization of what poetry on its deepest levels *is*. It is just as ridiculous to attempt the evaluation of a work of art *purely* in formal terms (considering only the Signature as Means), as it would be to evaluate it purely in terms of the "marvelous" or the archetypal. The question, for instance, of whether Mona Lisa is just a bourgeoise or whether she "as Leda, was the mother of Helen of Troy, and, as St. Anne, was the mother of Mary" is just as vital to a final estimate of the picture's worth as any matter of control of the medium or handling of light and shadow.

The Romantics seem to have realized this, and to have reacted, in their distinction between Fancy and Imagination°, with a search for rubrics to distinguish between the poetic method that touched the archetypal deeply and that which merely skirts it. Even the Arnoldian° description of Pope as "a classic of our prose," right or wrong, was feeling toward a similar standard of discrimination. It is typical and ironic

---

°*without the reduction of the poem:* Psychological criticism of literature is often accused of reducing a poem to a lower order of psychiatric comment.

°*Fancy and Imagination:* the Romantics, particularly Coleridge, used "Imagination" as a term to describe the faculty which produced poetry drawing upon the deepest parts of mind and spirit; "Fancy" was applied to a more mechanical faculty which, essentially, played with words °*Arnoldian:* Matthew Arnold (1822-1888), English poet and critic, complained that Alexander Pope's regular and witty verse was prosaic, not properly poetic in the Romantic sense; Fiedler suggests that Arnold, in praising poetry which has "high seriousness," is actually admiring poetry which contains Archetypal and Imaginative Depths.

that Arnold in a moralizing age should have felt obliged to call the daemonic power of evoking the Archetype "High Seriousness." Certainly, the complete abandonment of any such criterion by the intrinsicist leaves him baffled before certain strong mythopoeic talents like Dickens or Stevenson; and it is the same lack in his system which prevents his understanding of the complementary relationship of the life and work of the poet.

II

The Archetype which makes literature itself possible in the first instance is the Archetype of the Poet. At the moment when myth is uncertainly becoming literature—that is, reaching tentatively toward a Signature—the poet is conceived of passively, as a mere vehicle. It is the Muse who is mythically bodied forth, the unconscious, collective source of the Archetypes, imagined as more than human, and, of course, female; it is she who mounts the Poet, as it were, in that position of feminine supremacy preferred in matriarchal societies. The Poet is still conceived more as Persona than Personality; the few characteristics with which he is endowed are borrowed from the prophet: he is a blind old man, impotent in his own right. That blindness (impotence as power, what Keats much later would call "negative capability") is the earliest version of the blessing-curse, without which the popular mind cannot conceive of the poet. His flaw is, in the early stages, at once the result and the precondition of his submitting himself to the dark powers of inspiration for the sake of the whole people.

But very soon the poet begins to assume a more individualized lifestyle, the lived Signature imposed on the Archetype, and we have no longer the featureless poet born in seven cities, his face a Mask through which a voice not his is heard, but Aeschylus, the Athenian citizen-poet; Sophocles, the spoiled darling of fate; or Euripides, the crowd-condemner in his Grotto. The mass mind, dimly resentful as the *Vates*° becomes *Poeta,*° the Seer a Maker, the Persona a Personality, composes a new Archetype, an image to punish the poet for detaching himself from the collective id—and the Poet, amused and baffled, accepts and elaborates the new image. The legend asserts that Euripides (the first completely self-conscious alienated artist?) dies torn to pieces by dogs or, even more to the point, by *women.* And behind the new, personalized application looms the more ancient *mythos* of the ritually dismembered Orpheus, ripped by the Maenads when he had withdrawn for lonely contemplation. The older myth suggests that a sacrifice is involved as well as a punishment—the casting-out and rending of the poet being reinterpreted as

---

°*Vates:* Seer, the poet as divinely inspired   °*Poeta:* Maker

a death suffered for the group, by one who has dared make the first forays out of collectivity toward personality and has endured the consequent revenge of the group as devotees of the unconscious.

In light of this, it is no longer possible to think of the *poète maudit*° as an unfortunate invention of the Romantics, or of the Alienated Artist as a by-product of mass communications. These are reinventions, as our archetypal history repeats itself before the breakdown of Christianity. Our newer names name only recent exacerbations of a situation as old as literature itself which in turn is coeval with the rise of personality. Only the conventional stigmata of the poet as Scape-Hero have changed with time: the Blind Man becomes the disreputable Player, the Atheist, the incestuous Lover, the Homosexual or (especially in America) the Drunkard; though, indeed, none of the older versions ever die, even the Homer-*typus* reasserting itself in Milton and James Joyce. Perhaps in recent times the poet has come to collaborate somewhat more enthusiastically in his own defamation and destruction, whether by drowning or tuberculosis or dissipation—or by a token suicide in the work (*cf.* Werther).° And he helps ever more consciously to compose himself and his fellow poets—Byron, for instance, the poet par excellence of the mid-nineteenth century, being the joint product of Byron and Goethe—and, though most of us forget, Harriet Beecher Stowe! Some dramatic version of the poet seems necessary to every age, and the people do not care whether the poet creates himself in his life or work or both. One thinks right now of Fitzgerald,° of course, *our* popular image of the artist.

The contemporary critic is likely to become very impatient with the lay indifference to the poetizing of life and the "biographizing" of poetry; for he proceeds on the false assumption that the poet's life is primarily "given" and only illegitimately "made," while his work is essentially "made" and scarcely "given" at all. This is the source of endless confusion.

In perhaps the greatest periods of world literature, the "given" element in poetry is made clear by the custom of supplying or, more precisely, of *imposing* on the poet certain traditional bodies of story. The poet in such periods can think of himself only as "working with" materials belonging to the whole community, amending by a dozen or sixteen lines the inherited plot. Greek myths, the fairy tales and *novelle* of the Elizabethans, the Christian body of legend available to Dante are examples of such material. (In our world a traditionally restricted body of story is found only in subart: the pulp Western, or the movie horse opera.) In such situations, Archetype and "story" are synonymous; one remembers that for Aristotle *mythos* was the word for "plot," and plot

---

°*poète maudit:* the "cursed" poet °*Werther:* Goethe's novel about alienation, *The Sorrows of Young Werther* °*Fitzgerald:* F. Scott Fitzgerald, the novelist, whose life as an artist has become more interesting than his art

was, he insisted, the most important element in tragedy. That Aristotle makes his assertions on rationalistic grounds, with no apparent awareness of the importance of the Archetype as such, does not matter; it does not even matter whether the poet himself is aware of the implications of his material. As long as he works with such an inherited gift, he can provide the ritual satisfaction necessary to great art without self-consciousness.

A Shakespeare, a Dante or a Sophocles, coming at a moment when the Archetypes of a period are still understood as "given," and yet are not considered too "sacred" for rendering through the individual Signature, possesses immense initial advantages over the poet who comes earlier or later in the process. But the great poet is not simply the mechanical result of such an occasion; he must be able to rise to it, to be capable (like Shakespeare) at once of realizing utterly the archetypal implications of his material and of formally embodying it in a lucid and unmistakable Signature. But the balance is delicate and incapable of being long maintained. The brief history of Athenian tragedy provides the classic instance. After the successes of Sophocles come the attempts of Euripides; and in Euripides one begins to feel the encounter of Signature and Archetype as a *conflict*—the poet and the collectivity have begun to lose touch with each other and with their common preconscious sources of value and behavior. Euripides seems to feel his inherited material as a burden, tucking it away in prologue and epilogue, so that he can get on with his proper business—the imitation of particulars. The poem begins to come apart; the acute critic finds it, however "tragic," sloppy, technically inept; and the audience raises the familiar cry of "incomprehensible and blasphemous!" Even the poet himself begins to distrust his own impulses, and writes, as Euripides did in his *Bacchae*, a mythic criticism of his own sacrilege. The poetry of the struggle against the Archetype is especially moving and poignant, but to prefer it to the poetry of the moment of balance is to commit a gross lapse of taste.

After the Euripidean crisis, the Archetypes survive only in fallen form: as inherited and scarcely understood structures (the seeds of the genres which are structural Archetypes become structural platitudes); as type characters, less complex than the masks that indicate them; as "popular" stock plots. The "Happy Ending" arises as a kind of ersatz of the true reconciliation of society and individual in Sophoclean tragedy; and the audience which can no longer find essential reassurance in its poetry that the superego and the id can live at peace with each other content themselves with the demonstration that at least Jack has his Jill, despite the comic opposition of the Old Man. Still later, even the tension in Euripidean tragedy and New Comedy is lost, and the Signature comes to be disregarded completely; poetry becomes either completely "realistic," rendering the struggle between ego and superego in terms of the imitation of particulars; or it strives to be "pure" in the contemporary sense—that is, to make the Signature its sole subject as well as its means.

Can the Archetype be redeemed after such a fall? There are various possibilities (short of the emergence of a new, ordered myth system): the writer can, like Graham Greene or Robert Penn Warren, capture for serious purposes—that is, rerender through complex and subtle Signatures—debased "popular" Archetypes: the thriller, the detective story, the Western or science fiction; or the poet can ironically manipulate the shreds and patches of outlived mythologies, fragments shored against our ruins.° Eliot, Joyce, Ezra Pound and Thomas Mann have all made attempts of the latter sort, writing finally not archetypal poetry but poetry *about* Archetypes, in which plot (anciently, *mythos* itself) founders under the burden of overt explication or disappears completely. Or the poet can, like Blake or Yeats or Hart Crane, invent a private myth system of his own. Neither of the last two expedients can reach the popular audience, which prefers its Archetypes rendered without self-consciousness of so intrusive a sort.

A final way back into the world of the Archetypes, available even in our atomized culture, is an extension of the way instinctively sought by the Romantics, down through the personality of the poet, past his particular foibles and eccentricities, to his unconscious core, where he becomes one with us all in the presence of our ancient Gods, the protagonists of fables we think we no longer believe. In fantasy and terror, we can return to our common source. It is a process to delight a Hegelian, the triple swing from a naïve communal to a personal to a sophisticated communal.

We must be aware of the differences between the thesis and the synthesis in our series. What cannot be re-created as Plot is reborn as Character—ultimately the character of the poet (what else is available to him?), whether directly or in projection. In the Mask of his life and the manifold masks of his work, the poet expresses for a whole society the ritual meaning of its inarticulate selves; the artist goes forth not to "recreate the conscience of his race,"° but to redeem its unconscious. We cannot get back into the primal Garden of the unfallen Archetypes, but we can yield ourselves to the dreams and images that mean paradise regained. For the critic, who cannot only yield but must also *understand*, there are available new methods of exploration. To understand

---

°*fragments . . . ruins:* see T. S. Eliot, *The Wasteland;* Joyce's *Ulysses*, Pound's *Cantos*, Mann's *Dr. Faustus* are examples. For an extended list of modern works based upon myth see John J. White, *Mythology in the Modern Novel*, Princeton, 1971. (A selection of titles is given in Part VIII.)   °*"recreate . . . race":* what Stephen Dedalus, the protagonist of Joyce's *A Portrait of the Artist as a Young Man*, said he was going to do

the Archetypes of Athenian drama, he needs (above and beyond semantics) anthropology; to understand those of recent poetry, he needs (beyond "close analysis") depth analysis, as defined by Freud and, particularly, by Jung.

The biographical approach, tempered by such findings, is just now coming into its own. We are achieving new ways of connecting (or, more precisely, of understanding a connection which has always existed) the Poet and the poem, the lived and the made, the Signature and the Archetype. It is in the focus of the poetic personality that *Dichtung und Wahrheit*° become one; and it is incumbent upon us, without surrendering our right to make useful distinctions, to seize the principle of that unity. "Only connect!"

QUESTIONS

1. Summarize the arguments Langer makes against the "genetic hypothesis."
2. Summarize the arguments of the "naturalist school" and the "religious school" about man's "higher" aims and desires. How have genetic psychologists explained ritual? What is the original purpose of speech in a child?
3. Evaluate and discuss the argument that symbol-making is as essential a part of human activities as "eating, looking, or moving about." What does Langer think makes symbolism and ritual necessary?
4. Make an argument on behalf of the superior adaptational endowment of Hobie Baker. What are the disadvantages of using language as a means of communication?
5. Do the views in this essay express optimism or pessimism about the condition of man? Discuss.
6. What further areas of research in behavior are suggested by Langer's essay, or would cast further light on the questions it discusses?
7. What does Yeats claim to be the original source of the emotions which symbols convey?
8. What do the lines quoted by Yeats have which calls them to his attention? What have they in common with each other?
9. How does Yeats distinguish between metaphor and symbol?
10. What does Yeats think is the purpose of rhythm in poetry?
11. What does Yeats mean when he says that war, religious excitement, or other popular movements may be "because of something a boy piped in Thessaly." Can such a view be taken seriously?
12. Like Langer, Yeats connects the humanizing power of the poet with the traditional function of the priest. What are the similarities in their activities?

°*Dichtung and Wahrheit:* Poetry and Truth

13. What attitudes or points of view does Yeats most oppose and reject? Why?
14. Fiedler defines the Archetype by relating it to Jung's idea of the Collective Unconscious and to Plato's idea of an Ideal World of Things. All three notions suggest the existence of some common basis of human experience and knowledge, some ideas or knowledge common to all men, prior to experience, to culture or learning. There is a contrary view, identified with John Locke, Jeremy Bentham, John Stuart Mill, and other philosophers, that denies the existence of innate ideas, and the possibility of knowledge without some experience supplying the knowledge. What kind of evidence is available to support each side? Does symbolism make a convincing illustration of the existence of "innate ideas" or at least some psychological quality common to all men?
15. Give a definition and some illustrations of art that can be called "realistic" or "naturalistic."
16. Why does Fiedler think Faulkner, Dickens, and Dostoevsky are thought of as realists? What are they really? How can an artist think he is doing one thing and actually be doing another?
17. What are the disadvantages of referring to literature as containing elements of the "marvelous"?
18. Make a statement about the *Mona Lisa*, or about *The Rime of the Ancient Mariner*, or about another poem that would satisfy an "intrinsicist," a historical critic, a "formalist," Leslie Fiedler?
19. What do early "less conscious" societies imagine the Poet to be? How does he gain his inspiration? What happens to the Poet when he becomes individualized? What are the strengths and weaknesses of each state?
20. What are some modern Archetypes of the Poet? How do they connect with earlier views?
21. Notice the theory Fiedler offers to explain the effect on the poet of the force and power of the tradition present at any given time. What historical conditions does he see as most important to the poet? What conditions prevailed for Sophocles, Dante, Shakespeare?
22. What happens after the "fall" of the Archetype? What are some of the strategies of modern writers in response to this condition?

PART II

Remythologizing

Remythologizing

We now can begin to look at some examples of the techniques writers employ to extend the significance of their narratives beyond the literal. Perhaps the simplest of these is by reference to stories or characters which are part of the common culture or history of readers, either a formal "cultivated" sense of history or the simpler analogies and references of folktales. Patience is represented by Job, beauty by Helen of Troy; moral lessons, such as the dangers of Pride, by Satan or Icarus; the mischances of Fate, by Oedipus. Such references are much more common in older writers because readers of Chaucer's time, or Spenser's, were fewer, were better educated in classical tradition, and their culture offered a deeper sense of these meanings than modern readers may possess. Indeed, the modern reader may find himself cut off from writers whose literary and mythological background is different and unable to understand the works in which references to these backgrounds are made.

The simplest strategy for a writer faced with readers of this kind is to signify both his awareness of the traditional uses and his independence of them. He can do this by taking an older work and extending, modifying, or adapting it, so that the old story becomes a pattern against which the new is seen. Indeed, some writers in the last century have used such remythologizing as their primary mode of work, taking worn-out threads of old stories, no longer active in the imaginations of readers, and reworking them in ways that animate the values again and bring active responses from modern readers. Such technique is common in 19th- and 20th-century poetry and fiction, and one finds more examples of it occurring almost daily.

Patterns from old stories—formal or not—can be extended so easily because in their archetypes they contain simple and universal human situations. Oedipus, for example, offers a pattern for work dealing with the theme of family strife or for the love-hate relationships of parents and children. A Quest Story (the Grail legend) or the Return to Home Story (the *Odyssey*) also suggests the simplest narrative model, and some form of this theme seems to emerge from almost any novel or story where search or travel is involved. Sometimes a literary or mythic character may be isolated from traditional contexts and used to represent a particular state of mind or mood, or the cultural or philosophic "problem" of a particular time or age: Tennyson's adaptations of Greek and Arthurian mythology do this (*Idylls of the King, Ulysses, Lucretius, Oenone, Merlin, Mariana*, and others. Tennyson, it should be noted, makes no distinction between the mythologies of gods, ancient philosophers, and "real" historical figures).

The relation between a modern writer and mythic materials has two general forms. In one, the writer begins with his own feelings of inner conflict, and in writing about them, discovers the mythic structure of which they are a part, the addition of which can afford his work a more universal aspect. In the other, the writer begins with a historical myth, considers its imaginative possibilities, and discovers the themes of his own art. A writer may work from inner feeling outward to representation or from representation inward to feeling.

An example of both relationships between a modern writer and old mythology is wittily given by the protagonist-narrator of John Barth's recent story "Bellerophoniad" from *Chimera*.°

My general interest in the wandering-hero myth dates from my thirtieth year, when reviewers of my novel *The Sot-Weed Factor* (1960) remarked that the vicissitudes of its hero—Ebenezer Cooke, Gentleman, Poet and Laureate of Maryland—follow in some detail the pattern of mythical heroic adventure as described by Lord Raglan, Joseph Campbell, and other comparative mythologists. The suggestion was that I had used this pattern as the basis for the novel's plot. In fact I'd been till then unaware of the pattern's existence; once apprised of it, I was struck enough by the coincidence (which I later came to regard as more inevitable than remarkable) to examine those works by which I'd allegedly been influenced, and my next novel, *Giles Goat-Boy* (1966), was for better or worse the conscious and ironic orchestration of the Ur-Myth which its predecessor had been represented as being. Several of my subsequent fictions—the long short story *Menelaiad* and the novella *Perseid*, for example— deal directly with particular manifestations of the myth of the wandering hero and address as well a number of their author's more current thematic concerns: the mortal desire for immortality, for instance, and its ironically qualified fulfillment—especially by the mythic hero's transformation, in the latter stages of his career, into the sound of his own voice, or the story of his life, or both. I am forty.

Since myths themselves are among other things poetic distillations of our ordinary psychic experience and therefore point always to daily reality, to write realistic fictions which point always to mythic archetypes is in my opinion to take the wrong end of the mythopoeic stick, however meritorious such fictions may be in other respects. Better to address the archetypes directly. To the objection that classical mythology, like the Bible, is no longer a staple of the average reader's education, and that, consequently the old agonies of Oedipus or Antigone are without effect on contemporary sensibility, I reply, hum, I forget what, something about comedy and self-explanatory context.

The Further Travels of Ulysses

The first group of poems that illustrate these categories are chosen because they use the *Odyssey* as their basic point of reference. It is interesting to speculate about the reasons for the longevity and popularity of this story: it represents a Quest Narrative, one with a variety of adventures along the way, each one of which offers a new situation and new set of characters. These situations reflect in turn a range of illustrations of human situations and dramatic and psychological possibilities. Through all these adventures comes the personality and character of Ulysses (Odysseus, in Greek), perhaps the most human and in some senses the least heroic of myth figures.

Each of the poets whose works follow seems to want to have the mighty warrior have something more to say, a last word about the meaning of his voyage and adventures, some "conclusion." For Homer, the Return to Ithaca emphasized domesticity and decline. Odysseus will, apparently, live out his age quietly, contented to fulfill Teiresias' prophecy:

"then death will drift upon me
from seaward, mild as air, mild as your hand
in my well-tended weariness of age,
contented folk around me on our island."

*   *   *

Two thousand years after Homer, Dante encounters the spirit of Ulysses in Hell and discovers that the traveler could not bear retirement. Appearing as an "ancient flame," Ulysses speaks of his death.

From THE INFERNO

Dante Alighieri (1265–1321)

THE DEATH OF ULYSSES

As if it fought the wind, the greater prong 40
   of the ancient flame began to quiver and hum;
   then moving its tip as if it were the tongue

that spoke, gave out a voice above the roar.
   'When I left Circe,'° it said, 'who more than a year
   detained me near Gaëta° long before 45

Aeneas° came and gave the place that name,
   not fondness for my son, nor reverence
   for my aged father, nor Penelope's° claim

to the joys of love, could drive out of my mind
   the lust to experience the far-flung world 50
   and the failings and felicities of mankind.

I put out on the high and open sea
   with a single ship and only those few souls
   who stayed true when the rest deserted me.

As far as Morocco and as far as Spain 55
   I saw both shores; and I saw Sardinia
   and the other islands of the open main.

I and my men were stiff and slow with age
   when we sailed at last into the narrow pass
   where, warning all men back from further voyage. 60

Hercules' Pillars° rose upon our sight.
   Already I had left Ceuta° on the left;
   Seville° now sank behind me on the right.

°*Circe:* who had changed Ulysses's men to swine and had prevented him from leaving her island for a time   °*Gaëta:* town on southwest coast of Italy   °*Aeneas:* hero of Virgil's *Aeneid*   °*Penelope:* Ulysses's wife   °*Hercules' Pillars:* the eastern end of the narrow Strait of Gibraltar; Hercules was supposed to have parted the land at this point.   °*Ceuta:* in Africa, opposite Gibraltar   °*Seville:* name given to Spain in general; Ulysses is now in the Atlantic

'Shipmates,' I said, 'who through a hundred thousand
    perils have reached the West, do not deny   65
    to the brief remaining watch our senses stand

experience of the world beyond the sun.°
    Greeks! You were not born to live like brutes,
    but to press on toward manhood and recognition!'

With this brief exhortation I made my crew   70
    so eager for the voyage I could hardly
    have held them back from it when I was through;

and turning our stern toward morning, our bow toward night,°
    we bore southwest out of the world of man;
    we made wings of our oars for our fool's flight.   75

That night we raised the other pole ahead
    with all its stars,° and ours° had so declined
    it did not rise out of its ocean bed.

Five times since we had dipped our bending oars
    beyond the world, the light beneath the moon   80
    had waxed and waned,° when dead upon our course.

we sighted, dark in space, a peak° so tall
    I doubted any man had seen the like.
    Our cheers were hardly sounded, when a squall

broke hard upon our bow from the new land: 85
    three times it sucked the ship and the sea about
    as it pleased Another° to order and command.

At the fourth, the poop rose and the bow went down
till the sea closed over us and the light was gone.' ''

*   *   *

Poets, not surprisingly, take the view that their mythologies, their
reconstructions of older stories, are more authentic, more accurate than

---

°*do not . . . beyond the sun:* i.e., let's not deny ourselves this last great experience of sailing into the unknown °*morning . . . night:* East and West
°*stars:* the Southern stars °*ours:* North Star °*Five . . . waned:* i.e., five
months passed °*peak:* Purgatory °*Another:* God

the record based upon a study of antique documents from a library or artifacts from an archeological dig. John Keats, for example, told his friend Leigh Hunt that Dante's additions to the story were entirely "classical." According to Hunt, Keats said "that whenever so great a poet as Dante told us anything in addition or continuation of an ancient story, he had a right to be regarded as classical authority. For instance, said he, when he tells us of that characteristic death of Ulysses in one of the books of his *Inferno*, we ought to receive the information as authentic, and be glad that we have more news of Ulysses than we looked for." (Quoted by Douglas Bush in *Mythology and the Romantic Tradition*, p. 118.)

Tennyson's poem, one of the most famous of its time, follows the Dantean view that a man with Ulysses' experience and ambition would not be content to sit home with an aged wife, watching the affairs of his people being handled with pedestrian competence by his son Telemachus. But Tennyson's particular point of view and the popularity of the poem as well arise from the "issue" of the poem: the conflict between social responsibility and heroic individualism, a theme which Tennyson himself and many Victorians felt deeply.

ULYSSES

Alfred, Lord Tennyson (1809–1892)

It little profits that an idle king,
By this still hearth, among these barren crags,
Matched with an agèd wife, I mete and dole
Unequal laws unto a savage race,
That hoard, and sleep, and feed, and know not me.   5
I cannot rest from travel; I will drink
Life to the lees. All times have I enjoyed
Greatly, have suffered greatly, both with those
That loved me, and alone; on shore, and when
Through scudding drifts the rainy Hyades°   10
Vext the dim sea. I am become a name;
For always roaming with a hungry heart
Much have I seen and known,—cities of men
And manners, climates, councils, governments,
Myself not least, but honoured of them all;   15
And drunk delight of battle with my peers,
Far on the ringing plains of windy Troy.
I am a part of all that I have met;

°*Hyades:* nymphs associated with rainy weather

For all experience is an arch wherethro'
Gleams that untraveled world, whose margin fades   20
For ever and for ever when I move.
How dull it is to pause, to make an end,
To rust unburnished, not to shine in use!
As though to breathe were life! Life piled on life
Were all too little, and of one to me   25
Little remains; but every hour is saved
From that eternal silence, something more,
A bringer of new things; and vile it were
For some three suns to store and hoard myself,
And this gray spirit yearning in desire   30
To follow knowledge like a sinking star,
Beyond the utmost bound of human thought.

This is my son, mine own Telemachus,
To whom I leave the sceptre and the isle—
Well-loved of me, discerning to fulfil   35
This labor, by slow prudence to make mild
A rugged people, and through soft degrees
Subdue them to the useful and the good.
Most blameless is he, centred in the sphere
Of common duties, decent not to fail   40
In offices of tenderness, and pay
Meet adoration to my household gods,
When I am gone. He works his work, I mine.

There lies the port; the vessel puffs her sail:
There gloom the dark, broad seas. My mariners,   45
Souls that have toiled, and wrought, and thought with me—
That ever with a frolic welcome took
The thunder and the sunshine, and opposed
Free hearts, free foreheads—you and I are old;
Old age hath yet his honour and his toil.   50
Death closes all; but something ere the end,
Some work of noble note, may yet be done,
Not unbecoming men that strove with Gods.
The lights begin to twinkle from the rocks;
The long day wanes; the slow moon climbs; the deep   55
Moans round with many voices. Come, my friends,
'Tis not too late to seek a newer world.
Push off, and sitting well in order smite
The sounding furrows; for my purpose holds
To sail beyond the sunset, and the baths   60

Of all the western stars, until I die.
It may be that the gulfs will wash us down;
It may be we shall touch the Happy Isles,
And see the great Achilles, whom we knew.
Though much is taken, much abides; and though   65
We are not now that strength which in old days
Moved earth and heaven, that which we are, we are;
One equal temper of heroic hearts,
Made weak by time and fate, but strong in will
To strive, to seek, to find, and not to yield.   70

*   *   *

The most famous remythologizing of Odysseus is the monumental
novel by James Joyce, *Ulysses*, published in 1922. Here, the heroic
dimensions and grand adventures of the Greek warrior are contrasted,
often ironically, with a day's travels through Dublin of an obscure Jewish advertising salesman named Leopold Bloom. Bloom represents a
smaller (though not entirely unheroic) version of his great predecessor,
an average Dubliner going about a day's affairs. Joyce discussed the question of his interest in this particular hero with an acquaintance of his in
Zurich, Frank Budgen, a painter. In his book, *James Joyce and The
Making of Ulysses*, Budgen records some of the things Joyce had in mind
in his choosing Ulysses.

From JAMES JOYCE AND THE MAKING OF ULYSSES

Frank Budgen (1882–1971)

It was shortly after our meeting at Taylor's pension that I again met
Joyce, by chance this time, and we strolled through the double avenue of
trees on the Utoquai from Bellevue towards Zurich Horn. To the left of
us were the solid houses of Zurich burgesses, on our right the lake, and
on the far shore of the lake the green slopes and elegant contours of
the Uetliberg ridge.

"I am not writing a book," said Joyce, "based on the wanderings of
Ulysses. The *Odyssey*, that is to say, serves me as a ground plan. Only my
time is recent time and all my hero's wanderings take no more than
eighteen hours."

Reprinted with permission of Indiana University Press from *James Joyce and
the Making of Ulysses* by Frank Budgen.

A train of vague thoughts arose in my mind, but failed to take shape definite enough for any comment. I drew with them in silence the shape of the Uetliberg-Albis line of hills. The *Odyssey* for me was just a long poem that might at any moment be illustrated by some Royal Academician. I could see his water-colour Greek heroes, book-opened, in an Oxford Street bookshop window.

Joyce spoke again more briskly:

"You seem to have read a lot, Mr. Budgen. Do you know of any complete all-round character presented by any writer?"

With quick interest I summoned up a whole population of invented persons. Of the fiction writers Balzac, perhaps, might supply him? No. Flaubert? No. Dostoevski or Tolstoi then? Their people are exciting, wonderful, but not complete. Shakespeare surely. But no, again. The footlights, the proscenium arch, the fatal curtain are all there to present to us not complete, all-round beings, but only three hours of passionate conflict. I came to rest on Goethe.

"What about Faust?" I said. And then, as a second shot, "or Hamlet?"

"Faust!" said Joyce. "Far from being a complete man, he isn't a man at all. Is he an old man or a young man? Where are his home and family? We don't know. And he can't be complete because he's never alone. Mephistopheles is always hanging round him at his side or heels. We see a lot of him, that's all."

It was easy to see the answer in Joyce's mind to his own question.

"Your complete man in literature is, I suppose, Ulysses?"

"Yes," said Joyce. "No-age Faust isn't a man. But you mentioned Hamlet. Hamlet is a human being, but he is a son only. Ulysses is son to Laertes, but he is father to Telemachus, husband to Penelope, lover of Calypso, companion in arms of the Greek warriors around Troy and King of Ithaca. He was subjected to many trials, but with wisdom and courage came through them all. Don't forget that he was a war dodger who tried to evade military service by simulating madness. He might never have taken up arms and gone to Troy, but the Greek recruiting sergeant was too clever for him and, while he was ploughing the sands, placed young Telemachus in front of his plough. But once at the war the conscientious objector became a *jusqu'auboutist.*° When the others wanted to abandon the siege he insisted on staying till Troy should fall."

I laughed at Ulysses as a leadswinger° and Joyce continued:

"Another thing, the history of Ulysses did not come to an end when the Trojan war was over. It began just when the other Greek heroes went back to live the rest of their lives in peace. And then"—Joyce laughed—"he was the first gentleman in Europe. When he advanced, naked, to

---

°*jusqu'auboutist:* bitter-ender   °*leadswinger:* malingerer meet the young princess he hid from her maidenly eyes the parts that mattered of his brine-soaked, barnacle-encrusted body.° He was an inventor too. The tank is his creation. Wooden horse or iron box—it doesn't matter. They are both shells containing armed warriors."

*   *   *

W. S. Merwin's poem makes a decisive contrast with Tennyson's: the contrast between an age which thought heroic aspiration to be difficult but noble, and a more modern view, in which time, change, and the running together of one adventure with the next cast doubt on the worth of the Quest itself. For *this* Odysseus, "home" is relative, a matter not of community and love, but of definition.

ODYSSEUS

W. S. Merwin (1927–   )

Always the setting forth was the same,
Same sea, same dangers waiting for him
As though he had got nowhere but older.
Behind him on the receding shore
The identical reproaches, and somewhere   5
Out before him, the unravelling patience
He was wedded to. There were the islands
Each with its woman and twining welcome
To be navigated, and one to call "home."
The knowledge of all that he betrayed   10
Grew till it was the same whether he stayed
Or went. Therefore he went. And what wonder
If sometimes he could not remember
Which was the one who wished on his departure
Perils that he could never sail through,   15
And which, improbable, remote, and true,
Was the one he kept sailing home to?

*   *   *

°*When . . . body:* see the gentlemanly Bloom encounter Gertie MacDowell on the beach in the "Nausicaa" section (13) of *Ulysses*

Reprinted by permission of Harold Ober Associates Incorporated. Copyright © 1957 by W. S. Merwin.

According to Homer, the homecoming of Ulysses could not be complete until he had satisfied the advice of Teiresias: put an oar over his shoulder and journey inland until he met someone who did not recognize what it was. There he was to plant the oar in the earth and offer a burnt sacrificial animal to Poseidon, god of the sea (*Odyssey*, Book XXIII). This event would bring about the transformation of Ulysses from the seafaring adventurer to the declining old man ashore. But, in Ciardi's view, the past keeps its hold on the hero's emotions. Like Tennyson and Dante, he cannot see Ulysses as a sentimental old man, yet he does not see him as capable of heroic new adventures either.

ULYSSES

John Ciardi (1916–   )

At the last mountain I stood to remember the sea
and it was not the sea of my remembering
but something from an augur's madness:
sheep guts, bird guts, ox guts, smoking
in a hot eye. Was this my life? Dull red,   5
dull green, blood black, the coils still writhing
the last of the living thing: a carnage
steaming into the smokes of a sick dawn.

I had planted the oar at the crossroads, there in the goat dust
where the oaf waited, chewing a stalk of garlic.   10
"Stranger," he said, "what have you on your shoulder?"
"A world," I said, and made a hole for it,
watched by the oaf and his goats. I gave him money
for the fattest goat and asked to be alone,
and he would not leave me. I gave him money again   15
for a peace-parting, and he would not go.
"Stranger," I said, "I have sailed to all lands,
killed in all lands, and come home poor. I think
blood buys nothing, and I think it buys
all that's bought. Leave me this goat and go."   20
Why should I want his blood on me? The goat
stared at me like an old man, and the oaf
sat chewing garlic. This much had been commanded.
Was the rest commanded, too? Was it my life
or the god's laughter foresaw me?   25

Reprinted by permission of the author.

I prayed in anger:
"O coupling gods, if from your lecheries
among the bloods of man, a prayer may move you
to spare one life, call off this last sad dog
you have set on me. Does Heaven need such meat?"   30
The heavens lurched on unheeding. The fool stayed:
would not be scared off, and would not be whipped off.
Then he raised his staff against me.

                                        Was it my life
or the gods' laughter answered? I hacked him sidearm   35
across the middle: almost a stunt for practice—
dead level, no body weight to it, all in the shoulder
and wrist, and not three feet to the whole swing.
But it halved him like a melon! A chop
the ships would have sung for a century!   40
. . . But there were no ships, and the oar was planted unknown
in a country of garlic and goat turds,
and what lay fallen was rags and bones.

                                    "Take him, then!" I cried.
"Who else could stomach such a dusty tripe?"
I made the pyre with the planted oar at its center,
and as it flamed, I raised the libation cup,
but mouthed the wine and spat it at the blaze.
The fire roared up like Etna. "At your pleasure!"
I shouted back, and threw the dead clown in,   50
first one piece, then the other. The horns of the flame
raped him whole and blew for more. The goats
stood watching, huddled like old crazy men
in a chorus round the fire, and one by one
I slit their throats and threw them to their master.   55
I say those goats were mad: they waited there
as if the fire were Medusa: the blood of the dead
ran down the legs of the living and they did not move,
not even to turn their heads. And in the center
the flame went blood-mad in a shaft to Heaven.   60

It was dark when I turned away. I lost my road
and slept the night in a grove. When I awoke
I found a shrine to Apollo, a marble peace
leaned on by cypresses, but across his belly
a crack grinned hip to hip, and the right hand   65
lay palm-up in the dust. On the road back

I came on many such, but that was the first
of the cracked gods and the dusty altars.

I returned to the sea, and at the last mountain
I stood to remember, and the memory   70
could not live in the fact. I had grown old
in the wrong world. Penelope wove for nothing
her fabric and delay. I could not return.
I was woven to my dead men. In the dust
of the dead shore by the dead sea I lay down   75
and named their names who had matched lives with me,
and won. And they were all I loved.

*   *   *

Many of Ulysses' other adventures have also provided a source for
remythologizing. Samuel Daniel imagines a dialogue between Ulysses
and the Siren which contains both the sophistication of Elizabethan love
lyrics and the notion that aspiration and questing are proper attributes
of a heroic warrior.

ULYSSES AND THE SIREN

Samuel Daniel (1562–1619)

Siren

Come, worthy Greek! Ulysses, come,
    Possess these shores with me:
The winds and seas are troublesome,
    And here we may be free.
Here we may sit and view their toil   5
    That travail in the deep,
And joy the day in mirth the while,
    And spend the night in sleep.

Ulysses

Fair Nymph, if fame or honour were
    To be attained with ease,   10
Then would I come and rest with thee,
    And leave such toils as these.

But here it dwells, and here must I
    With danger seek it forth:
To spend the time luxuriously   15
    Becomes not men of worth.

Siren

Ulysses, oh, be not deceived
    With that unreal name!
This honour is a thing conceived,
    And rests on others' fame;   20
Begotten only to molest
    Our peace, and to beguile
The best of our life—our rest,
    And give us up to toil.

Ulysses

Delicious Nymph, suppose there were   25
    Nor honour nor report,
Yet manliness would scorn to wear
    The time in idle sport:
For toil doth give a better touch
    To make us feel our joy,   30
And ease finds tediousness as much
    As labour yields annoy.

Siren

Then pleasure likewise seems the shore,
    Whereto tends all your toil,
Which you forego, to make it more,   35
    And perish oft the while.
Who may disport them diversely
    Find never tedious day,
And ease may have variety
    As well as action may.   40

Ulysses

But natures of the noblest frame
    These toils and dangers please;
And they take comfort in the same
    As much as you in ease;

And with the thought of actions past   45
  Are recreated still;
When pleasure leaves a touch, at last,
  To show that it was ill.

   Siren

That doth opinion only cause
  That's out of custom bred,   50
Which makes us many other laws
  Than ever nature did,
No widows wail for our delights,
  Our sports are without blood;
The world, we see, by warlike wights   55
  Receives more hurt than good.

   Ulysses

But yet the state of things require
  These motions of unrest;
And these great spirits of high desire
  Seem born to turn them best;   60
To purge the mischiefs that increase
  And all good order mar;
For oft we see a wicked peace,
  To be well changed for war.

   Siren

Well, well, Ulysses, then I see   65
  I shall not have thee here;
And therefore I will come to thee,
  And make my fortune there.
I must be won, that cannot win,
  Yet lost were I not won;   70
For beauty hath created bin
  To undo, or be undone.

*   *   *

The Further Travels of the Magi

The following selections show that Christian mythology can be as easily adapted by modern writers as classical mythology: that it too can be studied to learn the way in which the particular aspects of the story—the images, the places, the "things" of the narrative—appeal to a writer, attract his interest, and represent some broader aspect of his culture or time. To Eliot, Yeats, Sylvia Plath, and George Garrett the essential interest in the story of the search of the Magi for the manger in Bethlehem lies in the contrast between the bright star shining in the sky—suggesting high and divine direction—and the lowly, daily humility of barnyard, straw, and dung. The story, even in the Biblical version, is about this contrast, the star and the straw standing for, symbolically, ways of searching and ways of living. This contrast is developed in much greater detail in the selection of Northrop Frye presented in Part V, where it is seen as a major aspect of modern mythology, occurring in many works, capable of marvelous transformation and extension.

From THE GOSPEL ACCORDING TO ST. MATTHEW

CHAPTER 2

1: Now when Jesus was born in Bethlehem of Judea in the days of Herod the king, behold, there came wise men from the east to Jerusalem,

2: Saying, Where is he that is born King of the Jews? For we have seen his star in the east, and are come to worship him.

3: When Herod the king had heard these things, he was troubled, and all Jerusalem with him.

4: And when he had gathered all the chief priests and scribes of the people together, he demanded of them where Christ should be born.

5: And they said unto him, In Bethlehem of Judea: for thus it is written by the prophet:

6: "And thou Bethelehem, in the land of Judea, art not the least among the princes of Juda, for out of thee shall come a Governor, that shall rule my people Israel."

7: Then Herod, when he had privily called the wise men, inquired of them diligently what time the star appeared.

8: And he sent them to Bethlehem and said, "Go and search diligently for the young child: and when ye have found him, bring me word again, that I may come and worship also."

9: When they had heard the king, they departed; and, lo, the star, which they saw in the east went before them, till it came and stood over where the young child was.

10: When they saw the star, they rejoiced with exceeding great joy.

11: And when they were come into the house, they saw the young child with Mary his mother, and fell down, and worshipped him; and when they had opened their treasures, they presented unto him gifts; gold, and frankincense, and myrrh.

12: And being warned of God in a dream that they should not return to Herod, they departed into their own country another way.

*   *   *

Eliot's poem shows that remythologizing may occur within the limits of Christian doctrine, for his "version" of the Nativity is from a Christian point of view and his changes in the mythology are an attempt to keep its stories and characters alive as an adjunct to faith. The poem is a dramatic monologue, giving the travelers' recollections of what they saw and felt along the way. The event which drew them is given less attention than the journey. There is no star, and the significance of the Birth is qualified by doubts. The quotation with which the poem begins is from a sermon given on Christmas Day, 1622, by Launcelot Andrews. It too offered sympathy for the hardships of the pilgrimage.

JOURNEY OF THE MAGI

T. S. Eliot (1888–1965)

"A cold coming we had of it,
Just the worst time of the year
For a journey, and such a long journey:
The ways deep and the weather sharp,

The very dead of winter."   5
And the camels galled, sore-footed, refractory,
Lying down in the melting snow,
There were times we regretted
The summer palaces on slopes, the terraces,
And the silken girls bringing sherbet.   10
Then the camel men cursing and grumbling
And running away, and wanting their liquor and women,
And the night-fires going out, and the lack of shelters,
And the cities hostile and the towns unfriendly
And the villages dirty and charging high prices: 15
A hard time we had of it.
At the end we preferred to travel all night,
Sleeping in snatches,
With the voices singing in our ears, saying
That this was all folly.   20

Then at dawn we came down to a temperate valley,
Wet, below the snow line, smelling of vegetation;
With a running stream and a water-mill beating the darkness,
And three trees on the low sky,
And an old white horse galloped away in the meadow.   25
Then we came to a tavern with vine-leaves over the lintel,
Six hands at an open door dicing for pieces of silver,
And feet kicking the empty wine-skins.
But there was no information, and so we continued
And arrived at evening, not a moment too soon   30
Finding the place; it was (you may say) satisfactory.

All this was a long time ago, I remember,
And I would do it again, but set down
This set down
This: were we led all that way for   35
Birth or Death? There was a Birth, certainly,
We had evidence and no doubt. I had seen birth and death,
But had thought they were different; this Birth was
Hard and bitter agony for us, like Death, our death.
We returned to our places, these Kingdoms,   40
But no longer at ease here, in the old dispensation,
With an alien people clutching their gods.
I should be glad of another death.

*   *   *

Yeats was the most self-conscious of modern mythmaking poets. Many of his poems call upon a kind of "vision," which is in effect a remythologizing of old mythic characters, stories, situations. In *The Magi*, the poet, like Eliot, is interested in the quality of faith, the psychological state which led the Magi to their quest. But Yeats is less sympathetic, and the poem treats the story not as history but as a vision, seen clearly but subjectively in "the mind's eye," that eye which sees through the old traditional images to their modern dress and forms.

THE MAGI

William Butler Yeats (1865–1939)

Now as at all times I can see in the mind's eye,
In their stiff, painted clothes, the pale unsatisfied ones
Appear and disappear in the blue depth of the sky
With all their ancient faces like rain-beaten stones,
And all their helms of silver hovering side by side,   5
And all their eyes still fixed, hoping to find once more,
Being by Calvary's turbulence unsatisfied,
The uncontrollable mystery on the bestial floor.

* * *

The influence of Yeats's mythology has been immense, and traces of it occur in the imagery of much modern literature. Illustrating the consistency and influence of these earlier poems is *Magi* by Sylvia Plath, in which the abstract and Platonic aspiration of the Magi is contrasted with the humble reality of a baby, not in a manger but in a crib.

MAGI

Sylvia Plath (1932–1963)

The abstracts hover like dull angels:
Nothing so vulgar as a nose or an eye
Bossing the ethereal blanks of their face-ovals.

Their whiteness bears no relation to laundry,
Snow, chalk or suchlike. They're   5
The real thing, all right: the Good, the True—

Salutary and pure as boiled water,
Loveless as the multiplication table.
While the child smiles into thin air.

Six months in the world, and she is able   10
To rock on all fours like a padded hammock.
For her, the heavy notion of Evil

Attending her cot is less than a bellyache,
And Love the mother of milk, no theory.
They mistake their star, these papery godfolk.   15

They want the crib of some lamp-headed Plato.
Let them astound his heart with their merit.
What girl ever flourished in such company?

*   *   *

Science, which discovers rational explanations for previous supernatural events, is a primary cause for the loss of faith in the older mythology. Sometimes the modern poet is more aware of the loss of the old
faith than the value of the new. Both George Garrett and Thomas
Hardy in the poems that follow demonstrate the cost of adult visions of
childish beliefs. Both connect their present lives with values of the past,
though both, at the same time, acknowledge that it is an act of belief and
faith, not of scientific fact. Hardy's poem is based on a folk belief that at
midnight on Christmas Eve, oxen can be found kneeling in their pens.

THE MAGI

George Garrett (1929–   )

First they were stiff and gaudy,
three painted wooden figures on the table,
bowing in a manger without any walls

Reprinted with permission of the University of Texas Press from *The Sleeping
Gypsy and Other Poems* by George Garrett, 1958.

among bland clay beasts and shepherds
who huddled where my mother always put them   5
in a perfect ring around the Holy Child.
At that season and by candlelight
it was easy for a child to believe in them.

Later on I *was* one. I brought gold,
ascended the platform in the Parish House   10
and muffed my lines, but left my gift
beside the cheap doll in its cradle,
knelt in my fancy costume trying to look wise
while the other two (my friends and rivals
for the girl who was chosen to be Mary)   15
never faltered with frankincense and myrrh.

Now that was a long time ago.
And now I know them for what they were,
moving across vague spaces on their camels,
visionaries, madmen, poor creatures possessed   20
by some slight deviation of the stars.
I know their gifts were shabby, if symbolic.
Their wisdom was a thing of waking dreams.
Their robes were dirty and their breath was bad.

Still, I would dream them back.   25
Let them be wooden and absurd again
in all the painted glory that a child
loved. Let me be one of them.
Let me step forward once more awkwardly
and stammer and choke on my prepared speech.   30
I will bring gold again and kneel
foolish and adoring in the dungy straw.

THE OXEN

Thomas Hardy (1840–1928)

Christmas Eve, and twelve of the clock.
　'Now they are all on their knees,'
An elder said as we sat in a flock
　By the embers in hearthside ease.

We pictured the meek mild creatures where   5
　They dwelt in their strawy pen,

Nor did it occur to one of there
    To doubt they were kneeling then.

So fair a fancy few would weave
    In these years! Yet, I feel,   10
If someone said on Christmas Eve,
    'Come; see the oxen kneel,

In the lonely barton° by yonder coomb°
    Our childhood used to know,'
I should go with him in the gloom,   15
    Hoping it might be so.

                        *   *   *

A Grim Fairy Tale

After Greece and Rome, and after Bethlehem, there is another
familiar source of mythological materials: huge amounts of folklore,
tale, legend, ballad, song, and story which descend through a simpler,
popular tradition. Though it is unconsciously wrought, it is often as
interesting and as rich in possibilities for the modern mythographer as
the more elaborate and more "literary" sources. In this remythologizing
of Hansel and Gretel's walk into the woods, we see an impressive use
of these materials.

THE GINGERBREAD HOUSE

Robert Coover (1932–   )

                            1

A pine forest in the midafternoon. Two children follow an old man,
dropping breadcrumbs, singing nursery tunes. Dense earthy greens seep
into the darkening distance, flecked and streaked with filtered sunlight.
Spots of red, violet, pale blue, gold, burnt orange. The girl carries a
basket for gathering flowers. The boy is occupied with the crumbs. Their
song tells of God's care for little ones.

°*barton:* farmyard   °*coomb:* valley

2

Poverty and resignation weigh on the old man. His cloth jacket is patched and threadbare, sunbleached white over the shoulders, worn through on the elbows. His feet do not lift, but shuffle through the dust. White hair. Parched skin. Secret forces of despair and guilt seem to pull him earthward.

3

The girl plucks a flower. The boy watches curiously. The old man stares impatiently into the forest's depths, where night seems already to crouch. The girl's apron is a bright orange, the gay color of freshly picked tangerines, and is stitched happily with blues and reds and greens; but her dress is simple and brown, tattered at the hem, and her feet are bare. Birds accompany the children in their singing and butterflies decorate the forest spaces.

4

The boy's gesture is furtive. His right hand trails behind him, letting a crumb fall. His face is half-turned toward his hand, but his eyes remain watchfully fixed on the old man's feet ahead. The old man wears heavy mud-spattered shoes, high-topped and leather-thonged. Like the old man's own skin, the shoes are dry and cracked and furrowed with wrinkles. The boy's pants are a bluish-brown, ragged at the cuffs, his jacket a faded red. He, like the girl, is barefoot.

5

The children sing nursery songs about May baskets and gingerbread houses and a saint who ate his own fleas. Perhaps they sing to lighten their young hearts, for puce wisps of dusk now coil through the trunks and branches of the thickening forest. Or perhaps they sing to conceal the boy's subterfuge. More likely, they sing for no reason at all, a thoughtless childish habit. To hear themselves. Or to admire their memories. Or to entertain the old man. To fill the silence. Conceal their thoughts. Their expectations.

6

The boy's hand and wrist, thrusting from the outgrown jacket (the faded red cuff is not a cuff at all, but the torn limits merely, the ragged edge of the soft worn sleeve), are tanned, a little soiled, childish. The fingers are short and plump, the palm soft, the wrist small. Three fingers curl under, holding back crumbs, kneading them, coaxing them into position, while the index finger and thumb flick them sparingly, one by one, to the ground, playing with them a moment, balling them, pinching them as if for luck or pleasure, before letting them go.

7

The old man's pale blue eyes float damply in deep dark pouches, half-shrouded by heavy upper lids and beetled over by shaggy white brows. Deep creases fan out from the moist corners, angle down past the nose, score the tanned cheeks and pinch the mouth. The old man's gaze is straight ahead, but at what? Perhaps at nothing. Some invisible destination. Some irrecoverable point of departure. One thing can be said about the eyes: they are tired. Whether they have seen too much or too little, they betray no will to see yet more.

8

The witch is wrapped in a tortured whirl of black rags. Her long face is drawn and livid, and her eyes glow like burning coals. Her angular body twists this way and that, flapping the black rags—flecks of blue and amethyst wink and flash in the black tangle. Her gnarled blue hands snatch greedily at space, shred her clothes, claw cruelly at her face and throat. She cackles silently, then suddenly screeches madly, seizes a passing dove, and tears its heart out.

9

The girl, younger than the boy, skips blithely down the forest path, her blonde curls flowing freely. Her brown dress is coarse and plain, but her apron is gay and white petticoats wink from beneath the tattered hem. Her skin is fresh and pink and soft, her knees and elbows dimpled, her cheeks rosy. Her young gaze flicks airily from flower to flower, bird to bird, tree to tree, from the boy to the old man, from the green grass to the encroaching darkness, and all of it seems to delight her equally. Her basket is full to overflowing. Does she even know the boy is dropping crumbs? or where the old man is leading them? Of course, but it's nothing! a game!

10

There is, in the forest, even now, a sunny place, with mintdrop trees and cotton candy bushes, an air as fresh and heady as lemonade. Rivulets of honey flow over gumdrop pebbles, and lollypops grow wild as daisies. This is the place of the gingerbread house. Children come here, but, they say, none leave.

11

The dove is a soft lustrous white, head high, breast filled, tip of the tail less than a feather's thickness off the ground. From above, it would be seen against the pale path—a mixture of umbers and grays and the sharp brown strokes of pine needles—but from its own level, in profile, its pure whiteness is set off glowingly against the obscure mallows and distant moss greens of the forest. Only its small beak moves. Around a bread crumb.

12

The song is about a great king who won many battles, but the girl sings alone. The old man has turned back, gazes curiously but dispassionately now at the boy. The boy, too, has turned, no longer furtive, hand poised but no crumb dropping from his fingertips. He stares back down the path by which they three have come, his mouth agape, his eyes startled. His left hand is raised, as if arrested a moment before striking out in protest. Doves are eating his bread crumbs. His ruse has failed. Perhaps the old man, not so ignorant in such matters after all, has known all along it would. The girl sings of pretty things sold in the market.

13

So huddled over her prey is the witch that she seems nothing more than a pile of black rags heaped on a post. Her pale long-nailed hands are curled inward toward her breast, massaging the object, her head lower than her hunched shoulders, wan beaked nose poked in among the restless fingers. She pauses, cackling softly, peers left, then right, then lifts the heart before her eyes. The burnished heart of the dove glitters like a ruby, a polished, cherry, a brilliant, heart-shaped bloodstone. It beats still. A soft radiant pulsing. The black bony shoulders of the witch quake with glee, with greed, with lust.

14

A wild blur of fluttering white: the dove's wings flapping! Hands clutch its body, its head, its throat, small hands with short plump fingers. Its wings flail against the dusky forest green, but it is forced down against the umber earth. The boy falls upon it, his hands bloodied by beak and claws.

15

The gingerbread house is approached by flagstones of variegated wafers, through a garden of candied fruits and all-day suckers in neat little rows.

16

No song now from the lips of the girl, but a cry of anguish. The basket of flowers is dropped, the kings and saints forgotten. She struggles with the boy for the bird. She kicks him, falls upon him, pulls his hair, tears at his red jacket. He huddles around the bird, trying to elbow free of the girl. Both children are weeping, the boy of anger and frustration, the girl of pain and pity and a bruised heart. Their legs entangle, their fists beat at each other, feathers fly.

The pale blue eyes of the old man stare not ahead, but down. The squint, the sorrow, the tedium are vanished; the eyes focus clearly. The deep creases fanning out from the damp corners pinch inward, a brief wince, as though at some inner hurt, some certain anguish, some old wisdom. He sighs.

The girl has captured the bird. The boy, small chest heaving, kneels in the path watching her, the anger largely drained out of him. His faded red jacket is torn; his pants are full of dust and pine needles. She has thrust the dove protectively beneath her skirt, and sits, knees apart, leaning over it, weeping softly. The old man stoops down, lifts her bright orange apron, her skirt, her petticoats. The boy turns away. The dove is nested in her small round thighs. It is dead.

19

Shadows have lengthened. Umbers and lavenders and greens have grayed. But the body of the dove glows yet in the gathering dusk. The whiteness of the ruffled breast seems to be fighting back against the threat of night. It is strewn with flowers, now beginning to wilt. The old man, the boy, and the girl have gone.

The beams of the gingerbread house are licorice sticks, cemented with taffy, weatherboarded with gingerbread, and coated with caramel. Peppermint-stick chimneys sprout randomly from its chocolate roof and its windows are laced with meringue. Oh, what a house! and the best thing of all is the door.

The forest is dense and deep. Branches reach forth like arms. Brown animals scurry. The boy makes no furtive gestures. The girl, carrying her flowerbasket, does not skip or sing. They walk, arms linked, eyes wide open and staring ahead into the forest. The old man plods on, leading the way, his heavy old leather-thonged shoes shuffling in the damp dust and undergrowth.

22

The old man's eyes, pale in the sunlight, now seem to glitter in the late twilight. Perhaps it is their wetness picking up the last flickering light of day. The squint has returned, but it is not the squint of weariness: resistance, rather. His mouth opens as though to speak, to rebuke, but his teeth are clenched. The witch twists and quivers, her black rags whirling, whipping, flapping. From her lean bosom, she withdraws the pulsing red heart of a dove. How it glows, how it rages, how it dances in the dusk! The old man now does not resist. Lust flattens his face and mists his old eyes, where glitter now reflections of the ruby heart. Grimacing, he plummets forward, covering the cackling witch, crashing through brambles that tear at his clothes.

23

A wild screech cleaves the silence of the dusky forest. Birds start up from branches and the undergrowth is alive with frightened animals. The old man stops short, one hand raised protectively in front of him, the other, as though part of the same instinct, reaching back to shield his children. Dropping her basket of flowers, the girl cries out in terror and springs forward into the old man's arms. The boy blanches, shivers as though a cold wind might be wetly wrapping his young body, but manfully holds his ground. Shapes seem to twist and coil, and vapors seep up from the forest floor. The girl whimpers and the old man holds her close.

24

The beds are simple but solid. The old man himself has made them. The sun is setting, the room is in shadows, the children tucked safely in. The old man tells them a story about a good fairy who granted a poor man three wishes. The wishes, he knows, were wasted, but so then is the story. He lengthens the tale with details about the good fairy, how sweet and kind and pretty she is, then lets the children complete the story with their own wishes, their own dreams. Below, a brutal demand is being forced upon him. Why must the goodness of all wishes come to nothing?

The flowerbasket lies, overturned, by the forest path, its wilting flowers strewn. Shadows darker than dried blood spread beneath its gaping mouth. The shadows are long, for night is falling.

26

The old man has fallen into the brambles. The children, weeping, help pull him free. He sits on the forest path staring at the boy and girl. It is as though he is unable to recognize them. Their weeping dies away. They huddle more closely together, stare back at the old man. His face is scratched, his clothes torn. He is breathing irregularly.

27

The sun, the songs, the breadcrumbs, the dove, the overturned basket, the long passage toward night: where, the old man wonders, have all the good fairies gone? He leads the way, pushing back the branches. The children follow, silent and frightened.

28

The boy pales and his heart pounds, but manfully he holds his ground. The witch writhes, her black rags fluttering, licking at the twisted branches. With a soft seductive cackle, she holds before him the burnished cherry-red heart of a dove. The boy licks his lips. She steps back. The glowing heart pulses gently, evenly, excitingly.

29

The good fairy has sparkling blue eyes and golden hair, a soft sweet mouth and gentle hands that caress and soothe. Gossamer wings sprout from her smooth back; from her flawless chest two firm breasts with tips bright as rubies.

30

The witch, holding the flaming pulsing heart out to the boy, steps back into the dark forest. The boy, in hesitation, follows. Back. Back. Swollen eyes aglitter, the witch draws the ruby heart close to her dark lean breast, then past her shoulder and away from the boy. Transfixed, he follows it, brushing by her. The witch's gnarled and bluish fingers claw at his poor garments, his pale red jacket and bluish-brown pants, surprising his soft young flesh.

31

The old man's shoulders are bowed earthward, his face is lined with sorrow, his neck bent forward with resignation, but his eyes glow like burning coals. He clutches his shredded shirt to his throat, stares intensely at the boy. The boy stands alone and trembling on the path, staring into the forest's terrible darkness. Shapes whisper and coil. The boy licks his lips, steps forward. A terrible shriek shreds the forest hush. The old man grimaces, pushes the whimpering girl away, strikes the boy.

No more breadcrumbs, no more pebbles, no more songs or flowers. The slap echoes through the terrible forest, doubles back on its own echoes, folding finally into a sound not unlike a whispering cackle.

The girl, weeping, kisses the struck boy and presses him close, shielding him from the tormented old man. The old man, taken aback, reaches out uncertainly, gently touches the girl's frail shoulder. She shakes his hand off—nearly a shudder—and shrinks toward the boy. The boy squares his shoulders, color returning to his face. The familiar creases of age and despair crinkle again the old man's face. His pale blue eyes mist over. He looks away. He leaves the children by the last light of day.

34

But the door! The door is shaped like a heart and is as red as a cherry, always half-open, whether lit by sun or moon, is sweeter than a sugar-plum, more enchanting than a peppermint stick. It is red as a poppy, red as an apple, red as a strawberry, red as a bloodstone, red as a rose. Oh, what a thing is the door of that house!

The children, alone in the strange black forest, huddle wretchedly under a great gnarled tree. Owls hoot and bats flick menacingly through the twisting branches. Strange shapes writhe and rustle before their weary eyes. They hold each other tight and, trembling, sing lullabyes, but they are not reassured.

The old man trudges heavily out of the black forest. His way is marked, not by breadcrumbs, but by dead doves, ghostly white in the empty night.

The girl prepares a mattress of leaves and flowers and pineneedles. The boy gathers branches to cover them, to hide them, to protect them. They make pillows of their poor garments. Bats screech as they work and owls blink down on their bodies, ghostly white, young, trembling. They creep under the branches, disappearing into the darkness.

38

Gloomily, the old man sits in the dark room and stares at the empty beds. The good fairy, though a mystery of the night, effuses her surroundings with a lustrous radiance. Is it the natural glow of her small nimble body or perhaps the star at the tip of her wand? Who can tell? Her gossamer wings flutter rapidly, and she floats, ruby-tipped breasts downward, legs dangling and dimpled knees bent slightly, glowing buttocks arched up in defiance of the night. How good she is! In the black empty room, the old man sighs and uses up a wish: he wishes his poor children well.

39

The children are nearing the gingerbread house. Passing under mint-drop trees, sticking their fingers in the cotton candy bushes, sampling the air as heady as lemonade, they skip along singing nursery songs. Nonsense songs about dappled horses and the slaying of dragons. Counting songs and idle riddles. They cross over rivulets of honey on gumdrop pebbles, picking the lollypops that grow as wild as daffodils.

40

The witch flicks and flutters through the blackened forest, her livid face twisted with hatred, her inscrutable condition. Her eyes burn like glowing coals and her black rags flap loosely. Her gnarled hands claw greedily at the branches, tangle in the night's webs, dig into tree trunks until the sap flows beneath her nails. Below, the boy and girl sleep an exhausted sleep. One ghostly white leg, with dimpled knee and soft round thigh, thrusts out from under the blanket of branches.

But wish again! Flowers and butterflies. Dense earthy greens seeping into the distance, flecked and streaked with midafternoon sunlight. Two children following an old man. They drop breadcrumbs, sing nursery songs. The old man walks leadenly. The boy's gesture is furtive. The girl—but it's no use, the doves will come again, there are no reasonable wishes.

The children approach the gingerbread house through a garden of candied fruits and all-day suckers, hopping along on flagstones of variegated wafers. They sample the gingerbread weatherboarding with its caramel coating, lick at the meringue on the windowsills, kiss each other's sweetened lips. The boy climbs up on the chocolate roof to break off a peppermint-stick chimney, comes sliding down into a rainbarrel full of vanilla pudding. The girl, reaching out to catch him in his fall, slips on a sugarplum and tumbles into a sticky rock garden of candied chestnuts. Laughing gaily, they lick each other clean. And how grand is the red-and-white striped chimney the boy holds up for her! how bright! how sweet! But the door: here they pause and catch their breath. It is heart-shaped and bloodstone-red, its burnished surface gleaming in the sunlight. Oh, what a thing is that door! Shining like a ruby, like hard cherry candy, and pulsing softly, radiantly. Yes, marvelous! delicious! insuperable! but beyond: what is that sound of black rags flapping?

*   *   *

QUESTIONS

1. What reasons can be suggested for the popularity of the Quest or Travel or Return to Home story? Why is it the commonest of mythic structures?
2. Contrast Homer's account of Odysseus' last days with the views of more modern poets. What indications does each view have of the time in which it was written?
3. Write a dialogue between the Hero and the Siren in terms of contemporary psychology, incorporating modern views of the proper roles of men and women toward each other.
4. What aspects of modern society make it difficult to have heroic action of the kind Homer's hero could achieve? Who do we think of as heroic? What sources of culture or art supply us with examples of high action?
5. What is the effect of the Journey on Eliot's Magi? What do the details of the travelers' difficulties add? Eliot seems to concentrate on the "realistic" details such a journey might have encountered. What is the effect of this attention? What kind of "voice" does the speaker have? What relationship does he have to other people? Explain the relationship between Birth and Death in the poem.
6. Yeats's poem begins with the evocation of the archetypal unconscious, with a vision that has "appeared" to the poet. What is the most striking aspect of this vision? What is most important about the appearance of the Magi? What is important about the "blue sky" where they are

seen? What aspects of the Biblical story are given emphasis? Which are omitted or altered?

7. What similarity exists between the poem by Sylvia Plath and the poems of Yeats and Eliot? What evidence is there that she knows these earlier works? What images represent the "high" and the "low" aspects of the story?

8. What is the effect of Garrett's connection of his own experience as a child with the Magi's experience? Does this more casual treatment of the story affect its seriousness? Why or why not?

9. Hardy's poem has no wise men, but draws instead on another folk tale of the Nativity. Both he and Garrett point to a more secular interpretation that "modernity" makes necessary. What difficulties offer themselves in these attempts to talk about old stories in new ways? To what extent can each of them properly be called "Christian"?

10. What archetypal elements are there in Coover's story? What are the particular reasons for his interest in this tale? What accounts for the longevity of the traditional story?

11. Discuss the points at which this story depends upon or changes the emphasis of the traditional tale. What aspects are added to and given greater weight and explicitness?

12. What do you think the theme of this story is? What passages support your position?

13. What is the meaning of the dominant images in the story: the dove, the dark woods, the innocent boy and girl, the old man, the witch?

14. What other fairy tales deal with the same theme as this tale?

15. Explain the ways in which fairy tales are true stories.

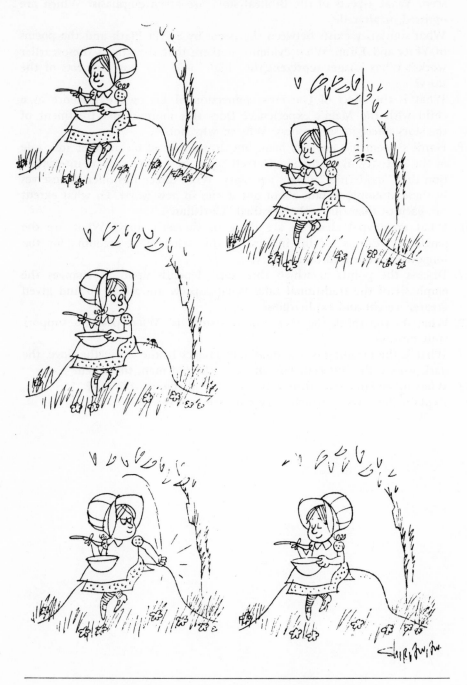

Reprinted by permission of the artist, Vahan Shirvanian

PART III

Voyages and Quests: The Landscape of the Mind

Voyages and Quests: The Landscape of the Mind

The *Odyssey*, the story of the Magi, and the Journey into the Forest are travel stories, Quest Tales, in which the protagonists travel through a land- or seascape, meeting adventures in different places. We need, therefore, to examine the countryside along the way, to observe that between Troy and Ithaca, between the meadow and the forest, between the Setting Out and the End, many things happen. We must learn to pay attention to geography, to the mountains, roads, islands, valleys, forests, woods, meadows through which or in which the journey occurs.

A journey is a process, taking place in time, locating and demonstrating cause and effect. A writer chooses a journey or quest form when he recognizes that growth, change, new insight, or any change in a state of mind worthy of recording in a serious work must be earned, that to be interesting to others, the means of its achievement and accomplishment must be demonstrated. Unless the writer shows us how he came to where he is, his assertion that he has arrived may not mean very much. Modern sensibility, as we have already seen, carries the notion that, to a degree, each man's journey is his private odyssey and that its account offers a particular, special story. We will not be surprised to see that the voyage or quest form has been used widely in the 19th and 20th centuries and that some of the most significant works of this period take this form: Melville's *Moby Dick*, Joyce's *Ulysses*, Conrad's *Heart of Darkness*.

We come, therefore, to another illustration of the need for symbolic, nonliteral language—the fact that we recognize the process, the journey, as a spiritual or psychological one; it is the growth or decline of a mind. It cannot be represented literally, and a resort to abstractions (Mind, Soul, Despair, Depression, Id, Ego, Identity Crisis, etc.) does not make a very good story. The solution is to employ figurative language in which both the journey and the incidents on the way represent psychological and emotional states of mind. To read such a work, we must learn to translate the events, encounters, and circumstances of the traveler—who he meets and where, the time of day, season of the year, condition of the weather—into interior terms. Finally, if we can learn the patterns of the geography, this landscape of the mind, we will have grasped an important key to modern literature, and a device by which we may better understand the psychological and spiritual events of our time.

Caves and Meadows

Keats, like Coleridge in the selection to follow, employs the strategy of a pseudo-antique form, the medieval ballad, in order to direct our attention away from the literal to the psychological and irrational. Keats's knight is the first of a series of modern travelers (an uneasy rider) whose direction on the road is not clear, who are stuck on a "cold hill side."

LA BELLE DAME SANS MERCI

John Keats (1795–1821)

O, what can ail thee, knight-at-arms,
    Alone and palely loitering?
The sedge has wither'd from the lake,
    And no birds sing.

O, what can ail thee, knight-at-arms,   5
    So haggard and so woe-begone?
The squirrel's granary is full,
    And the harvest's done.

I see a lily on thy brow,
    With anguish moist and fever dew,   10
And on thy cheeks a fading rose
    Fast withereth too.

I met a lady in the meads,
    Full beautiful—a faery's child,
Her hair was long, her foot was light,   15
    And her eyes were wild.

I made a garland for her head,
    And bracelets too, and fragrant zone;
She look'd at me as she did love,
    And made sweet moan.   20

I set her on my pacing steed,
    And nothing else saw all day long,
For sidelong would she bend and sing
    A faery's song.

She found me roots of relish sweet,   25
   And honey wild, and manna dew,
And sure in language strange she said
   "I love thee true."

She took me to her elfin grot,
   And there she wept and sigh'd full sore,   30
And there I shut her wild wild eyes
   With kisses four.

And there she lulled me asleep,
   And there I dream'd—Ah! woe betide!
The latest dream I ever dream'd   35
   On the cold hill side.

I saw pale kings and princes too,
   Pale warriors, death-pale were they all;
They cried, "La Belle Dame sans Merci
   Hath thee in thrall!"   40

I saw their starved lips in the gloam,
   With horrid warning gaped wide,
And I awoke, and found me here,
   On the cold hill's side.

And this is why I sojourn here,   45
   Alone and palely loitering,
Though the sedge is wither'd from the lake,
   And no birds sing.

*   *   *

Seas and Snakes

    The voyage of the Mariner from his simple home community through polar regions to his lonely encounter on a lonely sea is the best known, and in some ways, the best of all Psychological Quest poems. It has seemed rich and inexhaustible in symbolic implication and in the insights it has to offer about the processes of spiritual growth. That we are to take the poem's subject to be the invisible—spiritual and psychological events—rather than a sailor's log book is made clear by the Latin motto that Coleridge put at the beginning of the poem. It is a passage by Thomas Burnet, an Anglican clergyman, written in 1692.

I can easily believe that there are more invisible things in the universe than visible. But who can tell us their categories and ranks and relationships and particular features and activities? What do they do? Where do they live? The human mind has always reached toward these things, but has never touched them. I do not doubt, however, that it is sometimes worthwhile to consider in the mind, as if in a picture, the idea of a greater and better world; otherwise, the mind, too accustomed to small daily aspects of life may become too small, and subsist entirely on trivial thoughts. But in the meantime, we must be vigilant for truth and observe proper proportions, that we may distinguish the certain from the uncertain, day from night.

THE RIME OF THE ANCIENT MARINER

Samuel Taylor Coleridge (1772–1834)

ARGUMENT

How a ship having passed the Line was driven by storms to the cold Country towards the South Pole; and how thence she made her course to the tropical Latitude of the Great Pacific Ocean; and of the strange things that befell; and in what manner the Ancient Mariner came back to his own Country.

I

An ancient Mariner meeteth three Gallants bidden to a wedding-feast, and detaineth one.

It is an ancient Mariner,
And he stoppeth one of three.
'By thy long grey beard and glittering eye,
Now wherefore stopp'st thou me?

The Bridegroom's doors are opened wide,   5
And I am next of kin;
The guests are met, the feast is set:
May'st hear the merry din.'

He holds him with his skinny hand,
'There was a ship,' quoth he.   10
'Hold off! unhand me, grey-beard loon!'
Eftsoons his hand dropt he.

The Wedding-Guest is spellbound by the eye of the old seafaring man, and constrained to hear his tale.

He holds him with his glittering eye—
The Wedding-Guest stood still,
And listens like a three years' child: 15
The Mariner hath his will.

The Wedding-Guest sat on a stone:
He cannot choose but hear;
And thus spake on that ancient man,
The bright-eyed Mariner.   20

'The ship was cheered, the harbour cleared,
Merrily did we drop
Below the kirk, below the hill,
Below the lighthouse top.

<table>
<tr><td>

The Mariner tells
how the ship
sailed southward
with a good wind
and fair weather,
till it reached the
line.

</td><td>

The Sun came up upon the left,   25
Out of the sea came he!
And he shone bright, and on the right
Went down into the sea.

</td></tr>
</table>

Higher and higher every day,
Till over the mast at noon—'   30
The Wedding-Guest here beat his breast,
For he heard the loud bassoon.

<table>
<tr><td>

The Wedding-
Guest heareth the
bridal music; but
the Mariner con-
tinueth his tale.

</td><td>

The bride hath paced into the hall,
Red as a rose is she;
Nodding their heads before her goes   35
The merry minstrelsy.

</td></tr>
</table>

The Wedding-Guest he beat his breast,
Yet he cannot choose but hear;
And thus spake on that ancient man,
The bright-eyed Mariner.   40

<table>
<tr><td>

The ship drawn
by a storm toward
the south pole.

</td><td>

'And now the STORM-BLAST came, and he
Was tyrannous and strong:
He struck with his o'ertaking wings,
And chased us south along.

</td></tr>
</table>

<table>
<tr><td>

The land of ice,
and of fearful
sounds where no
living thing was
to be seen.

</td><td>

With sloping masts and dipping prow,   45
As who pursued with yell and blow
Still treads the shadow of his foe,
And forward bends his head,
The ship drove fast, loud roared the blast,
And southward aye we fled.   50

</td></tr>
</table>

And now there came both mist and snow,
And it grew wondrous cold:

And ice, mast-high, came floating by,
As green as emerald.

And through the drifts the snowy clifts   55
Did send a dismal sheen:
Nor shapes of men nor beasts we ken—
The ice was all between.

The ice was here, the ice was there,
The ice was all around: 60
It cracked and growled, and roared and howled,
Like noises in a swound!°

Till a great sea-bird, called the Albatross, came through the snow-fog, and was received with great joy and hospitality.

At length did cross an Albatross,
Thorough the fog it came;
As if it had been a Christian soul,   65
We hailed it in God's name.

It ate the food it ne'er had eat,
and round and round it flew,
The ice did split with a thunder-fit;
The helmsman steered us through!   70

And lo! the Albatross proveth a bird of good omen, and followeth the ship as it returned northward through fog and floating ice.

And a good south wind sprung up behind;
The Albatross did follow,
And every day, for food or play,
Came to the mariners' hollo!

In mist or cloud, on mast or shroud,   75
It perched for vespers nine;
Whiles all the night, through fog-smoke white,
Glimmered the white Moon-shine.'

The ancient Mariner inhospitably killeth the pious bird of good omen.

'God save thee, ancient Mariner!
From the fiends, that plague thee thus!—   80
Why look'st thou so?'—With my cross-bow
I shot the ALBATROSS.'

II

'The Sun now rose upon the right:
Out of the sea came he,

°*swound:* swoon

Still hid in mist, and on the left   85
Went down into the sea.

And the good south wind still blew behind,
But no sweet bird did follow,
Nor any day for food or play
Came to the mariners' hollo!   90

His shipmates cry
out against the
ancient Mariner
for killing the
bird of good luck.

And I had done a hellish thing,
And it would work 'em woe:
For all averred, I had killed the bird
That made the breeze to blow.
Ah wretch! said they, the bird to slay,   95
That made the breeze to blow!

But when the fog
cleared off, they
justify the same,
and thus make
themselves accom-
plices in the
crime.

Nor dim nor red, like God's own head,
The glorious Sun uprist:
Then all averred, I had killed the bird
That brought the fog and mist.   100
'Twas right, said they, such birds to slay,
That bring the fog and mist.

The fair breeze
continues; the
ship enters the
Pacific Ocean, and
sails northward,
even till it reaches
the line.

The fair breeze blew, the white foam flew,
The furrow followed free;
We were the first that ever burst   105
Into that silent sea.

Down dropt the breeze, the sails dropt down,
'Twas sad as sad could be;
And we did speak only to break
The silence of the sea!   110

The ship hath
been suddenly be-
calmed.

All in a hot and copper sky,
The bloody Sun, at noon,
Right up above the mast did stand,
No bigger than the Moon.

Day after day, day after day,   115
We stuck, nor breath nor motion;
As idle as a painted ship
Upon a painted ocean.

And the Albatross begins to be avenged.

Water, water, every where,
And all the boards did shrink; 120
Water, water, every where,
Nor any drop to drink.

The very deep did rot: O Christ!
That ever this should be!
Yea, slimy things did crawl with legs 125
Upon the slimy sea.

About, about, in reel and rout
The death-fires danced at night;
The water, like a witch's oils,
Burnt green, and blue and white. 130

And some in dreams assuréd were
Of the Spirit that plagued us so;
Nine fathom deep he had followed us
From the land of mist and snow.

A Spirit had followed them; one of the invisible inhabitants of this planet, neither departed souls nor angels; concerning whom the learned Jew, Josephus, and the Platonic Constantinopolitan, Michael Psellus, may be consulted. They are very numerous, and there is no climate or element without one or more. The shipmates, in their sore distress, would fain throw the whole guilt on the ancient Mariner: in sign whereof they hang the dead seabird round his neck.

And every tongue, through utter drought, 135
Was withered at the root;
We could not speak, no more than if
We had been choked with soot.

Ah! well a-day! what evil looks
Had I from old and young! 140
Instead of the cross, the Albatross
About my neck was hung.'

III

The ancient Mariner beholdeth a sign in the element afar off.

'There passed a weary time. Each throat
Was parched, and glazed each eye.
A weary time! a weary time! 145
How glazed each weary eye,
When looking westward, I beheld
A something in the sky.

At first it seemed a little speck,
And then it seemed a mist; 150

It moved and moved, and took at last
A certain shape, I wist.°

A speck, a mist, a shape, I wist!
And still it neared and neared:
As if it dodged a water-sprite,   155
It plunged and tacked and veered.

At its nearer approach, it seemeth him to be a ship; and at a dear ransom he freeth his speech from the bonds of thirst. A flash of joy;

With throats unslaked, with black lips baked,
We could nor laugh nor wail;
Through utter drought all dumb we stood!
I bit my arm, I sucked the blood,   160
And cried, "A sail! a sail!"

With throats unslaked, with black lips baked,
Agape they heard me call:
Gramercy! they for joy did grin,
And all at once their breath drew in,   165
As they were drinking all.

And horror follows. For can it be a ship that comes onward without wind or tide?

"See! see!" (I cried) "she tacks no more!
Hither to work us weal;°
Without a breeze, without a tide,
She steadies with upright keel!"   170

The western wave was all a-flame.
The day was well nigh done!
Almost upon the western wave
Rested the broad bright Sun;
When that strange shape drove suddenly   175
Betwixt us and the Sun.

It seemeth him but the skeleton of a ship.

And straight the Sun was flecked with bars,
(Heaven's Mother send us grace!)
As if through a dungeon-grate he peered
With broad and burning face.   180

Alas! (thought I, and my heart beat loud)
How fast she nears and nears!
Are those *her* sails that glance in the Sun,
Like restless gossameres?

°*wist:* knew   °*weal:* good

And its ribs are seen as bars on the face of the setting sun.

Are those *her* ribs through which the Sun   185
Did peer, as through a grate?
And is that Woman all her crew?
Is that a DEATH? and are there two?
Is DEATH that woman's mate?

The Spectre-Woman and her Death-mate, and no other on board the skeleton-ship. Like vessel, like crew!

Her lips were red, *her* looks were free,   190
Her locks were yellow as gold:
Her skin was as white as leprosy,
The Night-mare LIFE-IN-DEATH was she,
Who thicks man's blood with cold.

Death and Life-in-Death have diced for the ship's crew, and she (the latter) winneth the ancient Mariner.

The naked hulk alongside came,   195
And the twain were casting dice;
"The game is done! I've won! I've won!"
Quoth she, and whistles thrice.

The Sun's rim dips; the stars rush out:
At one stride comes the dark;   200
With far-heard whisper, o'er the sea,
Off shot the spectre-bark.

We listened and looked sideways up!
Fear at my heart, as at a cup,
My life-blood seemed to sip!   205
No twilight within the courts of the sun.
The stars were dim, and thick the night,
The steersman's face by his lamp gleamed white;
From the sails the dew did drip—
Till clomb above the eastern bar
At the rising of the moon
The hornéd Moon, with one bright star   210
Within the nether tip.°

One after another, His shipmates drop down dead.

One after one, by the star-dogged Moon,
Too quick for groan or sigh,
Each turned his face with a ghastly pang,
And cursed me with his eye.   215

Four times fifty living men,
(And I heard nor sigh nor groan)
With heavy thump, a lifeless lump,
They dropped down one by one.

°*Moon . . . tip:* "It is a common superstition among sailors that something evil is about to happen whenever a star dogs the moon" [Coleridge's note].

But Life-in-Death begins her work on the ancient Mariner.	The souls did from their bodies fly,— 220 They fled to bliss or woe! And every soul, it passed me by, Like the whizz of my cross-bow!'

IV

The Wedding-Guest feareth that a spirit is talking to him;	'I fear thee, ancient Mariner! I fear thy skinny hand! 225 And thou art long, and lank, and brown, As is the ribbed sea-sand.

I fear thee and thy glittering eye,
And thy skinny hand, so brown.'—

But the ancient Mariner assureth him of his bodily life, and proceedeth to relate his horrible penance.	'Fear not, fear not, thou Wedding-Guest! 230 This body dropt not down.

Alone, alone, all, all alone,
Alone on a wide wide sea!
And never a saint took pity on
My soul in agony.   235

He despiseth the creatures of the calm,	The many men, so beautiful! And they all dead did lie: And a thousand thousand slimy things Lived on; and so did I.

And envieth that they should live, and so many be dead.	I looked upon the rotting sea, 240 And drew my eyes away; I looked upon the rotting deck, And there the dead men lay.

I looked to heaven, and tried to pray;
But or ever a prayer had gusht,   245
A wicked whisper came, and made
My heart as dry as dust.

I closed my lids, and kept them close,
And the balls like pulses beat;
For the sky and the sea, and the sea and the sky   250
Lay like a load on my weary eye,
And the dead were at my feet.

But the curse liv-
eth for him in the
eye of the dead
men.
The cold sweat melted from their limbs,
Nor rot nor reek did they:
The look with which they looked on me   255
Had never passed away.

An orphan's curse would drag to hell
A spirit from on high;
But oh! more horrible than that
Is the curse in a dead man's eye!   260
Seven days, seven nights, I saw that curse,
And yet I could not die.

The moving Moon went up the sky,
And no where did abide:
In his loneliness
and fixedness he
yearneth towards
the journeying
moon, and the
stars that still so-
journ, yet still
move onward;
and every where
the blue sky be-
longs to them,
and is their ap-
pointed rest, and their native country and their own natural homes, which they
enter unannounced, as lords that are certainly expected and yet there is a silent
joy at their arrival.
By the light of the
moon he behold-
eth God's crea-
tures of the great
calm.
Softly she was going up,
And a star or two beside—   265

Her beams bemocked the sultry main,
Like April hoar-frost spread;
But where the ship's huge shadow lay,
The charméd water burnt alway
A still and awful red.   270

Beyond the shadow of the ship,
I watched the water-snakes:
They moved in tracks of shining white,
And when they reared, the elfish light   275
Fell off in hoary flakes.

Within the shadow of the ship
I watched their rich attire:
Blue, glossy green, and velvet black,
They coiled and swam; and every track   280
Was a flash of golden fire.

O happy living things! no tongue
Their beauty might declare:
A spring of love gushed from my heart,
And I blessed them unaware: 285
Sure my kind saint took pity on me,
And I blessed them unaware.

The spell begins to break.

The self-same moment I could pray;
And from my neck so free
The Albatross fell off, and sank   290
Like lead into the sea.'

V

'Oh sleep! it is a gentle thing.
Beloved from pole to pole!
To Mary Queen the praise be given!
She sent the gentle sleep from Heaven,   295
That slid into my soul.

By grace of the holy Mother, the ancient Mariner is refreshed with rain.

The silly buckets on the deck,
That had so long remained,
I dreamt that they were filled with dew;
And when I awoke, it rained.   300

My lips were wet, my throat was cold,
My garments all were dank;
Sure I had drunken in my dreams,
And still my body drank.

I moved, and could not feel my limbs: 305
I was so light—almost
I thought that I had died in sleep,
And was a blessèd ghost.

He heareth sounds and seeth strange sights and commotions in the sky and the element.

And soon I heard a roaring wind:
It did not come anear;   310
But with its sound it shook the sails,
That were so thin and sere.

The upper air burst into life!
And a hundred fire-flags sheen,
To and fro they were hurried about!   315
And to and fro, and in and out,
The wan stars danced between.

And the coming wind did roar more loud,
And the sails did sigh like sedge;
And the rain poured down from one black cloud; 320
The Moon was at its edge.

The thick black cloud was cleft, and still
The Moon was at its side:
Like waters shot from some high crag,
The lightning fell with never a jag,   325
A river steep and wide.

The bodies of the ship's crew are inspired, and the ship moves on.

The loud wind never reached the ship,
Yet now the ship moved on!
Beneath the lightning and the Moon
The dead men gave a groan.   330

They groaned, they stirred, they all uprose,
Nor spake, nor moved their eyes;
It had been strange, even in a dream,
To have seen those dead men rise.

The helmsman steered, the ship moved on;   335
Yet never a breeze up-blew;
The mariners all 'gan work the ropes,
Where they were wont to do;
They raised their limbs like lifeless tools—
We were a ghastly crew.   340

The body of my brother's son
Stood by me, knee to knee:
The body and I pulled at one rope,
But he said nought to me.'

'I fear thee, ancient Mariner!'   345
'Be calm, thou Wedding-Guest!
'Twas not those souls that fled in pain,

But not by the souls of the men, nor by demons of earth or middle air, but by a blessed troop of angelic spirits, sent down by the invocation of the guardian saint.

Which to their corses came again,
But a troop of spirits blest:

For when it dawned—they dropped their arms,   350
And clustered round the mast;
Sweet sounds rose slowly through their mouths,
And from their bodies passed.

Around, around, flew each sweet sound,
Then darted to the Sun;   355
Slowly the sounds came back again,
Now mixed, now one by one.

Sometimes a-dropping from the sky
I heard the sky-lark sing;
Sometimes all little birds that are,
How they seemed to fill the sea and air
With their sweet jargoning!

And now 'twas like all instruments,
Now like a lonely flute;
And now it is an angel's song,
That makes the heavens be mute.

It ceased; yet still the sails made on
A pleasant noise till noon,
A noise like of a hidden brook
In the leafy month of June,
That to the sleeping woods all night
Singeth a quiet tune.

Till noon we quietly sailed on,
Yet never a breeze did breathe:
Slowly and smoothly went the ship,
Moved onward from beneath.

The lonesome Spirit from the south pole carries on the ship as far as the line, in obedience to the angelic troop, but still requireth vengeance.

Under the keel nine fathom deep,
From the land of mist and snow,
The spirit slid: and it was he
That made the ship to go.
The sails at noon left off their tune,
And the ship stood still also.

The Sun, right up above the mast,
Had fixed her to the ocean:
But in a minute she 'gan stir,
With a short uneasy motion—
Backwards and forwards half her length
With a short uneasy motion.

Then like a pawing horse let go,
She made a sudden bound:
It flung the blood into my head,
And I fell down in a swound.

How long in that same fit I lay,
I have not to declare;

But ere my living life returned,   395
I heard and in my soul discerned
Two voices in the air.

"Is it he?" quoth one, "Is this the man?
By him who died on cross,
With his cruel bow he laid full low   400
The harmless Albatross.

The spirit who bideth by himself
In the land of mist and snow,
He loved the bird that loved the man
Who shot him with his bow."   405

The other was a softer voice,
As soft as honey-dew:
Quoth he, "The man hath penance done,
And penance more will do." '

VI

First Voice

' "But tell me, tell me! speak again,   410
Thy soft response renewing—
What makes that ship drive on so fast?
What is the ocean doing?"

Second Voice

"Still as a slave before his lord,
The ocean hath no blast;   415
His great bright eye most silently
Up to the Moon is cast—

If he may know which way to go;
For she guides him smooth or grim.
See, brother, see! how graciously
She looketh down on him."   420

First Voice

"But why drives on that ship so fast,
Without or wave or wind?"

"The air is cut away before,
And closes from behind.   425

Fly, brother, fly! more high, more high!
Or we shall be belated:
For slow and slow that ship will go,
When the Mariner's trance is abated."

The supernatural motion is retarded; the Mariner awakes and his penance begins anew.

I woke, and we were sailing on   430
As in a gentle weather:
'Twas night, calm night, the moon was high;
The dead men stood together.

All stood together on the deck,
For a charnel-dungeon fitter: 435
All fixed on me their stony eyes,
That in the Moon did glitter.

The pang, the curse, with which they died,
Had never passed away:
I could not draw my eyes from theirs,   440
Nor turn them up to pray.

The curse is finally expiated.

And now this spell was snapt: once more
I viewed the ocean green,
And looked far forth, yet little saw
Of what had else been seen—   445

Like one, that on a lonesome road
Doth walk in fear and dread,
And having once turned round walks on,
And turns no more his head;
Because he knows, a frightful fiend   450
Doth close behind him tread.

But soon there breathed a wind on me,
Nor sound nor motion made:
Its path was not upon the sea,
In ripple or in shade.   455

It raised my hair, it fanned my cheek
Like a meadow-gale of spring—

It mingled strangely with my fears,
Yet it felt like a welcoming.

Swiftly, swiftly flew the ship,   460
Yet she sailed softly too:
Sweetly, sweetly blew the breeze—
On me alone it blew.

And the ancient Mariner beholdeth his native country.

Oh! dream of joy! is this indeed
The light-house top I see?   465
Is this the hill? is this the kirk?
Is this mine own countree?

We drifted o'er the harbour-bar,
And I with sobs did pray—
O let me be awake, my God!   470
Or let me sleep alway.

The harbour-bay was clear as glass,
So smoothly it was strewn!
And on the bay the moonlight lay,
And the shadow of the Moon.   475

The rock shone bright, the kirk no less,
That stands above the rock:
The moonlight steeped in silentness
The steady weathercock.

The angelic spirits leave the dead bodies.

And the bay was white with silent light,   480
Till rising from the same,
Full many shapes, that shadows were,
In crimson colours came.

And appear in their own forms of light.

A little distance from the prow
Those crimson shadows were: 485
I turned my eyes upon the deck—
Oh, Christ! what saw I there!

Each corse lay flat, lifeless and flat,
And, by the holy rood!°
A man all light, a seraph-man,   490
On every corse there stood.

°*rood:* cross

This seraph-band, each waved his hand:
It was a heavenly sight!
They stood as signals to the land,
Each one a lovely light;   495

This seraph-band, each waved his hand,
No voice did they impart—
No voice; but oh! the silence sank
Like music on my heart.

But soon I heard the dash of oars,   500
I heard the Pilot's cheer;
My head was turned perforce away
And I saw a boat appear.

The Pilot and the Pilot's boy,
I heard them coming fast: 505
Dear Lord in Heaven! it was a joy
The dead men could not blast.

I saw a third—I heard his voice:
It is the Hermit good!
He singeth loud his godly hymns   510
That he makes in the wood.
He'll shrieve my soul, he'll wash away
The Albatross's blood.'

VII

The Hermit of the
wood,

'This Hermit good lives in that wood
Which slopes down to the sea.   515
How loudly his sweet voice he rears!
He loves to talk with marineres
That come from a far countree.

He kneels at morn, and noon, and eve—
He hath a cushion plump: 520
It is the moss that wholly hides
The rotted old oak-stump.

The skiff-boat neared: I heard them talk,
"Why, this is strange, I trow!
Where are those lights so many and fair,   525
That signal made but now?"

"Strange, by my faith!" the Hermit said—
"And they answered not our cheer!
The planks looked warped! and see those sails,
How thin they are and sere!   530
I never saw aught like to them,
Unless perchance it were

Brown skeletons of leaves that lag
My forest-brook along;
When the ivy-tod is heavy with snow,   535
And the owlet whoops to the wolf below,
That eats the she-wolf's young."

"Dear Lord! it hath a fiendish look—
(The Pilot made reply)
"I am a-feared"—"Push on, push on!"   540
Said the Hermit cheerily.

The boat came closer to the ship,
But I nor spake nor stirred;
The boat came close beneath the ship,
And straight a sound was heard.   545

Under the water it rumbled on,
Still louder and more dread:
It reached the ship, it split the bay;
The ship went down like lead.

Stunned by that loud and dreadful sound,   550
Which sky and ocean smote,
Like one that hath been seven days drowned
My body lay afloat;
The ancient Mari-
ner is saved in the
pilot's boat.
But swift as dreams, myself I found
Within the Pilot's boat.   555

Upon the whirl, where sank the ship,
The boat spun round and round;
And all was still, save that the hill
Was telling of the sound.

I moved my lips—the Pilot shrieked   560
And fell down in a fit;
The holy hermit raised his eyes,
And prayed where he did sit.

I took the oars: the Pilot's boy,
Who now doth crazy go,   565
Laughed loud and long, and all the while
His eyes went to and fro.
"Ha! ha!" quoth he, "full plain I see,
The Devil knows how to row."

And now, all in my own countree,   570
I stood on the firm land!
The Hermit stepped forth from the boat,
And scarcely he could stand.

"O shrieve me, shrieve me, holy man!"
The Hermit crossed his brow.   575
"Say quick," quoth he, "I bid thee say—
What manner of man art thou?"

Forthwith this frame of mine was wrenched
With a woful agony,
Which forced me to begin my tale;   580
And then it left me free.

Since then, at an uncertain hour,
That agony returns:
And till my ghastly tale is told,
This heart within me burns.   585

I pass, like night, from land to land;
I have strange power of speech;
That moment that his face I see,
I know the man that must hear me:
To him my tale I teach.   590

What loud uproar bursts from that door!
The wedding-guests are there:
But in the garden-bower the bride
And bride-maids singing are:
And hark the little vesper bell,   595
Which biddeth me to prayer!

O Wedding-Guest! this soul hath been
Alone on a wide wide sea:
So lonely 'twas, that God himself
Scarce seeméd there to be.   600

O sweeter than the marriage-feast,
'Tis sweeter far to me,
To walk together to the kirk
With a goodly company!—

To walk together to the kirk,   605
And all together pray,
While each to his great Father bends,
Old men, and babes, and loving friends
And youths and maidens gay!

Farewell, farewell! but this I tell   610
To thee, thou Wedding-Guest!

And to teach, by his own example, love and reverence to all things that God made and loveth.

He prayeth well, who loveth well
Both man and bird and beast.

He prayeth best, who loveth best
All things both great and small;   615
For the dear God who loveth us,
He made and loveth all.'

The Mariner, whose eye is bright,
Whose beard with age is hoar,
Is gone: and now the Wedding-Guest   620
Turned from the bridegroom's door.

He went like one that hath been stunned,
And is of sense forlorn:
A sadder and a wiser man,
He rose the morrow morn.   625

*   *   *

Mountains and the Moon

Wordsworth gave his long autobiographical poem *The Prelude* the subtitle "The Growth of a Poet's Mind." In both the passages given here, he makes a specific connection between an outward event in his life and the inner psychological and spiritual meaning it represented. It is as if Wordsworth, less at ease with symbolic discourse than Keats and Coleridge, feels a need to "explain" more fully, to draw a more explicit connection between event and meaning. In the first passage, Wordsworth describes how, as he rows his stolen boat away from the shore, his changing angle of vision causes the closer ridge of the mountain to recede to reveal the summit of higher peaks behind. The experience colors his state of mind "for many days," though we are left to wonder as to the specific nature of that influence. In the second passage, beginning at line 63, he makes a specific "interpretation."

From THE PRELUDE

William Wordsworth (1770–1850)

Book First: A HUGE PEAK

Dust as we are, the immortal spirit grows   340
Like harmony in music; there is a dark
Inscrutable workmanship that reconciles
Discordant elements, makes them cling together
In one society. How strange that all
The terrors, pains, and early miseries,   345
Regrets, vexations, lassitudes interfused
Within my mind, should e'er have borne a part,
And that a needful part, in making up
The calm existence that is mine when I
Am worthy of myself! Praise to the end!   350
Thanks to the means which Nature deigned to employ;
Whether her fearless visiting, or those
That came with soft alarm, like hurtless light
Opening the peaceful clouds; or she may use
Severer interventions, ministry   355
More palpable, as best might suit her aim.

One summer evening (led by her)° I found
A little boat tied to a willow tree
Within a rocky cave, its usual home.
Straight I unloosed her chain, and stepping in   360
Pushed from the shore. It was an act of stealth
And troubled pleasure, nor without the voice
Of mountain-echoes did my boat move on;
Leaving behind her still, on either side,
Small circles glittering idly in the moon,   365
Until they melted all into one track
Of sparkling light. But now, like one who rows,

°*her:* Nature

Proud of his skill, to reach a chosen point
With an unswerving line, I fixed my view
Upon the summit of a craggy ridge,   370
The horizon's utmost boundary; for above
Was nothing but the stars and the grey sky.
She was an elfin pinnace; lustily
I dipped my oars into the silent lake,
And, as I rose upon the stroke, my boat   375
Went heaving through the water like a swan;
When, from behind that craggy steep till then
The horizon's bound, a huge peak, black and huge,
As if with voluntary power instinct
Upreared its head. I struck and struck again,   380
And growing still in stature the grim shape
Towered up between me and the stars, and still,
For so it seemed, with purpose of its own
And measured motion like a living thing,
Strode after me. With trembling oars I turned,   385
And through the silent water stole my way
Back to the covert of the willow tree;
There in her mooring-place I left my bark,—
And through the meadows homeward went, in grave
And serious mood; but after I had seen   390
That spectacle, for many days, my brain
Worked with a dim and undetermined sense
Of unknown modes of being; o'er my thoughts
There hung a darkness, call it solitude
Or blank desertion. No familiar shapes   395
Remained, no pleasant images of trees,
Of sea or sky, no colours of green fields;
But huge and mighty forms, that do not live
Like living men, moved slowly through the mind
By day, and were a trouble to my dreams.   400

Book Fourteenth: MOUNT SNOWDON

In one of those excursions (may they ne'er
Fade from remembrance!) through the Northern tracts
Of Cambria° ranging with a youthful friend,
I left Bethgelert's° huts at couching-time,
And westward took my way, to see the sun   5
Rise, from the top of Snowdon.° To the door

°*Cambria:* Wales   °*Bethgelert:* a village   °*Snowdon:* the highest mountain in
England and Wales

Of a rude cottage at the mountain's base
We came, and roused the shepherd who attends
The adventurous stranger's steps, a trusty guide;
Then, cheered by short refreshment, sallied forth.   10

It was a close, warm, breezeless summer night,
Wan, dull, and glaring, with a dripping fog
Low-hung and thick that covered all the sky;
But, undiscouraged, we began to climb
The mountain-side. The mist soon girt us round,   15
And, after ordinary travellers' talk
With our conductor, pensively we sank
Each into commerce with his private thoughts:
Thus did we breast the ascent, and by myself
Was nothing either seen or heard that checked   20
Those musings or diverted, save that once
The shepherd's lurcher,° who, among the crags,
Had to his joy unearthed a hedgehog, teased
His coiled-up prey with barkings turbulent.
This small adventure, for even such it seemed   25
In that wild place and at the dead of night,
Being over and forgotten, on we wound
In silence as before. With forehead bent
Earthward, as if in opposition set
Against an enemy, I panted up   30
With eager pace, and no less eager thoughts.
Thus might we wear a midnight hour away,
Ascending at loose distance each from each,
And I, as chanced, the foremost of the band;
When at my feet the ground appeared to brighten,   35
And with a step or two seemed brighter still;
Nor was time given to ask or learn the cause,
For instantly a light upon the turf
Fell like a flash, and lo! as I looked up
The Moon hung naked in a firmament   40
Of azure without cloud, and at my feet
Rested a silent sea of hoary mist.
A hundred hills their dusky backs upheaved
All over this still ocean; and beyond,
Far, far beyond, the solid vapours stretched,   45
In headlands, tongues, and promontory shapes,
Into the main Atlantic, that appeared

°*lurcher:* hunting dog

To dwindle, and give up his majesty,
Usurped upon far as the sight could reach.
Not so the ethereal vault; encroachment none   50
Was there, nor loss; only the inferior stars
Had disappeared, or shed a fainter light
In the clear presence of the full-orbed Moon,
Who, from her sovereign elevation, gazed
Upon the billowy ocean, as it lay   55
All meek and silent, save that through a rift—
Not distant from the shore whereon we stood,
A fixed, abysmal, gloomy, breathing-place—
Mounted the roar of waters, torrents, streams
Innumerable, roaring with one voice!   60
Heard over earth and sea, and, in that hour,
For so it seemed, felt by the starry heavens.

   When into air had partially dissolved
That vision, given to spirits of the night
And three chance human wanderers, in calm thought   65
Reflected, it appeared to me the type
Of a majestic intellect, its acts
And its possessions, what it has and craves,
What in itself it is, and would become.
There I beheld the emblem of a mind   70
That feeds upon infinity, that broods
Over the dark abyss, intent to hear
Its voices issuing forth to silent light
In one continuous stream; a mind sustained   *The mind of god*
By recognitions of transcendent power,   75   *is discovered in all*
In sense conducting to ideal form,   *things.*
In soul of more than mortal privilege.
One function, above all, of such a mind
Had Nature shadowed there, by putting forth,
'Mid circumstances awful and sublime,   80
That mutual domination which she loves
To exert upon the face of outward things,
So moulded, joined, abstracted, so endowed
With interchangeable supremacy,
That men, least sensitive, see, hear, perceive,   85
And cannot choose but feel.

Geography of
the mind

The archetype of
the self

*   *   *

QUESTIONS

1. Why is it difficult to make literal sense of *La Belle Dame sans Merci*? What does Keats do to emphasize the mysterious and the irrational?

2. What changes occur in the knight's state of mind? What are some of the possible meanings of his Encounter with La Belle Dame? Is his experience pleasant or unpleasant? What are the most important aspects of the experience?

3. What is the effect of having a third person "interview" the loiterer?

4. Explain the significance of details: the squirrel's granary, the absence of birds, the cold hill side.

5. One device in *La Belle Dame sans Merci* present also in *The Rime of the Ancient Mariner* is the use of dream visions, that is, of the offering of some special insight in a dream. What are the implications of this kind of "knowing"?

6. What stages does the Mariner's journey contain? What is the problem he faces at various points? What are the major turning points in his voyage? What events or circumstances lead to change?

7. Look carefully at the aspects of nature which the Mariner encounters: the Wind, the Lack of Wind, Rain, Sun, Moon, Stars, Heat, Cold, Rain, and Sea Water. What events in the voyage are connected with natural events?

8. The Albatross and the Water Snakes, air and water creatures, are important to the Mariner. What attitude does he take toward these creatures? What attitude do the shipmates take?

9. As a Quest Narrative, what is the Mariner seeking? What is the "purpose" of his voyage? How would the meaning be different if the journey had taken place on land instead of sea?

10. What does Coleridge do to direct the reader's attention away from literal interpretation? What is the effect of having the Mariner tell his story to passersby? Why, in this case, a Wedding Guest?

11. The marginal gloss, the intentionally antique language, the simple ballad meter are striking contrivances of Coleridge. What is his purpose in the use of these devices?

12. Coleridge told an acquaintance that he was afraid that the poem "had too much moral." What could he have meant by this remark?

13. Paraphrase the analogy made by Wordsworth between external natural scenery and internal spiritual meanings.

14. Contrast the point of vision in both selections from *The Prelude*. What events are required for a new insight to be gained?

PART IV

Learning the Mind's Geography

How to Read: Some Practical Suggestions

Learning why mythology and symbolism are so important to the understanding of modern literature may help us to approach it more intelligently, but it will not remove all difficulties. Each poem is its own particular case, and theoretical considerations, however helpful, are not enough; we have to learn to read poems and stories. The crucial question which faces readers, experienced or not, is this: if the poem or passage before us does not mean what it says in a simple literal sense, then what does it mean? Or, more practically, if it does not mean what it says, what is to keep us from attributing any and all meanings to it, at our whim?

A correct sense of the "proper" ways of extending meanings is one of the most important and subtle of skills, and its acquisition no simple task, as the excesses of even the most experienced critics too often witness. One must avoid excesses on both sides: "reading in" too much impressionistic subjectivity, too much cleverness; and, being too narrow, skeptical, and stingily literal, missing thereby richness and range of feeling and meaning. Obviously, no simple formula for avoiding these extremes exists. But, although differences among readings will occur and disagreements remain in spite of our best efforts, some rules and general procedures can help.

Most of the suggestions which follow have to do with the attitude of the reader toward these questions and with certain assumptions to be made and certain prejudices to be avoided.

1. Eliminate hostility: cultivate an attitude of reasonable and tolerant open-mindedness toward all possible meanings and readings. On the other hand, do not give assent to a "reading" merely because it is asserted with authority or by authority. One needs to be convinced. An understanding which depends entirely on someone else's say-so is not useful. Better readers need humility; less knowledgeable ones, confidence.

2. Assume that the artist is intelligent, earnest, honest, and that he knows what he is doing. Serious artists take their art seriously, spending a lifetime studying and thinking about their craft. Therefore, especially in the case of the great poets of the past, a degree of humility on the part of the reader is desirable, and an accompanying presumption on behalf of the writer's ability, along with a sense that difficulties, and obscurities, and uncertainties may be necessary, and are the task of the reader to overcome as well as he can. Not that poets are not sometimes guilty of lapses, of unnecessary obscurity, of confusion of mind. But the chances are that most poets well enough known to be anthologized have already been subjected to the critical passage of time, which has win-

nowed away the chaff, leaving us with the best works. (It might be remembered that even Shakespeare, Milton, Keats, Dickens, and Yeats wrote a good deal that we do not read: fragments and pieces classified as minor works, often all but forgotten.) In short, the initial assumption of the reader should be in favor of the artist, that he is capable of more complexity than the reader and that his vision is worth the reader's attempt to achieve.

That it is necessary to argue this point is itself evidence of the lamentably small part serious art plays in the lives of most people, even the "well educated." To give the proper kind of assent to the artist does not, of course, require our believing that everything he says is right, or even sensible or proper. But we must accept the seriousness of art and its importance, if not the worth of every idea or doctrine.

3. Intention: trust the tale, not the teller. The best source of information about the meaning of a work of art is the work itself. Next best are other works by the same writer. To go beyond text, to biography, to history, to critical commentary, even to commentary by the artist himself, in order to gauge better the intention of the work, is to be on very uncertain ground and to encounter sticky theoretical questions. In most cases, especially for the student with limited time and energy for the works at hand, the best policy is to consider that the intention of the writer was to write the poem he wrote, and not something else, and to remember that efforts to obtain additional accounts of intention from sources other than the text itself is a presumption of failure against the text.

We do not mean to say that intention is a fully conscious act on the part of the artist. Artists vary a good deal in their degree of self-consciousness. Some are quite self-aware, in possession of an exact sense of what they are doing; others less so. But it is perfectly possible, and not infrequent, for a writer to manifest clear symbolic elements in his work, to have them be generated directly out of his unconscious, and for these elements to be the source of the special power and force which the work may contain. The lack of conscious awareness by the writer of these elements is not an argument for or against their existence. For various reasons a writer may wish to create a public image of himself which is at variance with the quality of his art. The commonest of these public stances is one suggesting simplicity, folksy innocence of literary or academic ways. A well-known case is Robert Frost's public manner, which implied a rustic Yankee simplicity and directness, quite at odds with the qualities of his poems, which are neither simple nor direct. Whenever poets begin to adorn their work with public comment, it is best to be wary.

The use of secondary sources, critical readings, and analyses is also a vexing question requiring delicacy and judgment. To make a simple statement, such sources are useful when (1) the time taken to use them does not replace time spent on the primary work, and (2) the insights they supply are insights into the work itself, not into a critic's reading of it. One should say: "Oh, now I see what Frost is talking about," not "Now I know what Trilling or Thompson thinks about that poem." Critics, of course, see things in their own terms, but where those terms are ones the reader understands and can use himself, the critic's clarity is useful.

4. Relativity: all readings of a work are not equally valid. Since readers differ in many ways—in their sensibility, their awareness of complexity, their verbal skills—and, since without reference to literature they are individuals with separate and particular talents and life experiences, they will necessarily reflect these differences in the ways they respond to a work of art. Because in some sense any understanding by the reader of the work is a meeting on a middle ground between his particular perceptions and the particularities of the work, these differences need to be encouraged, recognized, and respected.

At the same time, some responses are better than others; and some are wrong. The poem, it should be kept in mind, does offer some basic form, some subject matter which must be respected in any statement of its meaning. Differences among readings ought not therefore to be contradictory: though a poem may be ambiguous, it probably is not capable of saying opposite things at the same time. Different interpretations should possess a measure of congruity, a similarity of pattern.

The four poems which follow employ various modes of travel in various countries to suggest connections between land- and seascapes and states of mind and conditions of consciousness. The connection is clear and explicit in the poems by Richard Blackmur and Daniel Hoffman, more ambiguous in the poems by Robert Browning and James Dickey. All of them offer the reader a chance to practice the "rules" and attitudes given above.

The short poem below by Richard Blackmur makes a simple and skillful connection between windlessness and the absence of will. When the last line asserts that the speaker has been "living" in a place he has never been, we see the simplest kind of extension of meaning from the literal to the figurative.

MIRAGE

Richard Blackmur (1904–1965)

The wind was in another country, and
the day had gathered to its heart of noon
the sum of silence, heat, and stricken time.
Not a ripple spread. The sea mirrored
perfectly all the nothing in the sky.   5
We had to walk about to keep our eyes
from seeing nothing, and our hearts from stopping
at nothing. Then most suddenly we saw
horizon on horizon lifting up
out of the sea's edge a shining mountain   10
sun-yellow and sea-green; against it surf
flung spray and spume into the miles of sky.
Somebody said mirage, and it was gone,
but there I have been living ever since.

(handwritten annotations: spirit; Dry, quiet, barren; mid Age; cond. of mind; Life in death; Nature has renewed man once again; life but bigger than life; Very Alive; The mystical center; change of heart; Metanoia; The vision stays with him.)

* * *

Daniel Hoffman is one of the most skillful and subtle modern poets
using mythic form. Many of his poems make telling connections between
simple events and ordinary places and adventures of the heart and mind,
adventures not only of the individual but of the collective experience of
modern consciousness. *The City of Satisfactions* is particularly interesting
because, in the fashion of traditional allegory and contrary to *Mirage*, it
begins with an abstraction which turns into a place. The poem also
contains an Encounter in the Wilderness and a Search for the Truth
Buried There.

THE CITY OF SATISFACTIONS

Daniel Hoffman (1923–   )

As I was travelling toward the city of satisfactions
On my employment, seeking the treasure of pleasure,   *(handwritten: Material)*
Laved in the superdome observation car by Muzak

Reprinted by permission of Joseph Frank.

From *The City of Satisfactions* (Oxford University Press, 1963), © 1963 by
Daniel Hoffman. Used by permission of the author.

Soothed by the cool conditioned and reconditioned air,
Sealed in from the smell of the heat and the spines   5
Of the sere mesquite and the seared windblast of the sand,
It was conjunction of a want of juicy fruit
And the train's slowdown and stopping at a depot
Not listed on the schedule, unnamed by platform sign,
That made me step down on the siding   10
With some change in hand. The newsstand, on inspection,
Proved a shed of greyed boards shading
A litter of stale rags.
Turning back, I blanched at the Silent Streak: a wink
Of the sun's reflection caught its rear-view window   15
Far down the desert track. I grabbed the crossbar
And the handcar clattered. Up and down
It pumped so fast I hardly could grab hold it,
His regal head proud despite the bending
Knees, back-knees, back-knees, back-knees propelling.   20
His eyes bulged beadier than a desert toad's eyes.
His huge hands shrank upon the handlebar,
His mighty shoulders shrivelled and his skin grew
Wrinkled while I watched the while we reeled
Over the mesquite till the train grew larger   25
And pumping knees, back-knees, we stood still and
Down on us the train bore,
The furious tipping of the levers unabated
Wrenched my sweating eyes and aching armpits,
He leapt on long webbed feet into the drainage   30
Dryditch and the car swung longside on a siding
Slowing down beside the Pullman diner
Where the napkined waiter held a tray of glasses.
The gamehen steamed crisp-crust behind the glass.
I let go of the tricycle and pulled my askew necktie,   35
Pushed through the diner door, a disused streetcar,
A Danish half devoured by flies beneath specked glass,
Dirty cups on the counter,
A menu, torn, too coffeestained for choices, told
In a map of rings my cryptic eyes unspelled   40
Of something worth the digging for right near by
Here just out beyond the two-door shed.
The tracks were gone now but I found a shovel,
Made one, that is, from a rusting oildrum cover,
A scrap of baling wire, a broken crutch,   45
And down I heaved on the giving earth and rockshards
And a frog drygasped once from a distant gulley

And up I spewed the debris in a range
Of peaks I sank beneath and sweated under till
One lunge sounded the clunk of iron on brass   50
And furious scratch and pawing of the dryrock
Uncovered the graven chest and the pile of earth downslid
While under a lowering sky, sweatwet, I grasped and wrestled
The huge chest, lunged and jerked and fought it upward
Till it toppled sideways on the sand. I smashed it   55
Open, and it held a barred box. My nails broke
On the bars that wouldn't open. I smashed it
Open and it held a locked box. I ripped my knuckles
But couldn't wrest that lock off till I smashed it
Open and it held a small box worked   60
In delicate filigree of silver with
A cunning keyhole. But there was no key.
I pried it, ripped my fingers underneath it
But couldn't get it open till I smashed it
Open and it held a little casket   65
Sealed tight with twisted wires or vines of shining
Thread. I bit and tugged and twisted, cracked my teeth
But couldn't loose the knot. I smashed it
Open and the top came off, revealing
A tiny casket made of jade. It had   70
No top, no seam, no turnkey. Thimblesmall
It winked unmoving near the skinbreak
Where steakjuice pulsed and oozed. I thought aroma
Sifted, thinning till the dark horizon
Seemed, and then no longer seemed, a trifle   75
Sweetened. I knelt before
A piece of desert stone. When I have fitted
That stone into its casket, and replaced
The lid and set that casket in its box,
Fitted the broken top and set that box within   80
The box it came in and bent back the bars
And put it in the chest, the chest back in the hole,
The peaks around the pit-edge piled back in the pit,
Replaced the baling wire and crutch and oildrum cover
And pushed back through the diner, will the train   85
Sealed in from the smell of heat and mesquite
Envelop me in Muzak while it swooshes
Past bleak sidings such as I wait on
Nonstop toward the city of satisfactions roaring?
If I could only make this broken top   90
Fit snug back on this casket

LEARNING THE MIND'S GEOGRAPHY   117

The *Rime of the Ancient Mariner* and *La Belle Dame sans Merci* both use pseudo-antique forms to encourage a nonliteral reading. Browning uses an opposite technique: a very exact description of place and detail and an assumption of intimacy on the part of the speaker which allows him to assume considerable knowledge on the part of the reader or listener. He, in turn, must study carefully for clues as to who is talking, where, when, and why: Cuthbert and Giles (lines 91 and 97) suggest other questing knights who have, in some past adventure, lost some unspecified faith. Yet, in spite of the "realism" of detail and circumstance, the purpose of the journey remains obscure, the meaning of the Dark Tower and the events to follow its discovery remain ambiguous.

"CHILDE ROLAND TO THE DARK TOWER CAME"°
Robert Browning (1812–1898)

I

My first thought was, he lied in every word,
   That hoary cripple, with malicious eye
   Askance to watch the working of his lie
On mine, and mouth scarce able to afford
Suppression of the glee, that pursed and scored   5
   Its edge, at one more victim gained thereby.

II

What else should he be set for, with his staff?
   What, save to waylay with his lies, ensnare
   All travellers who might find him posted there,
And ask the road? I guessed what skull-like laugh   10
Would break, what crutch 'gin write my epitaph
   For pastime in the dusty thoroughfare,

°The title refers to the end of Act III, scene iv, of *King Lear*. Edgar, disguised as a madman, greets the wandering Lear with snatches of old songs: "Childe Rowland to the dark tower came;/ His word was still, 'Fie, foh, and fum,/ I smell the blood of a British man.'" A "childe" is a well-born youth, not yet a knight.

III

If at his counsel I should turn aside
   Into that ominous tract which, all agree,
   Hides the Dark Tower. Yet acquiescingly   15
I did turn as he pointed: neither pride
Nor hope rekindling at the end descried,
   So much as gladness that some end might be.

IV

For, what with my whole world-wide wandering,
   What with my search drawn out thro' years, my hope   20
   Dwindled into a ghost not fit to cope
With that obstreperous joy success would bring,
I hardly tried now to rebuke the spring
   My heart made, finding failure in its scope.°

V

As when a sick man very near to death   25
   Seems dead indeed, and feels begin and end
   The tears and takes the farewell of each friend,
And hears one bid the other go, draw breath
Freelier outside, ("since all is o'er," he saith,
   "And the blow fallen no grieving can amend";)   30

VI

While some discuss if near the other graves
   Be room enough for this, and when a day
   Suits best for carrying the corpse away,
With care about the banners, scarves and staves;
And still the man hears all, and only craves   35
   He may not shame such tender love and stay.

VII

Thus, I had so long suffered in this quest,
   Heard failure prophesied so oft, been writ
   So many times among "The Band"—to wit,
The knights who to the Dark Tower's search addressed   40
Their steps—that just to fail as they, seemed best,
   And all the doubt was now—should I be fit?

°*finding . . . scope:* able to accept failure

VIII

So, quiet as despair, I turned from him,
    That hateful cripple, out of his highway
    Into the path he pointed. All the day   45
Had been a dreary one at best, and dim
Was settling to its close, yet shot one grim,
    Red leer to see the plain catch its estray.°

IX

For mark! no sooner was I fairly found
    Pledged to the plain, after a pace or two,   50
    Than, pausing to throw backward a last view
O'er the safe road, 'twas gone; gray plain all round:
Nothing but plain to the horizon's bound.
    I might go on; naught else remained to do.

X

So, on I went. I think I never saw   55
    Such starved ignoble nature; nothing throve:
    For flowers—as well expect a cedar grove!
But cockle, spurge, according to their law
Might propagate their kind, with none to awe,
    You'd think; a burr had been a treasure-trove.   60

XI

No! penury, inertness and grimace,
    In some strange sort, were the land's portion. "See
    Or shut your eyes," said Nature peevishly,
"It nothing skills: I cannot help my case:
'Tis the Last Judgment's fire must cure this place,   65
    Calcine° its clods and set my prisoners free."

XII

If there pushed any ragged thistle-stalk
    Above its mates, the head was chopped; the bents°
    Were jealous else. What made those holes and rents
In the dock's harsh swarth leaves, bruised as to balk   70

°*estray:* a strange person, i.e. Roland   °*Calcine:* pulverize by intense heat
 °*bents:* coarse grasses

All hope of greenness? 'tis a brute must walk
   . Pashing° their life out, with a brute's intents.

XIII

As for the grass, it grew as scant as hair
   In leprosy; thin dry blades pricked the mud
   Which underneath looked kneaded up with blood.   75
One stiff blind horse, his every bone a-stare,
Stood stupefied, however he came there:
   Thrust out past service from the devil's stud!

XIV

Alive? he might be dead for aught I know,
   With that red gaunt and colloped° neck a-strain,   80
   And shut eyes underneath the rusty mane;
Seldom went such grotesqueness with such woe;
I never saw a brute I hated so;
   He must be wicked to deserve such pain.

XV

I shut my eyes and turned them on my heart.   85
   As a man calls for wine before he fights,
   I asked one draught of earlier, happier sights,
Ere fitly I could hope to play my part.
Think first, fight afterwards—the soldier's art:
   One taste of the old time sets all to rights.   90

XVI

Not it! I fancied Cuthbert's reddening face
   Beneath its garniture of curly gold,
   Dear fellow, till I almost felt him fold
An arm in mine to fix me to the place,
That way he used. Alas, one night's disgrace!   95
   Out went my heart's new fire and left it cold.

XVII

Giles then, the soul of honour—there he stands
   Frank as ten years ago when knighted first.
   What honest man should dare (he said) he durst.

°*Pashing:* squashing   °*colloped:* folded

Good—but the scene shifts—faugh! what hangman hands   100
   Pin to his breast a parchment? His own bands
      Read it. Poor traitor, spit upon and curst!

XVIII

Better this present than a past like that;
   Back therefore to my darkening path again!
      No sound, no sight, as far as eye could strain.   105
Will the night send a howlet or a bat?
I asked: when something on the dismal flat
   Came to arrest my thoughts and change their train.

XIX

A sudden little river crossed my path
   As unexpected as a serpent comes.   110
      No sluggish tide congenial to the glooms;
This, as it frothed by, might have been a bath
For the fiend's glowing hoof—to see the wrath
   Of its black eddy bespate° with flakes and spumes.

XX

So petty yet so spiteful! All along,   115
   Low scrubby alders kneeled down over it;
      Drenched willows flung them headlong in a fit
Of mute despair, a suicidal throng:
The river which had done them all the wrong,
   Whate'er that was, rolled by, deterred no whit.   120

XXI

Which, while I forded,—good saints, how I feared
   To set my foot upon a dead man's cheek,
      Each step, or feel the spear I thrust to seek
For hollows, tangled in his hair or beard!
—It may have been a water-rat I speared,   125
   But, ugh! it sounded like a baby's shriek.

XXII

Glad was I when I reached the other bank.
   Now for a better country. Vain presage!

°*bespate:* spattered

Who were the strugglers, what war did they wage,
Whose savage trample thus could pad the dank
   Soil to a plash?° Toads in a poisoned tank,
     Or wild cats in a red-hot iron cage—

XXIII

The fight must so have seemed in that fell cirque.°
   What penned them there, with all the plain to choose?
   No foot-print leading to that horrid mews,°
None out of it. Mad brewage set to work
Their brains, no doubt, like galley-slaves the Turk
   Pits for his pastime, Christians against Jews.

XXIV

And more than that—a furlong on—why, there!
   What bad use was that engine for, that wheel,
   Or brake, not wheel—that harrow fit to reel
Men's bodies out like silk? with all the air
Of Tophet's° tool, on earth left unaware,
   Or brought to sharpen its rusty teeth of steel.

XXV

Then came a bit of stubbed ground, once a wood,
   Next a marsh, it would seem, and now mere earth
   Desperate and done with; (so a fool finds mirth,
Makes a thing and then mars it, till his mood
Changes and off he goes!) within a rood—
   Bog, clay and rubble, sand and stark black death.

XXVI

Now blotches rankling, colored gay and grim,
   Now patches where some leanness of the soil's
   Broke into moss or substances like boils;
Then came some palsied oak, a cleft in him
Like a distorted mouth that splits its rim
   Gaping at death, and dies while it recoils.

130

135

140

145

150

155

°*plash:* puddle   °*fell cirque:* deadly arena   °*mews:* enclosure   °*Tophet's:*
Hell's

XXVII

And just as far as ever from the end!
  Naught in the distance but the evening, naught
  To point my footstep further! At the thought,
A great black bird, Apollyon's° bosom-friend,
Sailed past, nor beat his wide wing dragon-penned°
  That brushed my cap—perchance the guide I sought.

XXVIII

For, looking up, aware I somehow grew,
  'Spite of the dusk, the plain had given place
  All round to mountains—with such name to grace   165
Mere ugly heights and heaps now stolen in view.
How thus they had surprised me,—solve it, you!
  How to get from them was no clearer case.

XXIX

Yet half I seemed to recognize some trick
  Of mischief happened to me, God knows when—   170
  In a bad dream perhaps. Here ended, then,
Progress this way. When, in the very nick
Of giving up, one time more, came a click
  As when a trap shuts—you're inside the den!

XXX

Burningly it came on me all at once,   175
  This was the place! those two hills on the right,
  Crouched like two bulls locked horn in horn in fight;
While to the left, a tall scalped mountain . . . Dunce,
Dotard, a-dozing at the very nonce,°
  After a life spent training for the sight!   180

XXXI

What in the midst lay but the Tower itself?
  The round squat turret, blind as the fool's heart,
  Built of brown stone, without a counterpart
In the whole world. The tempest's mocking elf

°*Apollyon:* a name for the devil   °*dragon-penned:* dragon-winged   °*nonce:*
moment

Points to the shipman thus the unseen shelf°
He strikes on, only when the timbers start.

XXXII

Not see? because of night perhaps?—why, day
　　Came back again for that! before it left,
　　The dying sunset kindled through a cleft:
The hills, like giants at a hunting, lay,
Chin upon hand, to see the game at bay,—
　　"Now stab and end the creature—to the heft!"°

XXXIII

Not hear? when noise was everywhere! it tolled
　　Increasing like a bell. Names in my ears
　　Of all the lost adventurers my peers,—
How such a one was strong, and such was bold,
And such was fortunate, yet each of old
　　Lost, lost! one moment knelled the woe of years.

XXXIV

There they stood, ranged along the hill-sides, met
　　To view the last of me, a living frame
　　For one more picture! in a sheet of flame
I saw them and I knew them all. And yet
Dauntless the slug-horn° to my lips I set,
　　And blew. *"Childe Roland to the Dark Tower came."*

*　　*　　*

Like Daniel Hoffman, James Dickey is extremely skillful at constructing "realistic" situations which direct our attention nonetheless to secondary symbolic meanings. In this poem, as well as in *Power and Light* and *Coming Back to America* (see below), object, place, and motion, though very "real" in their literal senses, convey symbolic meanings with the ease and lack of artifice that is the mark of the authentic mythmaker.

°*shelf:* rock　°*heft:* handle　°*slug-horn:* trumpet

CHERRYLOG ROAD

James Dickey (1923–   )

Off Highway 106
At Cherrylog Road I entered
The '34 Ford without wheels,
Smothered in kudzu,°
With a seat pulled out to run   5
Corn whiskey down from the hills,

And then from the other side
Crept into an Essex
With a rumble seat of red leather
And then out again, aboard   10
A blue Chevrolet, releasing
The rust from its other color,

Reared up on three building blocks.
None had the same body heat;
I changed with them inward, toward   15
The weedy heart of the junkyard,
For I knew that Doris Holbrook
Would escape from her father at noon

And would come from the farm
To seek parts owned by the sun   20
Among the abandoned chassis,
Sitting in each in turn
As I did, leaning forward
As in a wild stock-car race

In the parking lot of the dead.   25
Time after time, I climbed in
And out the other side, like
An envoy or movie star
Met at the station by crickets.
A radiator cap raised its head,   30

°*kudzu:*   a species of vine or creeper that spreads very rapidly

Become a real toad or a kingsnake
As I neared the hub of the yard,
Passing through many states,
Many lives, to reach
Some grandmother's long Pierce-Arrow   35
Sending platters of blindness forth

From its nickel hubcaps
And spilling its tender upholstery
On sleepy roaches,
The glass panel in between   40
Lady and colored driver
Not all the way broken out,

The back-seat phone
Still on its hook.
I got in as though to exclaim,   45
"Let us go to the orphan asylum
John; I have some old toys
For children who say their prayers."

I popped with sweat as I thought
I heard Doris Holbrook scrape   50
Like a mouse in the southern-state sun
That was eating the paint in blisters
From a hundred car tops and hoods.
She was tapping like code,

Loosening the screws,   55
Carrying off headlights,
Sparkplugs, bumpers,
Cracked mirrors and gear-knobs,
Getting ready, already,
To go back with something to show   60

Other than her lips' new trembling
I would hold to me soon, soon.
Where I sat in the ripped back seat
Talking over the interphone,
Praying for Doris Holbrook   65
To come from her father's farm

And to get back there
With no trace of me on her face

To be seen by her red-haired father
Who would change, in the squalling barn,   70
Her back's pale skin with a strop,
Then lay for me

In a bootlegger's roasting car
With a string-triggered 12-gauge shotgun
To blast the breath from the air.   75
Not cut by the jagged windshields,
Through the acres of wrecks she came
With a wrench in her hand,

Through dust where the blacksnake dies
Of boredom, and the beetle knows   80
The compost has no more life.
Someone outside would have seen
The oldest car's door inexplicably
Close from within:

I held her and held her and held her,   85
Convoyed at terrific speed
By the stalled, dreaming traffic around us,
So the blacksnake, stiff
With inaction, curved back
Into life, and hunted the mouse   90

With deadly overexcitement,
The beetles reclaimed their field
As we clung, glued together,
With the hooks of the seat springs
Working through to catch us red-handed   95
Amidst the gray, breathless batting

That burst from the seat at our backs.
We left by separate doors
Into the changed, other bodies
Of cars, she down Cherrylog Road   100
And I to my motorcycle
Parked like the soul of the junkyard

Restored, a bicycle fleshed
With power, and tore off
Up Highway 106, continually   105
Drunk on the wind in my mouth,

Wringing the handlebar for speed,
Wild to be wreckage forever.

* * *

QUESTIONS

1. What are the main elements of the psychological states of mind described in *Mirage*? How are the elements of the land and sea used to represent states of mind?
2. What is the connection between "seeing nothing" and "stopping at nothing"?
3. What brings about the vision of the mountain?
4. Who said "mirage"? In general, who offers such explanations? What kind of evidence would such a person give to support his statement?
5. Explain the paradox of the last two lines.
6. Notice that the use of windlessness in *Mirage* is similar to the calm in which the Ancient Mariner suffers. Are there other points where the poet uses "weather" in the same way that Coleridge does?
7. What is the City of Satisfactions? who lives there? where is it located?
8. What state of existence is suggested by the Muzak-soothed, cool-conditioned car, the wasteland, the diner, the place where the treasure is buried?
9. Think about various ways in which the following phrases may be understood: "conditioned and reconditioned" (ln. 4), "juicy fruit" (ln. 7), "some change" (ln. 11), "crossbar" (ln. 16), "tricycle" (ln. 35).
10. What change in the horizon occurs at the discovery of the casket without key or seam? What does kneeling before desert stone signify?
11. Is this Journey a successful one? Is the discovery beneficial or painful? Why is it on a side track?
12. John Bunyan's *The Pilgrim's Progress* and Dante's *The Divine Comedy* both begin with analogies between the processes of life and travel. Hoffman probably has consciously in mind both these works. Compare his first line with Bunyan's, "As I walked through the wilderness of this world. . . ." Another excellent "train" poem is X. J. Kennedy's *Cross Ties*.
13. What details of landscape seem most vivid in Browning's poem, most exactly described? What details are missing that might be useful?
14. Where does the search being undertaken by the speaker take place? What historical period does the speaker seem to represent? Is he a knight on traditional knightly quest or can his search be put in more modern terms? What do modern knights search for? Why is the goal, the end of the search, so unexpected to the speaker?

15. What is added to the encounter between the speaker and Doris Holbrook by the location and the process of reaching the "hub of the yard"?
16. What stages does the speaker go through in his movement through the various wrecked cars?
17. Lovers are accustomed, at least in poetry, to meet in more attractive places than the one described here. What attitude does the speaker take toward the unusual location of his rendezvous?

PART V

The Structure of Modern Mythology

The Structure of Modern Mythology

The structure of modern mythology consists of the patterns of imagery which run through much modern literature and the meanings which can be given to these images. Scholars and critics, such as Northrop Frye, M. H. Abrams, and Harold Bloom, have given interesting accounts of the patterns in which these images occur, and with their aid and a careful study of the literature itself, we can learn an important technique for thinking about these works. Like any technique, the study of the structure of this mythology is important not for its own "system," but for the insights the system gives to the study of individual works and writers.

As we have suggested, the simplest and most basic symbolic materials are the commonest stuff of nature, in its daily forms. The essential elements of modern mythology are, therefore, the essential elements themselves: gas, liquid, and matter—air, ocean, and earth. The various specific forms of these materials are arranged in a cosmological scale, running vertically from underground or underwater, through the surfaces of earth and sea, to the sky. Generally, the location (height or depth) on this scale represents particular meaning: "up" represents Ideality, Perfection, Divinity, pure Form; "down" signifies the absence of these qualities—baseness and degradation. At the top of the scale is Light and Heaven and God; at the bottom, Darkness, Hell, and Satan. Between these extremes is man's place, the surface of the earth, between the moral and ideological extremes represented by God and Satan, Heaven and Hell, Sky and Underground, Consciousness and Ignorance. Movement upward, therefore, represents movement toward Perfection and Ideality, toward Godliness or Higher Qualities, away from earth, with its concrete and specific Things. Movement upward is toward the abstract, toward the disembodied Idea, away from human particulars and incarnation, toward inhuman categories and forms, away from body and flesh toward spiritual essences, away from reality and fact toward imagination and fancy. Vertical movement represents movement away from the physical world, away from animal, vegetable, and mineral toward celestial, airy purities, away from content toward form.

Downward movement from sky toward earth or from the surface of the earth to depths and caves represents opposite qualities and suggests the forces of instinct of raw animal energy, of libido, of the powers of the unconscious, of the id. It is movement away from the powers of rationality and the light of reason (away from sun and moon) toward subterranean caverns, toward more primitive powers. If heaven is the place of divinity, and earth of human, then lower places are for the sub-human, the primitive, the biological lower, toward apes and downward to amino acids and the primeval proteinic stuff of matter. Evolutionarily, movement downward is also a movement backward in time, toward the darkness of prehistory, before the dawn (light) of time, toward the preliterate, the nonverbal, the blind, raw, unformed energies and matter.

Man lives in the middle of these opposite sets of images and forces, and the essential energies of his life are generated by the conflict in his consciousness between sky ideas (the Ideal) and earth ideas (the Real) or between his "higher" nature and his darker, "lower" instinctive background and heritage. In the work of a poet, these images come to represent a modern sense of the human condition, of psychological conflict, of dialectical pressures upon human behavior, of the paradoxes and ambiguities of life. Whether we take the traditional view of the human condition in which man, created in God's image, falls from divinity into the human world, or whether we see man as struggling upward out of elemental matter and animal ancestry toward earthly rationality, we notice the conflict between extremes: between reason and instinct, between love and aggression, between grandeur and folly, between elegant formality and destructive chaos, between nobility and baseness.

Because of the dependency of all life upon water, modern mythology sees water as an image of natural energy, of passionate sensual drives, as an aspect of the basic and vital processes of animated life, as a reflection of psycho-biological forces of birth, growth, sexuality, and instinctive change. By the fact of its movement in natural tidal rhythms, water represents energies and forces which are common yet general, intimately affecting all living creatures, yet impersonal and vast. Like the tides, sensual motives move through the forms of organic life, dwarfing at times individual agency and control. To man, such forces are irrational, separate from his knowledge and higher faculties, yet as his life comes from water and as his body is sustained by it, so water suggests the dependence of human existence on irrational forces, and the degree to which we remain bound to and moved by the instinctual forces of life.

We mean this account to be sufficiently broad and general to indicate that no image offers a single symbolic translation. "Meaning" is complex and variable and will vary with a number of factors: the poet's and the poem's point of view, the associated contexts, and the relationship of images to other images. For example, we frequently encounter what we will call the dialectical situation, where nothing can be valued by itself, but all meaning and images are derived from the place of the image among others. Water may represent positive ideas and feelings (water may sustain or revive a life) or negative ideas and feelings (a person may drown in water, and salt water is less healthful than fresh and requires better sailors and swimmers). Water may thereby reflect the sensual energies of life, the creative possibilities, or it may pull down (drown) higher powers and lead to bondage to tidal forces. Thus, nothing is good or evil by itself, but rather in degree and balance with other forces, between extremes, dialectically balancing opposites.

Indeed, one of the central ideas of modern mythology is *mediation*: the sense that meaning (or even truth) lies always between, within the process of life, experienced as a tension or pressure between conflicting attractions, rarely clear and distinct and unalloyed. The geographical aspects of the symbolic landscape offer a variety of ways in which the poet may dramatize this idea of mediation, this tension between opposites that is one of the basic conditions of human life. We may, as suggested, have too much water or too little, too pure or too salty; we may have the shallow pool or the dangerous depth; water may be tranquil or agitated; it may fall as the gentle rain from heaven or descend torrentially. If it is deep, it may be filled with fearful things: snakes, monsters, sharks, or whales; it may pound against the shore or flow gently down the mountainside. And in all these cases people may be found in intermediate positions: beside the waters, on a beach, on the riverside, on the edge of a pool, or on a bridge over troubled waters.

Similarly, sky and earth images offer varieties of meaning in mediation: sky may be clear or cloudy, dark or bright; in it may be shining sun, moon, or stars. Earth may be flat or hilly, a sterile desert wasteland or a green Edenic garden; it may be laid out in city squares, a green country plot, a rural sea, farm or forest, plantation or frontier.

If, as we have suggested above, vertical movement toward the sky, away from the earth, represents the movement away from nature toward art, away from the real toward the ideal, away from Content toward Form, then vertical and horizontal movement may be combined as journeys, voyages, roads, paths, or walks, leading one upward or downward. Thus visions of God are often obtained on mountain tops. Struggle upward may represent the difficulties of moral improvement or the attainment of virtue, while descent into caves, caverns, and grottoes or into the interior of a continent may represent motion toward the interior of the self or toward the unconscious, natural forces of instinct.

Similarly, towers or trees mediate. Trees, rooted in the earth, grow toward the sky, offer their blossoms to the air and their fruit to the ground; towers are similar in location to trees, but are man-made, not natural. Other images of mediation occur in bridges and thresholds or doorways. Birds also mediate: between air and earth or, in the case of seabirds, between water and air. Some birds fly higher than others; some sing well, some badly; some are friends to man, others eaters of carrion. Beaches and strands and seashores, the margins of islands, represent mediation also, as do mixtures of earth and water which form mud or clay, from which one can either build houses, grow crops, or get dirty.

Many additional modifications and extensions of these basic patterns will occur to the careful reader, and the texts which follow give both specific illustration of these ideas and ample opportunity for tracing the outlines of modern mythology. The poems will sustain continued thought and close study. By taking these works with this degree of seriousness, the reader will be joining his own intelligence and awareness to one of the major events and achievements in the evolution of poetic consciousness. It may be that the consistency of these patterns is created by historical or psychological forces or both, by some energy which produces changes in consciousness itself and in the culture which consciousness produces. Poets "know" or reflect these changes sooner and more profoundly than most of us. Our efforts to learn the poet's lesson will, if successful, give all of us a clearer sense of our time and place.

High and Low Cosmology

Northrop Frye is probably the most eminent literary critic and theorist of our time. Besides his *Anatomy of Criticism*, he has written books on general aspects of mythology and its relationship to literary history and to popular culture. His immense range of knowledge need not intimidate the reader who may not recognize all his references and illustrations. What is important is the connection he makes between the structure of modern mythology and traditional mythology, both Classical and Christian, and the crucial changes, particularly in the notions of "up" and "down," made by romantic literature.

TOPOCOSM

Northrop Frye (1912–   )

In its use of images and symbols, as in its use of ideas, poetry seeks the typical and recurring. That is one reason why throughout the history of poetry the basis for organizing the imagery of the physical world has been the natural cycle. The sequence of seasons, times of day, periods of life and death, have helped to provide for literature the combination of movement and order, of change and regularity, that is needed in all the arts. Hence the importance, in poetic symbolism, of the mythical figure known as the dying god°, whether Adonis or Proserpine or their innumerable allotropic° forms, who represents the cycle of nature.

°*the dying god:* a metaphor for the dialectical relationship of life to death in nature   °*allotropic:* variations on the basic substance or form

From "New Directions from Old" by Northrop Frye from *Myths and Mythmaking*, edited by Henry A. Murray: reprinted with the permission of the publisher. Copyright © 1960 by George Braziller.

Again, for poets, the physical world has usually been not only a cyclical world but a "middle earth," situated between an upper and a lower world. These two worlds reflect in their form the heavens and hells of the religions contemporary with the poet, and are normally thought of as abodes of unchanging being, not as cyclical. The upper world is reached by some form of ascent, and is a world of gods or happy souls. The most frequent images of ascent are the mountain, the tower, the winding staircase or ladder, or a tree of cosmological dimensions. The upper world is often symbolized by the heavenly bodies, of which the one nearest us is the moon. The lower world, reached by descent through a cave or under water, is more oracular and sinister, and as a rule is or includes a place of torment and punishment. It follows that there would be two points of particular significance in poetic symbolism. One is the point, usually the top of a mountain just below the moon, where the upper world and this one come into alignment, where we look up to the heavenly world and down on the turning cycle of nature. The other is the point, usually in a mysterious labyrinthine cave, where the lower world and this one come into alignment, where we look down to a world of pain and up to the turning cycle of nature. This upward perspective sees the same world, though from the opposite pole, as the downward perspective in the vision of ascent, and hence the same cyclical symbols may be employed for it.

The definitive literary example of the journey of ascent is in the last half-dozen cantos of Dante's *Purgatorio*.° Here Dante, climbing a mountain in the form of a winding stair, purges himself of his last sin at the end of Canto 26, and then finds that he has recovered his lost youth, not his individual but his generic youth as a child of Adam, and hence is in the garden of Eden, the Golden Age of Classical mythology, a lower Paradise directly below the moon, where Paradise proper begins. This point is as far up as Virgil can go, and after Virgil leaves Dante the great apocalyptic vision of the Word and the Church begins. We are told in Canto 28 that Eden is a *locus amoenus*°, a place of perpetually temperate climate, from which the seeds of vegetable life in the world below proceed, and to which they return—in other words Eden is at the apex of the natural cycle. In Eden Dante sees the maiden Matilda, who, he says in the same canto, makes him remember where and what Proserpine was, when her mother lost her and she lost the spring flowers. Earlier, in Canto 27, the dying god's conventional emblem, the red or purple flower, is dropped into the imagery with a reference to Pyramus and Thisbe. As a garden is a place of trees, the tree itself is, like the mountain-top, a natural symbol of the vision of ascent, and enters Dante's vision, first in

---

°*Purgatorio:* the middle of the three books of *The Divine Comedy*　°*locus amoenus:* "pleasant place"

Canto 29 in the form of the seven candlesticks, which look like golden trees at a distance, and later in Canto 32 as the tree of knowledge, which turns purple in color.

The Gardens of Adonis episode in Book Three of *The Faerie Queene*° is a familiar English example of *locus amoenus* symbolism. The Gardens of Adonis are spoken of as a "Paradise," and are, again, a place of seed from which the forms of life in the cycle of nature proceed, and to which they return. In Spenser we have the dying god Adonis, the purple flower amaranthus (associated with Sidney,° whose fatal thigh-wound made him a favorite historical embodiment of Adonis) and a grove of myrtle trees on top of a mountain. One of Spenser's earliest and acutest critics, Henry Reynolds, suggests, in the easy-going fashion of his time, an etymological connection between Adonis and Eden, but Spenser does not make any explicit link between this garden and Eden, which is the kingdom of Una's parents in Book One. Nor does he explicitly locate the Gardens at the apex of the cyclical world just below the moon, though he does speak of Adonis as "eterne in mutabilitie," which reminds us of the *Mutabilitie Cantoes* and of the dispute between Mutability and Jove, held in the sphere of the moon at the boundary of Jove's world. In this poem the evidence brought forward by Mutability in her favor, which consists of various aspects of the natural cycle, proves Jove's case instead, because it is evidence of a principle of stability in flux. In any case the upper location of the Gardens of Adonis seems to be in Milton's mind when in *Comus*° he introduces the Attendant Spirit as coming from the Gardens of Adonis, which according to the opening line are "Before the starry threshold of Jove's Court." Milton also places Eden on a mountain-top, protected by a "verdurous wall," and the world into which Adam is exiled is spoken of as a "subjected plain."

In Biblical typology° the relation between Eden and the wilderness of Adam's exile is closely parallel to the relation between the Promised Land and the wilderness of the law. Here again the Promised Land is thought of as being "above" the wilderness, its capital being Jerusalem, the center of the world and the city on the mountain, "whither the tribes go up." The same kind of language enters the prophetic visions: Ezekiel's wilderness vision of dry bones is in a valley, while the panorama of the restored Jerusalem with which the prophecy concludes begins with the prophet seated "upon a very high mountain." In *Paradise Regained*° Christ's temptation in the wilderness is really a descent into hell, or the domain of Satan, terminated by his successful stand on the pinnacle of

---

°*The Faerie Queene:* a long symbolic poem by Edmund Spenser (1552–1599)
°*Sidney:* Sir Philip Sidney (1554–1586), courtier, warrior, and poet   °*Comus:* an allegory or "masque" written in 1634   °*typology:* the study of "types," i.e., of image patterns   °*Paradise Regained:* a long poem by John Milton (1608-1674)

Jerusalem, which prefigures his later conquest of the lower world of death and hell, much as Satan prefigures his own success, in Eden when he sits "like a cormorant," in the tree of life, the highest point in the garden. Christ's victory over Satan also, Milton says, "raised" Eden in the wilderness. The forty days of the temptation are commemorated in Lent, which is immediately followed in the calendar by Easter; they also correspond to the forty years of wilderness wandering under the law, which was terminated by the conquest of the Promised Land by Joshua, who has the same name as Jesus (cf. *Paradise Lost* xii, 307-314).

T. S. Eliot's *Ash Wednesday* is a poem founded on Dante's *Purgatorio* which at the same time glances at these Biblical and liturgical typologies. The central image of the poem is the winding stair of Dante's mountain, which leads to a Paradisal garden. Overtones of Israel in the wilderness ("This is the land. We have our inheritance."), of Ezekiel's valley of dry bones, and of course of Lent, are also present. As the poet is preoccupied with ascent, we get only fitful glimpses of the natural cycle on the way up: "a slotted window bellied like the fig's fruit," "hawthorn blossom," and a "broadbacked figure drest in blue and green," the last reappearing in a subdued form as a silent "garden god" in the *locus amoenus* above. In the final section the poet returns from the universal past to the individual past, from "the violet and the violet" of the garden to a nostalgia symbolized among other things by "lost lilacs."

In view of the explicit and avowed debt of this poem to the *Purgatorio*, the parallels in imagery may not seem very significant. It is all the more interesting to compare the treatment of the "winding stair" image in Yeats, as there, whatever influence from Dante there may be, the attitude taken towards the ascent is radically different. Two of Yeats's poems, *A Dialogue of Self and Soul* and *Vacillation*, turn on a debate between a "soul" who wants only to ascend the stair to some ineffable communion beyond, and a "self" or "heart" who is fascinated by the downward vision into nature, even to the point of accepting rebirth in its cycle. In the former poem the "self" focuses its gaze on the dying-god symbol of the Japanese ceremonial sword wrapped in silk embroidered with flowers of "heart's purple." In *Vacillation* the symbol of ascent and separation from the cycle, the uncorrupted body of the saint, is contrasted with the cycle itself of death and corruption and rebirth, represented by the lion and honeycomb of Samson's riddle. Here, however, it is the symbol of the tree, associated with "Attis' image" and somewhat like Dante's candlestick vision, "half all glittering flame and half all green," that dominates the poem, and that seems to combine in itself the images of ascent and cycle. Similarly in *Among School Children* the contrast between the nun and the mother, the "bronze repose" of direct ascent and the cyclical "honey of generation," is resolved in the image of the chestnut tree.

There are other examples of the green world at the top of the natural cycle in modern poetry. Wallace Stevens, for instance, gives us a very clear description of it in *Credences of Summer*:

> It is the natural tower of all the world,
> The point of survey, green's green apogee,
> But a tower more precious than the view beyond,
> A point of survey squatting like a throne,
> Axis of everything.

But in the twentieth century, on the whole, images of descent are, so to speak, in the ascendant. These derive mainly from the sixth book of the Aeneid, and its progenitor in the eleventh book of the Odyssey. Here also one is confronted with two levels, a lower world of unending pain, the world of Tantalus and Sisyphus and Ixion, and an upper world more closely connected with the natural cycle. In Virgil there is a most elaborate development of cyclical and rebirth symbolism, introducing speculations of a type that are rarely encountered again in Western poetry before at least Romantic times. In the vision of descent, where we enter a world of darkness and mystery, there is more emphasis on initiation, on learning the proper rites, on acquiring effective talismans like the golden bough. The main figures have a strongly parental aura about them: in Virgil the prophet of the future of Rome is Aeneas' father, and the maternal figure is represented by the Sibyl. In Homer, Odysseus' mother appears, and the figure corresponding to Virgil's Sibyl is Circe, whom Homer calls *potnia*, which means something like reverend. At the top of the winding stair one normally attains direct knowledge or vision, but the reward of descent is usually oracular or esoteric knowledge, concealed or forbidden to most people, often the knowledge of the future.

In romance, where descent themes are very common, the hero often has to kill or pacify a dragon who guards a secret hoard of wealth or wisdom. The descent is also often portrayed as a mimic, temporary or actual death of the hero; or he may be swallowed by the dragon, so that his descent is into the monster's belly. In medieval treatments of the Christian story some of these themes reappear. Between his death on the cross and his resurrection Jesus descends into hell, often portrayed, especially in fresco, as the body of a huge dragon or shark, which he enters by the mouth, like his prototype Jonah. Again there are two levels in the lower world: hell proper, a world of endless torment, and the upper limbo which is "harrowed," and from which the redeemed, among whom the parental figures Adam and Eve have an honored place, return to the upper world. The monster's open mouth recurs in *Ash Wednesday*° as

---

°*Ash Wednesday:* a symbolic poem by T. S. Eliot (1888–1965)

"the toothed gullet of an agèd shark," and as the symbol of the "blue rocks" or Symplegades, whose clashing together has similar overtones.

For obvious reasons, visions of descent in medieval and Renaissance poetry are usually infernal visions, based on Virgil but ignoring his interest in rebirth. Only with Romantic poetry do we begin to get once more the oracular or quest descent, where the hero gets something more from his descent than a tragic tale or an inspection of torments. In Keats's *Endymion* there are adventures in both upward and downward directions, the upward ones being mainly quests for beauty and the downward ones quests for truth. The Gardens of Adonis in this poem seem to be down rather than up, as they do at the conclusion of Blake's *Book of Thel*, though in that conclusion there is a sudden reversal of perspective. Shelley's *Prometheus Unbound°* is a more striking example of a cosmology in which the beneficial comes mainly from below, and the sinister from above. The contrast here with the cosmology of Dante and Milton is so striking that it deserves more examination.

In Dante, in Spenser, in Milton, the foreground of symbols and images seems to be portrayed against a background of roughly four levels of existence. I need a word for this background, and am strongly tempted to steal "topocosm" from Theodor H. Gaster's *Thespis*, though he uses it in a quite different sense. The top level is the place of the presence of God, the empyreal heaven, which operates in this world as the order of grace and providence. The next level is that of human nature properly speaking, represented by the garden of Eden or the Golden Age before the Fall, and now a world to be regained internally by moral and intellectual effort. Third is the level of physical nature, morally neutral but theologically fallen, which man is born into but can never adjust to, and fourth is the level of sin, death and corruption, which since the Fall has permeated the third level too. Throughout this period it was traditional to symbolize the top level by the starry spheres, the spiritual by the physical heaven. Dante's upper Paradise is located in the planetary spheres, and in Milton's *Nativity Ode* the music of the spheres, symbol of the understanding of unfallen man, is in counterpoint to the chorus of descending angels.

After the rise of Copernican astronomy and Newtonian physics, the starry sky becomes a less natural and a more perfunctory and literary metaphor for the spiritual world. The stars look increasingly less like vehicles of angelic intelligences, and come to suggest rather a mechanical and mindless revolution. This shift of perspective is of course already present in a famous passage in Pascal,° but it does not make its full

---

°*Prometheus Unbound:* a long poem by Percy Bysshe Shelley (1792–1822) in which the hero frees mankind for human love by defying the tyrannical gods
°*Pascal:* French philosopher, mathematician, and physicist (1623–1662)

impact on poetry until much later. A deity at home in such a world would seem stupid or malignant, at best a kind of self-hypnotized Pangloss.° Hence the variety of stupid sky-gods in Romantic poetry: Blake's Urizen, Shelley's Jupiter, Byron's Arimanes, Hardy's Immanent Will, perhaps the God of the Prologue to *Faust.*° Blake, the closest of this group to the orthodox Christian tradition, points out that there is more Scriptural evidence for Satan as a sky god than for Jesus. Even more significant for poetic symbolism is the sense of the mechanical complications of starry movement as the projection or reflection of something mechanical and malignant in human nature. In other words, the Frankenstein theme of actualizing human death-impulses in some form of fateful mechanism has a strong natural connection with the sky or "outer space," and in modern science fiction is regularly attached to it. At the same time poets in the Romantic period tend to think of nature less as a structure or system, set over against the conscious mind as an object, and more as a body of organisms from which the human organism proceeds, nature being the underlying source of humanity, as the seed is of the plant.

Hence with Romanticism another "topocosm," almost the reverse of the traditional one, begins to take shape. On top is the bleak and frightening world of outer space. Next comes the level of ordinary human experience, with all its anomalies and injustices. Below, in the only place left for any *locus amoenus,* is the buried original form of society, now concealed under the historical layers of civilization. With a modern Christian poet this would be the old unfallen world, or its equivalent: thus in Auden's *For the Time Being* the "garden" world is hidden within or concealed by the "wilderness" of ordinary life. With a poet closer to Rousseau° this buried society would be the primitive society of nature and reason, the sleeping beauty that a revolutionary act of sufficient courage would awaken. On the fourth level, corresponding to the traditional hell or world of death, is the mysterious reservoir of power and life out of which both nature and humanity proceed. This world is morally ambivalent, being too archaic for distinctions of good and evil, and so retains some of the sinister qualities of its predecessor. Hence the insistence in Romantic culture of the ambivalent nature of "genius," or an unusual degree of natural creative power, which may destroy the poet's personality or drive him to various forms of evil or suffering, as in the Byronic hero, the *poète maudit,* the compulsive sinner of contempo-

---

°*Pangloss:* a character in Voltaire's *Candide* who insisted, in the face of all evidence to the contrary, that this was the best of all possible worlds   °*Faust:* by Johann Wolfgang von Goethe (1749–1832), noted German poet and dramatist   °*Rousseau:* Jean Jacques Rousseau (1712–1778), French philosopher who held that society contributes to man's unhappiness by it artificiality

rary Christian and existential fiction, and other varieties of Romantic agony.

Against this "topocosm," the action of *Prometheus Unbound* seems logical enough. In the sky is Jupiter, the projection of human superstition with its tendency to deify a mechanical and subhuman order. Below is the martyred Prometheus; below him Mother Earth (in whose domain is included the world of death, which has a mysterious but recurring connection with the *locus amoenus* in Shelley), and at the bottom of the whole action is the oracular cave of Demogorgon, who calls himself Eternity, and from whom the power proceeds that rejuvenates Earth, liberates Prometheus, and annihilates Jupiter.

The Romantic "topocosm," like its predecessor, is, for the poet, simply a way of arranging metaphors, and does not in itself imply any particular attitudes or beliefs or conceptions. The traditional infernal journey naturally persists: Eliot's *Waste Land* and the first of Pound's *Cantos* are closely related examples, the former having many Aeneid echoes and the latter being based on the Odyssey. In Pound the characteristic parental figure is Aphrodite, called "venerendam," an echo of Homer's *potnia*, who bears the "golden bough of Argicida," in other words of Hermes the psychopomp. In Eliot the parallel figure to this combination of Hermes and Aphrodite is the hermaphroditic Teiresias, the seer who was the object of Odysseus' descent.

The "topocosm" of Dante was closely related to contemporary religious and scientific constructs, and to a much lesser degree the same is true of the post-Romantic one. We get our "up" metaphors from the traditional forms: everything that is uplifting or aspiring about the spiritual quest, such as the wings of angels or the ascension of Christ or the phrase "lift up your hearts," is derived from the metaphorical association of God and the sky. Even as late as the nineteenth century, progress and evolution were still going up as well as on. In the last century or so there has been a considerable increase in the use of approving "down" metaphors: to get "down" to bedrock or brass tacks or the basic facts is now the sign of a proper empirical procedure. Descent myths are also deeply involved in the social sciences, especially psychology, where we have a subconscious or unconscious mind assumed, by a spatial metaphor, to be underneath the consciousness, and into this mind we descend in quest of parental figures. The Virgilian inspiration of modern scientific mythology is not hard to see: the golden bough of the sixth book of the *Aeneid* supplies the title and theme for *Frazer*,° and the

---

°*Frazer:* Sir James Frazer, (1890–1915), whose book, *The Golden Bough* was an early survey of mythology, drawing connections between various cultures and historical periods. This book has been credited with giving encouragement and ideas to modern "myth" poets, particularly T. S. Eliot.

famous line spoken by Juno in the seventh, that if she cannot prevail on the high gods, she will stir up Hell (*fletere si nequeo superos, Acheronta movebo*), is the apt motto of Freud's *Interpretation of Dreams*. But now that politics and science at least are beginning to focus once more on the moon, it is possible that a new construct will be formed, and a new table of metaphors will organize the imagery of our poets.

*   *   *

Sky and Water I (1938), by M. C. Escher. (*Reprinted by permission of the Escher Foundation, Haags Gemeentemuseum, The Hague.*)

Motion between the Elements

The following selection of poems suggests only a few of the hundreds of sources and illustrations of romantic topography of the kind described by Northrop Frye. These poems have been chosen to illustrate the meanings to which "up" and "down" images have been put, and to suggest the variety of consistent and congruent meanings which modern poetic symbolism contains.

THE WORLD BELOW THE BRINE

Walt Whitman (1819–1892)

The world below the brine,
Forests at the bottom of the sea, the branches and leaves,
Sea-lettuce, vast lichens, strange flowers and seeds, the
    thick tangle, openings, and pink turf,
Different colors, pale gray and green, purple, white, and
    gold, the play of light through the water,
Dumb swimmers there among the rocks, coral, gluten,
    grass, rushes, and the aliment of the swimmers,   5
Sluggish existences grazing there suspended, or slowly
    crawling close to the bottom,
The sperm-whale at the surface blowing air and spray,
    or disporting with his flukes,
The leaden-eyed shark, the walrus, the turtle, the hairy
    sea-leopard, and the sting-ray,
Passions there, wars, pursuits, tribes, sight in those
    ocean-depths, breathing that thick-breathing air, as
    so many do,
The change thence to the sight here, and to the subtle
    air breathed by beings like us who walk this sphere,   10
The change onward from ours to that of beings who
    walk other spheres.

THE SEA-FAIRIES

Alfred, Lord Tennyson (1809–1892)

Slow sail'd the weary mariners and saw,
Betwixt the green brink and the running foam,
Sweet faces, rounded arms, and bosoms prest
To little harps of gold; and while they mused,

Whispering to each other half in fear,
Shrill music reach'd them on the middle sea.

Whither away, whither away, whither away?
    fly no more.
Whither away from the high green field, and the happy
    blossoming shore?
Day and night to the billow the fountain calls;
Down shower the gambolling waterfalls
From wandering over the lea;
Out of the live-green heart of the dells
They freshen the silvery-crimson shells,
And thick with white bells the clover-hill swells
High over the full-toned sea.
O, hither, come hither and furl your sails.

Come hither to me and to me;
Hither, come hither and frolic and play;
Here it is only the mew that wails;
We will sing to you all the day.
Mariner, mariner, furl your sails,
For here are the blissful downs and dales,
And merrily, merrily carol the gales,
And the spangle dances in bight and bay,
And the rainbow forms and flies on the land
Over the islands free;
And the rainbow lives in the curve of the sand;
Hither, come hither and see;
And the rainbow hangs on the poising wave,
And sweet is the color of cove and cave,
And sweet shall your welcome be,
O, hither, come hither, and be our lords,
For merry brides are we.
We will kiss sweet kisses, and speak sweet words;
O, listen, listen, your eyes shall glisten
With pleasure and love and jubilee.
O, listen, listen, your eyes shall glisten
When the sharp clear twang of the golden chords
Runs up the ridged sea.
Who can light on as happy a shore
All the world o'er, all the world o'er?
Whither away? Listen and stay; mariner, mariner,
    fly no more.

THE FORSAKEN MERMAN

Matthew Arnold (1822–1888)

Come, dear children, let us away;
Down and away below!
Now my brothers call from the bay,
Now the great winds shoreward blow,
Now the salt tides seaward flow;   5
Now the wild white horses play,
Champ and chafe and toss in the spray.
Children dear, let us away!
This way, this way!

Call her once before you go—   10
Call once yet!
In a voice that she will know:
'Margaret! Margaret!'
Children's voices should be dear
(Call once more) to a mother's ear;   15
Children's voices, wild with pain—
Surely she will come again!
Call her once and come away;
This way, this way!
'Mother dear, we cannot stay!   20
The wild white horses foam and fret.'
Margaret, Margaret!

Come, dear children, come away down;
Call no more!
One last look at the white-wall'd town,   25
And the little grey church on the windy shore,
Then come down!
She will not come though you call all day;
Come away, come away!

Children dear, was it yesterday   30
We heard the sweet bells over the bay?
In the caverns where we lay,
Through the surf and through the swell,
The far-off sound of a silver bell?
Sand-strewn caverns, cool and deep,   35
Where the winds are all asleep;
Where the spent lights quiver and gleam,
Where the salt weed sways in the stream,

Where the sea-beasts, ranged all round,
Feed in the ooze of their pasture-ground;   40
Where the sea-snakes coil and twine,
Dry their mail and bask in the brine;
Where great whales come sailing by,
Sail and sail, with unshut eye,
Round the world for ever and aye?   45
When did music come this way?
Children dear, was it yesterday?

Children dear, was it yesterday
(Call yet once) that she went away?
Once she sate with you and me,   50
On a red gold throne in the heart of the sea,
And the youngest sate on her knee.
She comb'd its bright hair, and she tended it well,
When down swung the sound of a far-off bell.
She sigh'd, she look'd up through the clear green sea;   55
She said: 'I must go, for my kinsfolk pray
In the little grey church on the shore to-day.
'Twill be Easter-time in the world—ah me!
And I lose my poor soul, Merman, here with thee.'
I said: 'Go up, dear heart, through the waves;   60
Say thy prayer, and come back to the kind sea-caves.'
She smiled, she went up through the surf in the bay.
Children dear, was it yesterday?

Children dear, were we long alone?
'The sea grows stormy, the little ones moan;   65
Long prayers,' I said, 'in the world they say;
Come!' I said; and we rose through the surf in the bay.
We went up the beach, by the sandy down
Where the sea-stocks bloom, to the white-wall'd town;
Through the narrow paved streets, where all was still,   70
To the little grey church on the windy hill.
From the church came a murmur of folk at their prayers,
But we stood without in the cold blowing airs.
We climb'd on the graves, on the stones worn with rains,
And we gazed up the aisle through the small leaded panes.   75
She sate by the pillar; we saw her clear;
'Margaret, hist! come quick, we are here!
Dear heart,' I said, 'we are long alone;
The sea grows stormy, the little ones moan.'
But, ah, she gave me never a look,   80

For her eyes were seal'd to the holy book!
Loud prays the priest; shut stands the door.
Come away, children, call no more!
Come away, come down, call no more!

Down, down, down!   85
Down to the depths of the sea!
She sits at her wheel in the humming town,
Singing most joyfully.
Hark what she sings: 'O joy, O joy,
For the humming street, and the child with its toy!   90
For the priest, and the bell, and the holy well;°
For the wheel where I spun,
And the blessed light of the sun!'
And so she sings her fill,
Singing most joyfully,   95
Till the spindle drops from her hand,
And the whizzing wheel stands still.
She steals to the window, and looks at the sand,
And over the sand at the sea;
And her eyes are set in a stare;   100
And anon there breaks a sigh,
And anon there drops a tear,
From a sorrow-clouded eye,
And a heart sorrow-laden,
A long, long sigh;   105
For the cold strange eyes of a little Mermaiden
And the gleam of her golden hair.

Come away, away children;
Come children, come down!
The hoarse wind blows coldly;   110
Lights shine in the town.
She will start from her slumber
When gusts shake the door;
She will hear the winds howling,
Will hear the waves roar.   115
We shall see, while above us
The waves roar and whirl,
A ceiling of amber,
A pavement of pearl.
Singing: 'Here came a mortal,   120

° *holy well:* church font

But faithless was she!
And alone dwell for ever
The kings of the sea.'

But, children, at midnight,
When soft the winds blow,   125
When clear falls the moonlight,
When spring-tides are low;
When sweet airs come seaward
From heaths starr'd with broom,
And high rocks throw mildly   130
On the blanch'd sands a gloom;
Up the still, glistening beaches,
Up the creeks we will hie,
Over banks of bright seaweed
The ebb-tide leaves dry.   135
We will gaze, from the sand-hills,
At the white, sleeping town;
At the church on the hill-side—
And then come back down.
Singing: 'There dwells a loved one,   140
But cruel is she!
She left lonely for ever
The kings of the sea.'

TO MARGUERITE

Matthew Arnold (1822–1888)

Yes! in the sea of life enisled,°
With echoing straits between us thrown,
Dotting the shoreless watery wild,
We mortal millions live *alone,*
The islands feel the enclasping flow,   5
And then their endless bounds they know.

But when the moon their hollows lights,
And they are swept by balms of spring,
And in their glens, on starry nights,
The nightingales divinely sing;   10
And lovely notes, from shore to shore,
Across the sounds and channels pour—

°*enisled:*   separated, as on an island

Oh! then a longing like despair
Is to their farthest caverns sent;
For surely once, they feel, we were   15
Parts of a single continent!
Now round us spreads the watery plain—
Oh might our marges meet again!

Who order'd, that their longing's fire
Should be, as soon as kindled, cool'd?   20
Who renders vain their deep desire?—
A God, a God their severance ruled!
And bade betwixt their shores to be
The unplumb'd, salt, estranging sea.

THE WINDHOVER

Gerard Manley Hopkins (1844–1889)

To Christ Our Lord

I caught this morning morning's minion, king-
   dom of daylight's dauphin, dapple-dawn-drawn Falcon,
     in his riding
   Of the rolling level underneath him steady air, and
     striding
High there, how he rung upon the rein of a wimpling wing
In his ecstasy! then off, off forth on swing,   5
   As a skate's heel sweeps smooth on a bow-bend: the
     hurl and gliding
   Rebuffed the big wind. My heart in hiding
Stirred for a bird,—the achieve of, the mastery of the thing!
Brute beauty and valor and act, oh, air, pride, plume, here
   Buckle! AND the fire that breaks from thee then,
     a billion
Times told lovelier, more dangerous, Oh my chevalier!   10

   No wonder of it; shéer plód makes plow down sillion
Shine, and blue-bleak embers, ah my dear,
   Fall, gall themselves, and gash gold-vermilion.

*   *   *

Leda was raped by Zeus, who had taken the form of a swan (a bird which both floats and flies). The story represents a point of intersection between antithetical elements, a favorite situation in Yeats's works. Here, a sky figure assumes the form of a water-bird in order to make love to an earth creature (another union of opposites).

LEDA AND THE SWAN

William Butler Yeats (1865–1939)

A sudden blow: the great wings beating still
Above the staggering girl, her thighs caressed
By the dark webs, her nape caught in his bill,
He holds her helpless breast upon his breast.

How can those terrified vague fingers push   5
The feathered glory from her loosening thighs?
And how can body, laid in that white rush,
But feel the strange heart beating where it lies?

A shudder in the loins engenders there
The broken wall, the burning roof and tower   10
And Agamemnon dead.°
                Being so caught up,
So mastered by the brute blood of the air,
Did she put on his knowledge with his power
Before the indifferent beak could let her drop?

THE WILD SWANS AT COOLE

William Butler Yeats (1865–1939)

The trees are in their autumn beauty,
The woodland paths are dry,
Under the October twilight the water
Mirrors a still sky;

°*The broken . . . dead:* Helen of Troy was the offspring of this union, and it was Helen's abduction that brought about the Trojan War ("The broken . . . tower") and the murder of the Greek leader, Agamemnon, by his wife on his victorious return from Troy.

Reprinted with permission of the Macmillan Company from *Collected Poems* by William Butler Yeats. Copyright 1928 by The Macmillan Company, renewed 1956 by Bertha Georgie Yeats.

Upon the brimming water among the stones   5
Are nine-and-fifty swans.

The nineteenth autumn has come upon me
Since I first made my count;
I saw, before I had well finished,
All suddenly mount   10
And scatter wheeling in great broken rings
Upon their clamorous wings.

I have looked upon those brilliant creatures,
And now my heart is sore.
All's changed since I, hearing at twilight,   15
The first time on this shore,
The bell-beat of their wings above my head,
Trod with a lighter tread.

Unwearied still, lover by lover,
They paddle in the cold   20
Companionable streams or climb the air;
Their hearts have not grown old;
Passion or conquest, wander where they will;
Attend upon them still.

But now they drift on the still water,   25
Mysterious, beautiful;
Among what rushes will they build,
By what lake's edge or pool
Delight men's eyes when I awake some day
To find they have flown away?   30

*   *   *

Mediation: High, Low, and Middle

Modern mythology recognizes both the upward and the downward impulse in human nature, the fact that man is attracted to or has psychological energy which leads him toward Idealism, God, and Heights, and a contrary impulse or appetite which leads him sensually toward the world of things, the organic processes of flesh and blood. We might recall that the original myth of the Judeo-Christian Bible is the *Fall* Myth, itself a drama in verticality of a kind, and that the New Testament offers as its central concern the Resurrection, that is, redemption by elevation from previous descent.

That there is some psychological dialectic between these directions is, it would seem, not a new idea. The poems which follow all use not only air and water and earth imagery, but also the movement between as ways of speaking more profoundly about these basic aspects of human experience than abstractions will allow.

The story of Daedalus and Icarus is told by Ovid in Book VIII of the *Metamorphoses* or "Stories of Changing Forms." Daedalus, famed for his powers of invention, was imprisoned by King Minos on Crete.

THE FALL OF ICARUS

Ovid (43 B.C.?–A.D. 17)

Daedalus came to loath his long exile in Crete, but though he longed to escape, the sea kept him prisoner. "Although Minos blocks escape by usual means," he said, "yet the sky remains open; that is the way we will go. Minos controls common things, but he does not control the sky." Thus saying, he turned his thoughts to unknown arts°, making new approaches to natural things. He placed small feathers in order, smaller then less small, the way the pipes of a rustic flute are arranged. Then he tied them with a string in the middle and with wax, and arranged them in a small curve, so that they took the shape of a bird's wing.

The son, Icarus, stood by, ignorant of the peril to himself that was being arranged, and with smiling face, chased the feathers in the breeze, and softened the wax with his thumb, the ways small boys interfere with the work of their fathers. After it was finished, the father hovered in the wind, waving his bird like feathers, as if they were his own body.

He told his son: "I give you warning, Icarus, fly a middle way; for if you fly too low, the feathers will become heavy with water, and if too high, the sun's heat will burn them. Fly between extremes. Avoid stargazing. Follow my example."

Having given lessons on the proper way to fly, he fitted the wings to the boy with trembling hand and tearful cheeks. He gave Icarus a last kiss. Then he rose on his wings, and encouraged his son to follow after, leading the way into the sky like a bird teaching the fledgling. Encouraging him to follow, to study the dangerous art, Daedalus moved his own wings, and looked back at his son.

°*he . . . arts:* "et ignotas animum dimittit in artes" is the epigraph for Joyce's *A Portrait of the Artist as a Young Man*, the story of Stephen Dedalus's attempts to learn appropriate arts. The novel is rich in allusions to Ovid's story, and uses "high-low" imagery throughout.

Under their flight, ordinary earthbound men pursued their lower occupations: the fisherman with his rod, the shepherd with his staff, the plowman with his plow. They all looked up in amazement, and believed the fliers to be gods.

Daedalus and Icarus passed over Samos, Jupiter's sacred island, and over Delos and Paros and Libeinthis and Calymne, rich in honey, and Icarus, being carried away with his power, deserted his father's guidance, and took a higher way, out of a lust for the sky. But as he flew higher, the sun melted the wax and the feathers it held. His naked arms, suited to earth, were useless in the air. Then his shouts to his father were drowned by the waters.

The miserable father, now no longer a father, called his name: "Where are you, Icarus? Where have you gone?" He recognized the feathers fallen onto the waves; he buried the body on the shore, and cursed the arts he had used.

BIRCHES

Robert Frost (1874–1963)

When I see birches bend to left and right
Across the lines of straighter darker trees,
I like to think some boy's been swinging them.
But swinging doesn't bend them down to stay
As ice storms do. Often you must have seen them   5
Loaded with ice a sunny winter morning
After a rain. They click upon themselves
As the breeze rises, and turn many-colored
As the stir cracks and crazes their enamel.
Soon the sun's warmth makes them shed crystal shells   10
Shattering and avalanching on the snow crust—
Such heaps of broken glass to sweep away
You'd think the inner dome of heaven had fallen.
They are dragged to the withered bracken by the load,
And they seem not to break; though once they are bowed   15
So low for long, they never right themselves:
You may see their trunks arching in the woods
Years afterwards, trailing their leaves on the ground
Like girls on hands and knees that throw their hair
Before them over their heads to dry in the sun.   20

But I was going to say when Truth broke in
With all her matter of fact about the ice storm,
I should prefer to have some boy bend them
As he went out and in to fetch the cows—
Some boy too far from town to learn baseball,   25
Whose only play was what he found himself,
Summer or winter, and could play alone.
One by one he subdued his father's trees
By riding them down over and over again
Until he took the stiffness out of them,   30
And not one but hung limp, not one was left
For him to conquer. He learned all there was
To learn about not launching out too soon
And so not carrying the tree away
Clear to the ground. He always kept his poise   35
To the top branches, climbing carefully
With the same pains you use to fill a cup
Up to the brim, and even above the brim.
Then he flung outward, feet first, with a swish,
Kicking his way down through the air to the ground.   40
So was I once myself a swinger of birches.
And so I dream of going back to be.
It's when I'm weary of considerations,
And life is too much like a pathless wood
Where your face burns and tickles with the cobwebs   45
Broken across it, and one eye is weeping
From a twig's having lashed across it open.
I'd like to get away from earth awhile
And then come back to it and begin over.
May no fate willfully misunderstand me   50
And half grant what I wish and snatch me away
Not to return. Earth's the right place for love:
I don't know where it's likely to go better.
I'd like to go by climbing a birch tree,
And climb black branches up a snow-white trunk   55
Toward heaven, till the tree could bear no more,
But dipped its top and set me down again.
That would be good both going and coming back.
One could do worse than be a swinger of birches.

JUGGLER

Richard Wilbur (1921–   )

A ball will bounce, but less and less. It's not
A light-hearted thing, resents its own resilience.
Falling is what it loves, and the earth falls
So in our hearts from brilliance,
Settles and is forgot.   5
It takes a skyblue juggler with five red balls

To shake our gravity up. Whee, in the air
The balls roll round, wheel on his wheeling hands,
Learning the ways of lightness, alter to spheres
Grazing his finger ends,   10
Cling to their courses there,
Swinging a small heaven about his ears.

But a heaven is easier made of nothing at all
Than the earth regained, and still and sole within
The spin of worlds, with a gesture sure and noble   15
He reels that heaven in,
Landing it ball by ball,
And trades it all for a broom, a plate, a table.

Oh, on his toe the table is turning, the broom's
Balancing up on his nose, and the plate whirls   20
On the tip of the broom! Damn, what a show, we cry:
The boys stamp, and the girls
Shriek, and the drum booms
And all comes down, and he bows and says goodbye.

If the juggler is tired now, if the broom stands   25
In the dust again, if the table starts to drop
Through the daily dark again, and though the plate
Lies flat on the table top,
For him we batter our hands
Who has won for once over the world's weight.   30

THE LADY AND THE BEAR

Theodore Roethke (1908–1963)

A Lady came to a Bear by a Stream.
"O why are you fishing that way?
Tell me, dear Bear there by the Stream,
Why are you fishing that way?"

"I am what is known as a Biddly Bear,—   5
That's why I'm fishing this way.
We Biddly's are Pee-culiar Bears.
And so,—I'm fishing this way.

"And besides, it seems there's a Law:
A most, most exactious Law   10
Says a Bear
Doesn't dare
Doesn't dare
Doesn't DARE
Use a Hook or a Line,   15
Or an old piece of Twine,
Not even the end of his Claw, Claw, Claw,
Not even the end of his Claw.
Yes, a Bear has to fish with his Paw, Paw, Paw.
A Bear has to fish with his Paw."   20

"O it's Wonderful how with a flick of your Wrist,
You can fish out a fish, out a fish, out a fish,
If *I* were a fish I just couldn't resist
You, when you are fishing that way, that way,
When you are fishing that way."   25

A Bear has to fish with his Paw."
And fell in the Stream still clutching a Plank,
But the Bear just sat there until she Sank;
As he went on fishing his way, his way,
As he went on fishing his way.   30

POWER AND LIGHT

James Dickey (1923–   )

> *. . . only connect . . .*
> *—E. M. Forster*

Going into the basement is slow, but the built-on smell of home
Beneath home gets better with age   the ground fermenting
And spilling through the barrel-cracks of plaster   the dark

I may even be
A man, I tell my wife: all day I climb myself   5
Bowlegged up those damned poles   rooster-heeled in all
Kinds of weather   and what is there when I get
Home? Yes, woman trailing ground-oil
Like a snail, home is where I climb down,
And this is the house I pass through on my way

                                                                                                10
To power and light.
Lying on the floor, ready for use   as I crack
The seal on the bottle   like I tell you it takes
A man to pour whiskey in the dark   and CLOSE THE DOOR
   between

The children and me.   15
The heads of nails drift deeper through their boards
And disappear. Years in the family dark have made me good
At this   nothing else.is so good   pure fires of the Self
Rise crooning in lively blackness   and the silence
   around them,
Like the silence inside a mouth, squirms with colors,   20
The marvellous worms of the eye float out into the real

World   sunspots
Dancing as though existence were
One huge closed eye   and I feel the wires running
Like the life-force along the limed rafters   and all connections   25
With poles   with the tarred naked belly-buckled black
Trees I hook to my heels   with the shrill phone calls leaping
Long distance   long distances through my hands   all connections

Even the one
With my wife, turn good   turn better than good   turn good   30
Not quite, but in the deep sway of underground   among the roots
That bend like branches   all things connect   and stream
Toward light and speech   tingle   rock like a powerline in wind,
Like a man working, drunk on pine-moves   the sun   in the socket
Of his shoulder   and on his neck dancing like dice-dots,   35

And I laugh
Like my own fate watching over me night and day   at home
Underground   or flung up on towers walking
Over mountains   my charged hair standing on end   crossing
The sickled, slaughtered alleys of timber   40
Where the lines loop and crackle on their gallows.
Far under the grass of my grave, I drink like a man

The night before
Resurrection Day. My watch glows with the time to rise
And shine. Never think I don't know my profession   45
Will lift me: why, all over hell the lights burn in your eyes,
People are calling each other   weeping with a hundred thousand
Volts   making deals   pleading   laughing like fate,
Far off, invulnerable   or with the right word pierced

To the heart   50
By wires I held, shooting off their ghostly mouths,
In my gloves. The house spins   I strap crampons to my shoes
To climb the basement stairs, sinking my heels in the tree-
life of the boards. Thorns! Thorns! I am bursting
Into the kitchen, into the sad way-station   55
Of my home, holding a double handful of wires

Spitting like sparklers
On the Fourth of July. Woman, I know the secret of sitting
In light   of eating a limp piece of bread   under
The red-veined eyeball of a bulb. It is all in how you are   60
Grounded. To bread I can see, I say, as it disappears and agrees
With me   the dark is drunk   and I am a man
Who turns on. I am a man.

* * *

Verticality in the Novel

The same enrichment which modern mythology gives to poetry is desirable for the novel as well. Themes from this mythology find their way into prose fiction in the setting and in the movements of characters, which illustrate symbolically the psychological events which are occurring in their lives. The three "descents" which follow illustrate important stages of insight and growth in the three protagonists.

The narrator in the passage below is Jack Burden, who finds in the course of a summer romance with Anne Stanton that he is being pulled by currents of time and maturity into "deeper waters" than he has the courage to enter. Anne's preparations for mature relationships and Jack's fear of them, a conflict which affects their future choices in crucial ways, is symbolized by this short account of Anne Stanton's diving tower exploits.

From ALL THE KING'S MEN

Robert Penn Warren (1905–   )

We went quite a long way, that summer, and there were times when I was perfectly sure I could have gone farther. When I could have gone the limit. For that fine, slender, compactly made, tight-muscled, soft-fleshed, golden-shouldered mechanism which fascinated Anne Stanton and me, which had dropped to us out of the blue, was a very sensitive and beautifully tuned-up contraption. But maybe I was wrong in that surmise, and maybe I could not have hurried the massive deliberation of that current in which we were caught and suspended, or hurried Anne Stanton's pensive and scholarly assimilation of each minute variation which had to be slowly absorbed into the body of our experience before another could be permitted. It was as though she was aware of a rhythm, a tune, a compulsion, outside of herself, and devoutly followed it in its subtle and winding progression. But wrong or not, I did not put my surmise to the test, for if I myself was not truly aware of that rhythm and compulsion which bemused her, I was aware of her devotion to it, and could find every moment with her full enough. Paradoxically enough, it was when I was away from her, when I was withdrawn from her context, back in my room at night or in the hot early afternoon, after lunch, that I was savagely impatient of the delays and discriminations. This would be especially true at those times when she wouldn't see me for a day, the times which seemed to mark, I came to understand, some stage, some milepost, we had passed. She would simply withdraw herself from me, as

---

she had done that night after we first kissed, and leave me, at first, confused and guilty, but later, as I came to grasp the pattern of things, merely impatient for the next day when she would appear at the court, swinging her racket, her face so smooth, young, healthy and apparently disinterested, though comradely, that I could not equate it with the face I remembered with the eyelids drooping and the damp, starlight-or-moonlight-glistening lips parted for the quick, shallow breath or the unashamed sigh.

But once, late in the summer, I didn't see her for two days. The night before, which was windless, with a full moon and an atmosphere that scarcely cooled or stirred with the coming on of evening, Anne and I had swum down to the hotel diving tower, late enough for everybody else to be out of the water. We lay on the big float for a while, not doing any talking, not touching each other, just lying on our backs and looking up at the sky. After a while she got up and began to climb the tower. I rolled over on my side to watch her. She went up to the twenty-foot board, poised a moment, and did a swan dive, a nice one. Then she went up to the next board. I don't know how many dives she made, but it was a lot. I drowsily watched them, watched her climb up, very slow, rung by rung, the moonlight on the wet fabric of the dark bathing suit making it look like metal, or lacquer, watched her poise at the verge, lift her arms out to the tingling extreme, rise on her toes, leave the board, and seem to hang there an instant, a dully gleaming form so slender and high up it blotted out only a star or two, just an instant before the heady swoop and the clean swishing rip into the water as though she had dived through a great circus hoop covered with black silk spangled with silver.

It happened when she took the highest dive I had ever seen her take, perhaps the highest she was ever to take in her life. I saw her climbing up, slow, then pass the board she had been using, the twenty-foot board, and go on up. I called to her, but she didn't even look down at me. I knew she had heard me. I also knew that she would go on where she was going, no matter what I said now, now that she had started. I didn't call again.

She made the dive. I knew it was a good one from the very instant she left the board, but I jumped to my feet, just the same, and stood at the edge of the float, holding my breath, my eyes fixed on her flight. Just as she entered the water, clean as a whistle, I plunged in, too, diving deep and drawing down with my stroke. I saw the silvery tangle and trail of bubbles and the glimmer of her legs and arms in the dark water when she turned. She had gone down deep. Not that she had to go down deep, for she could whisk out shallow if she wanted. But that time—and other times—she went in deep, as if to continue the flight as long as possible through the denser medium. I pulled deep and met her as she began to rise. I put my arms around her waist and drew her to me and put our lips together. She let her arms trail down, loose, not making a motion, while I held her body to me and pressed her face back and our legs trailed down together as we rose slowly and waveringly through the blackness of the water and the silver of ascending bubbles. We rose very slowly, or at least it seemed very slowly, and I was holding my breath so long there was a pain in my chest and a whirling dizziness in my head, but the pain and the dizziness had passed the line over into a rapture like that I had had in my room the night I had first taken her to a movie and had stopped on the way home. I thought we would never reach the surface, we rose so slowly.

Then we were there, with the moonlight brittle and fractured on the water all about our eyes. We hung there together, still not breathing, for another moment, then I released her and we fell apart to float on our backs and gaspingly draw the air in and stare up at the high, whirling, star-stung sky.

After a little while I realized that she was swimming away. I thought that she would be taking a few strokes to the float. But when I did finally roll over and swim to the float, she was already at the beach. I saw her pick up her robe, wrap it around her, and stoop to put on her sandals. I called to her. She waved back, then shaking her hair loose out of the cap, began to run up the beach toward home. I swam in, but by the time I reached the beach she was near her house. I knew I couldn't catch her. So I walked on up the beach, taking my time.

* * *

The strongly sensual relationship between Paul Morel and Clara Dawes in Lawrence's *Sons and Lovers* is portrayed in a carefully constructed scene in which the river, the flood tide, the flowers, the mud are all used to emphasize the archetypal significance of this event in the lives of the lovers.

From SONS AND LOVERS

D. H. Lawrence (1885–1930)

As they sat in the tramcar, she leaned her heavy shoulder against him, and he took her hand. He felt himself coming round from the anaesthetic, beginning to breathe. Her ear, half-hidden among her blonde hair, was near to him. The temptation to kiss it was almost too great. But there were other people on top of the car. It still remained to him to kiss it. After all, he was not himself, he was some attribute of hers, like the sunshine that fell on her.

He looked quickly away. It had been raining. The big bluff of the Castle rock was streaked with rain, as it reared above the flat of the town. They crossed the wide, black space of the Midland Railway, and passed the cattle enclosure that stood out white. Then they ran down sordid Wilford Road.

She rocked slightly to the tram's motion, and as she leaned against him, rocked upon him. He was a vigorous, slender man, with exhaustless energy. His face was rough, with rough-hewn features, like the common people's; but his eyes under the deep brows were so full of life that they fascinated her. They seemed to dance, and yet they were still trembling on the finest balance of laughter. His mouth the same was just going to spring into a laugh of triumph, yet did not. There was a sharp suspense about him. She bit her lip moodily. His hand was hard clenched over hers.

They paid their two halfpennies at the turnstile and crossed the bridge. The Trent was very full. It swept silent and insidious under the bridge, travelling in a soft body. There had been a great of rain. On the river levels were flat gleams of flood water. The sky was grey, with glisten of silver here and there. In Wilford churchyard the dahlias were sodden with rain—wet black-crimson balls. No one was on the path that went along the green river meadow, along the elm-tree colonnade.

There was the faintest haze over the silvery-dark water and the green meadow-bank, and the elm-trees that were spangled with gold. The river slid by in a body, utterly silent and swift, intertwining among itself like some subtle, complex creature. Clara walked moodily beside him.

"Why," she asked at length, in rather a jarring tone, "did you leave Miriam?"

He frowned.

"Because I *wante*d to leave her," he said.

"Why?"

"Because I didn't want to go on with her. And I didn't want to marry."

She was silent for a moment. They picked their way down the muddy path. Drops of water fell from the elm-trees.

"You didn't want to marry Miriam, or you didn't want to marry at all?" she asked.

"Both," he answered—"both!"

They had to manoeuvre to get to the stile, because of the pools of water.

"And what did she say?" Clara asked.

"Miriam? She said I was a baby of four, and that I always *had* battled her off."

Clara pondered over this for a time.

"But you have really been going with her for some time?" she asked.

"Yes."

"And now you don't want any more of her?"

"No. I know it's no good."

She pondered again.

"Don't you think you've treated her rather badly?" she asked.

"Yes; I ought to have dropped it years back. But it would have been no good going on. Two wrongs don't make a right."

"How old *are* you?" Clara asked.

"Twenty-five."

"And I am thirty," she said.

"I know you are."

"I shall be thirty-one—or *am* I thirty-one?"

"I neither know nor care. What does it matter!"

They were at the entrance to the Grove. The wet, red track, already sticky with fallen leaves, went up the steep bank between the grass. On either side stood the elm-trees like pillars along a great aisle, arching over and making high up a roof from which the dead leaves fell. All was empty and silent and wet. She stood on top of the stile, and he held both her hands. Laughing, she looked down into his eyes. Then she leaped. Her breast came against his; he held her, and covered her face with kisses.

They went on up the slippery, steep red path. Presently she released his hand and put it round her waist.

"You press the vein in my arm, holding it so tightly," she said.

They walked along. His finger-tips felt the rocking of her breast. All was silent and deserted. On the left the red wet plough-land showed through the doorways between the elm-boles° and their branches. On the right, looking down, they could see the tree-tops of elms growing far beneath them, hear occasionally the gurgle of the river. Sometimes there below they caught glimpses of the full, soft-sliding Trent, and of water-meadows dotted with small cattle.

"It has scarcely altered since little Kirke White used to come," he said.

But he was watching her throat below the ear, where the flush was fusing into the honey-white, and her mouth that pouted disconsolate. She stirred against him as she walked, and his body was like a taut string.

Half-way up the big colonnade of elms, where the Grove rose highest above the river, their forward movement faltered to an end. He led

---

°*boles:* trunks

her across to the grass, under the trees at the edge of the path. The cliff of red earth sloped swiftly down, through trees and bushes, to the river that glimmered and was dark between the foliage. The far-below water-meadows were very green. He and she stood leaning against one another, silent, afraid, their bodies touching all along. There came a quick gurgle from the river below.

"Why," he asked at length, "did you hate Baxter Dawes?"

She turned to him with a splendid movement. Her mouth was offered him, and her throat; her eyes were half-shut; her breast was tilted as if it asked for him. He flashed with a small laugh, shut his eyes, and met her in a long, whole kiss. Her mouth fused with his; their bodies were sealed and annealed. It was some minutes before they withdrew. They were standing beside the public path.

"Will you go down to the river?" he asked.

She looked at him, leaving herself in his hands. He went over the brim of the declivity and began to climb down.

"It is slippery," he said.

"Never mind," she replied.

The red clay went down almost sheer. He slid, went from one tuft of grass to the next, hanging on to the bushes, making for a little platform at the foot of a tree. There he waited for her, laughing with excitement. Her shoes were clogged with red earth. It was hard for her. He frowned. At last he caught her hand, and she stood beside him. The cliff rose above them and fell away below. Her colour was up, her eyes flashed. He looked at the big drop below them.

"It's risky," he said; "or messy, at any rate. Shall we go back?"

"Not for my sake," she said quickly.

"All right. You see, I can't help you; I should only hinder. Give me that little parcel and your gloves. Your poor shoes!"

They stood perched on the face of the declivity, under the trees.

"Well, I'll go again," he said.

Away he went, slipping, staggering, sliding to the next tree, into which he fell with a slam that nearly shook the breath out of him. She came after cautiously, hanging on to the twigs and grasses. So they descended, stage by stage, to the river's brink. There, to his disgust, the flood had eaten away the path and the red decline ran straight into the water. He dug in his heels and brought himself up violently. The string of the parcel broke with a snap; the brown parcel bounded down, leaped into the water, and sailed smoothly away. He hung on to his tree.

"Well, I'll be damned!" he cried crossly. Then he laughed. She was coming perilously down.

"Mind!" he warned her. He stood with his back to the tree, waiting. "Come now," he called, opening his arms.

She let herself run. He caught her, and together they stood watching the dark water scoop at the raw edge of the bank. The parcel had sailed out of sight.

"It doesn't matter," she said.

He held her close and kissed her. There was only room for their four feet.

"It's a swindle!" he said. "But there's a rut where a man has been, so if we go on I guess we shall find the path again."

The river slid and twined its great volume. On the other bank cattle were feeding on the desolate flats. The cliff rose high above Paul and Clara on their right hand. They stood against the tree in the watery silence.

"Let us try going forward," he said; and they struggled in the red clay along the groove a man's nailed boots had made. They were hot and flushed. Their barkled° shoes hung heavy on their steps. At last they found the broken path. It was littered with rubble from the water, but at any rate it was easier. They cleaned their boots with twigs. His heart was beating thick and fast.

Suddenly, coming on to the little level, he saw two figures of men standing silent at the water's edge. His heart leaped. They were fishing. He turned and put his hand up warningly to Clara. She hesitated, buttoned her coat. The two went on together.

The fishermen turned curiously to watch the two intruders on their privacy and solitude. They had had a fire, but it was nearly out. All kept perfectly still. The men turned again to their fishing, stood over the grey glinting river like statues. Clara went with bowed head, flushing; he was laughing to himself. Directly they passed out of sight behind the willows.

"Now they ought to be drowned," said Paul softly.

Clara did not answer. They toiled forward along a tiny path on the river's lip. Suddenly it vanished. The bank was sheer red solid clay in front of them, sloping straight into the river. He stood and cursed beneath his breath, setting his teeth.

"It's impossible!'" said Clara.

He stood erect, looking round. Just ahead were two islets in the stream, covered with osiers. But they were unattainable. The cliff came down like a sloping wall from far above their heads. Behind, not far back, were the fishermen. Across the river the distant cattle fed silently in the desolate afternoon. He cursed again deeply under his breath. He gazed up the great steep bank. Was there no hope but to scale back to the public path?

"Stop a minute," he said, and, digging his heels sideways into the steep bank of red clay, he began nimbly to mount. He looked across at

---

°*barkled:* caked

every tree-foot. At last he found what he wanted. Two beech-trees side by side on the hill held a little level on the upper face between their roots. It was littered with damp leaves, but it would do. The fishermen were perhaps sufficiently out of sight. He threw down his rainproof and waved to her to come.

She toiled to his side. Arriving there, she looked at him heavily, dumbly, and laid her head on his shoulder. He held her fast as he looked round. They were safe enough from all but the small, lonely cows over the river. He sunk his mouth on her throat, where he felt her heavy pulse beat under his lips. Everything was perfectly still. There was nothing in the afternoon but themselves.

When she arose, he, looking on the ground all the time, saw suddenly sprinkled on the black wet beech-roots many scarlet carnation petals, like splashed drops of blood; and red, small splashes fell from her bosom, streaming down her dress to her feet.

"Your flowers are smashed," he said.

She looked at him heavily as she put back her hair. Suddenly he put his finger-tips on her cheek.

"Why dost look so heavy?" he reproached her.

She smiled sadly, as if she felt alone in herself. He caressed her cheek with his fingers, and kissed her.

"Nay!" he said. "Never thee bother!"

She gripped his fingers tight, and laughed shakily. Then she dropped her hand. He put the hair back from her brows, stroking her temples, kissing them lightly.

"But tha shouldna worrit!" he said softly, pleading.

"No, I don't worry!" she laughed tenderly and resigned.

"Yea, tha does! Dunna thee worrit," he implored, caressing.

"No!" she consoled him, kissing him.

They had a stiff climb to get to the top again. It took them a quarter of an hour. When he got on to the level grass, he threw off his cap, wiped the sweat from his forehead, and sighed.

"Now we're back at the ordinary level," he said.

She sat down, panting, on the tussocky grass. Her cheeks were flushed pink. He kissed her, and she gave way to joy.

"And now I'll clean thy boots and make thee fit for respectable folk," he said.

He kneeled at her feet, worked away with a stick and tufts of grass. She put her fingers in his hair, drew his head to her, and kissed it.

"What am I supposed to be doing," he said, looking at her laughing; "cleaning shoes or dibbling with love? Answer me that!"

"Just whichever I please," she replied.

"I'm your boot-boy for the time being, and nothing else!" But they remained looking into each other's eyes and laughing. Then they kissed with little nibbling kisses.

"T-t-t-t!" he went with his tongue, like his mother. "I tell you, nothing gets done when there's a woman about."

And he returned to his boot-cleaning, singing softly. She touched his thick hair, and he kissed her fingers. He worked away at her shoes. At last they were quite presentable.

"There you are, you see!" he said. "Aren't I a great hand at restoring you to respectability? Stand up! There, you look as irreproachable as Britannia herself!"

He cleaned his own boots a little, washed his hands in a puddle, and sang. They went on into Clifton village. He was madly in love with her; every movement she made, every crease in her garments, sent a hot flash through him and seemed adorable.

The old lady at whose house they had tea was roused into gaiety by them.

"I could wish you'd had something of a better day," she said, hovering round.

"Nay!" he laughed. "We've been saying how nice it is."

The old lady looked at him curiously. There was a peculiar glow and charm about him. His eyes were dark and laughing. He rubbed his moustache with a glad movement.

"Have you been saying so!" she exclaimed, a light rousing in her old eyes.

"Truly!" he laughed.

"Then I'm sure the day's good enough," said the old lady.

She fussed about, and did not want to leave them.

"I don't know whether you'd like some radishes as well," she said to Clara; "but I've got some in the garden—*and* a cucumber."

Clara flushed. She looked very handsome.

"I should like some radishes," she answered.

And the old lady pottered off gleefully.

"If she knew!" said Clara quietly to him.

"Well, she doesn't know; and it shows we're nice in ourselves, at any rate. You look quite enough to satisfy an archangel, and I'm sure I feel harmless—so—if it makes you look nice, and makes folk happy when they have us, and makes us happy—why, we're not cheating them out of much!"

They went on with the meal. When they were going away, the old lady came timidly with three tiny dahlias in full blow, neat as bees, and speckled scarlet and white. She stood before Clara, pleased with herself, saying:

"I don't know whether——" and holding the flowers forward in her old hand.

"Oh, how pretty!" cried Clara, accepting the flowers.

"Shall she have them all?" asked Paul reproachfully of the old woman.

"Yes, she shall have them all," she replied, beaming with joy. "You have got enough for your share."

"Ah, but I shall ask her to give me one!" he teased.

"Then she does as she pleases," said the old lady, smiling. And she bobbed a little curtsey of delight.

Clara was rather quiet and uncomfortable. As they walked along, he said:

"You don't feel criminal, do you?"

She looked at him with startled grey eyes.

"Criminal!" she said. "No"

"But you seem to feel you have done a wrong?"

"No," she said. "I only think, 'If they knew!' "

"If they knew, they'd cease to understand. As it is, they do understand, and they like it. What do they matter? Here, with only the trees and me, you don't feel not the least bit wrong, do you?"

He took her by the arm, held her facing him, holding her eyes with his. Something fretted him.

"Not sinners, are we?" he said, with an uneasy little frown.

"No," she replied.

He kissed her, laughing.

"You like your little bit of guiltiness, I believe," he said. "I believe Eve enjoyed it, when she went cowering out of Paradise."

But there was a certain glow and quietness about her that made him glad. When he was alone in the railway-carriage, he found himself tumultuously happy, and the people exceedingly nice, and the night lovely, and everything good.

* * *

The invisibility of the unnamed narrator of this novel is a metaphor for Ralph Ellison's view of the situation which faces his Black protagonist when he attempts to achieve a place in a society dominated by White values. This first excursion to the "basement" of the "white" paint factory uses "depth" to represent an aspect of the development of the protagonist's experience (he ends living "underground"—literally and figuratively) and an aspect of the way in which the public or "higher" parts of American society depend upon "lower" or hidden forces, often forces unacknowledged, or concealed. The passage leads to a "breakdown" in the protagonist and suggests also that the depth represents an aspect of his own sense of himself.

From INVISIBLE MAN

Ralph Ellison (1914–   )

It was a deep basement. Three levels underground I pushed upon a heavy metal door marked "Danger" and descended into a noisy, dimly lit room. There was something familiar about the fumes that filled the air and I had just thought *pine*, when a high-pitched Negro voice rang out above the machine sounds.

"Who you looking for down here?"

"I'm looking for the man in charge," I called, straining to locate the voice.

"You talkin' to him. What you want?"

The man who moved out of the shadow and looked at me sullenly was small, wiry and very natty in his dirty overalls. And as I approached him I saw his drawn face and the cottony white hair showing beneath his tight, striped engineer's cap. His manner puzzled me. I couldn't tell whether he felt guilty about something himself, or thought I had committed some crime. I came closer, staring. He was barely five feet tall, his overalls looking now as though he had been dipped in pitch.

"All right," he said. "I'm a busy man. What you want?"

"I'm looking for Lucius," I said.

He frowned. "That's me—and don't come calling me by my first name. To you and all like you I'm *Mister* Brockway . . ."

"You. . . ?" I began.

"Yeah, me! Who sent you down here anyway?"

"The personnel office," I said. "I was told to tell you that Mr. Sparland said for you to be given an assistant."

"Assistant!" he said. "I don't need no damn assistant! Old Man Sparland must think I'm getting old as him. Here I been running things by myself all these years and now they keep trying to send me some assistant. You get on back up there and tell 'em that when I want an assistant I'll ask for one!"

I was so disgusted to find such a man in charge that I turned without a word and started back up the stairs. First Kimbro, I thought, and now this old . . .

"Hey! wait a minute!"

I turned, seeing him beckon.

"Come on back here a minute," he called, his voice cutting sharply through the roar of the furnaces.

I went back, seeing him remove a white cloth from his hip pocket and wipe the glass face of a pressure gauge, then bend close to squint at the position of the needle.

"Here," he said, straightening and handing me the cloth, "you can stay 'til I can get in touch with the Old Man. These here have to be kept clean so's I can see how much pressure I'm getting."

I took the cloth without a word and began rubbing the glasses. He watched me critically.

"What's your name?" he said.

I told him, shouting it in the roar of the furnaces.

"Wait a minute," he called, going over and turning a valve in an intricate network of pipes. I heard the noise rise to a higher, almost hysterical pitch, somehow making it possible to hear without yelling, our voices moving blurrily underneath.

Returning, he looked at me sharply, his withered face an animated black walnut with shrewd, reddish eyes.

"This here's the first time they ever sent me anybody like you," he said as though puzzled. "That's how come I called you back. Usually they sends down some young white fellow who thinks he's going to watch me a few days and ask me a heap of questions and then take over. Some folks is too damn simple to even talk about," he said, grimacing and waving his hand in a violent gesture of dismissal. "You an engineer?" he said, looking quickly at me.

"An *engineer?*"

"Yeah, that's what I asked you," he said challengingly.

"Why, no, sir, I'm no engineer."

"You sho?"

"Of course I'm sure. Why shouldn't I be?"

He seemed to relax. "That's all right then. I have to watch them personnel fellows. One of them thinks he's going to git me out of here, when he ought to know by now he's wasting his time. Lucius Brockway not only intends to protect hisself, he *knows how* to do it! Everybody knows I been here ever since there's been a here—even helped dig the first foundation. The Old Man hired me, nobody else; and, by God, it'll take the Old Man to fire me!"

I rubbed away at the gauges, wondering what had brought on this outburst, and was somewhat relieved that he seemed to hold nothing against me personally.

"Where you go to school?" he said.

I told him.

"Is that so? What you learning down there?"

"Just general subjects, a regular college course," I said.

"Mechanics?"

"Oh no, nothing like that, just a liberal arts course. No trades."

"Is that so?" he said doubtfully. Then suddenly, "How much pressure I got on that gauge right there?"

"Which?"

"You see it," he pointed. "That one right there!"

I looked, calling off, "Forty-three and two-tenths pounds."

"Uh huh, uh huh, that's right." He squinted at the gauge and back at me. "Where you learn to read a gauge so good?"

"In my high-school physics class. It's like reading a clock."

"They teach you that in *high* school?"

"That's right."

"Well, that's going to be one of your jobs. These here gauges have to be checked every fifteen minutes. You ought to be able to do that."

"I think I can," I said.

"Some kin, some caint. By the way, who hired you?"

"Mr. MacDuffy," I said, wondering why all the questions.

"Yeah, then where you been all morning?"

"I was working over in Building No. 1."

"That there's a heap of building. Where'bouts?"

"For Mr. Kimbro."

"I see, I see. I knowed they oughtn't to be hiring anybody this late in the day. What Kimbro have you doing?"

"Putting dope in some paint that went bad," I said wearily, annoyed with all the questions.

His lips shot out belligerently. "What paint went bad?"

"I think it was some for the government . . ."

He cocked his head. "I wonder how come nobody said nothing to me about it," he said thoughtfully. "Was it in buckets or them little biddy cans?"

"Buckets."

"Oh, that ain't so bad, them little ones is a heap of work." He gave me a high dry laugh. "How you hear about this job?" he snapped suddenly, as though trying to catch me off guard.

"Look," I said slowly, "a man I know told me about the job; Mac-Duffy hired me; I worked this morning for Mr. Kimbro; and I was sent to you by Mr. MacDuffy."

His face tightened. "You friends to one of those colored fellows?"

"Who?"

"Up in the lab?"

"No," I said. "Anything else you want to know?"

He gave me a long, suspicious look and spat upon a hot pipe, causing it to steam furiously. I watched him remove a heavy engineer's watch from his breast pocket and squint at the dial importantly, then turn to check it with an electric clock that glowed from the wall. "You keep on wiping them gauges," he said. "I got to look at my soup. And look here." He pointed to one of the gauges. "I wants you to keep a 'specially sharp eye on this here sonofabitch. The last couple of days he's 'veloped a habit of building up too fast. Causes me a heap of trouble. You see him gitting past 75, you yell, and yell loud!"

He went back into the shadows and I saw a shaft of brightness mark the opening of a door.

Running the rag over a gauge I wondered how an apparently uneducated old man could gain such a responsible job. He certainly didn't sound like an engineer; yet he alone was on duty. And you could never be sure, for at home an old man employed as a janitor at the Water Works was the only one who knew the location of all of the water mains. He had been employed at the beginning, before any records were kept, and actually functioned as an engineer though he drew a janitor's pay. Perhaps this old Brockway was protecting himself from something. After all, there was antagonism to our being employed. Maybe he was dissimulating, like some of the teachers at the college, who, to avoid trouble when driving through the small surrounding towns, wore chauffeur caps and pretended that their cars belonged to white men. But why was he pretending with me? And what was his job?

I looked around me. It was not just an engine room; I knew, for I had been in several, the last at college. It was something more. For one thing, the furnaces were made differently and the flames that flared through the cracks of the fire chambers were too intense and too blue. And there were the odors. No, he was *making* something down here, something that had to do with paint, and probably something too filthy and dangerous for white men to be willing to do even for money. It was not paint because I had been told that the paint was made on the floors above, where, passing through, I had seen men in splattered aprons working over large vats filled with whirling pigment. One thing was certain: I had to be careful with this crazy Brockway; he didn't like my being here . . . And there he was, entering the room now from the stairs.

"How's it going?" he asked.

"All right," I said. "Only it seems to have gotten louder."

"Oh, it gets pretty loud down here, all right; this here's the uproar department and I'm in charge . . . Did she go over the mark?"

"No, it's holding steady," I said.

"That's good. I been having plenty trouble with it lately. Haveta bust it down and give it a good going over soon as I can get the tank clear."

Perhaps he *is* the engineer, I thought, watching him inspect the gauges and go to another part of the room to adjust a series of valves. Then he went and said a few words into a wall phone and called me, pointing to the valves.

"I'm fixing to shoot it to 'em upstairs," he said gravely. "When I give you the signal I want you to turn 'em wide open. 'N when I give you the second signal I want you to close 'em up again. Start with this here red one and work right straight across . . ."

I took my position and waited, as he took a stand near the gauge.

"Let her go," he called. I opened the valves, hearing the sound of liquids rushing through the huge pipes. At the sound of a buzzer I looked up . . .

"Start closing," he yelled. "What you looking at? Close them valves!"

"What's wrong with you?" he asked when the last valve was closed.

"I expected you to call."

"I said I'd *signal* you. Caint you tell the difference between a signal and a call? Hell, I buzzed you. You don't want to do that no more. When I buzz you I want you to do something and do it quick!"

"You're the boss," I said sarcastically.

"You mighty right, I'm the boss, and don't forget it. Now come on back here, we got work to do."

We came to a strange-looking machine consisting of a huge set of gears connecting a series of drum-like rollers. Brockway took a shovel and scooped up a load of brown crystals from a pile on the floor, pitching them skillfully into a receptacle on top of the machine.

"Grab a scoop and let's git going," he ordered briskly. "You ever done this before?" he asked as I scooped into the pile.

"It's been a long time," I said. "What is this material?"

He stopped shoveling and gave me a long, black stare, then returned to the pile, his scoop ringing on the floor. You'll have to remember not to ask this suspicious old bastard any questions, I thought, scooping into the brown pile.

Soon I was perspiring freely. My hands were sore and I began to tire. Brockway watched me out of the corner of his eye, snickering noiselessly.

"You don't want to overwork yourself, young feller," he said blandly.

"I'll get used to it," I said, scooping up a heavy load.

"Oh, sho, sho," he said. "Sho. But you better take a rest when you git tired."

I didn't stop. I piled on the material until he said, "That there's the scoop we been trying to find. That's what we want. You better stand back a little, 'cause I'm fixing to start her up."

I backed away, watching him go over and push a switch. Shuddering into motion, the machine gave a sudden scream like a circular saw, and sent a tattoo of sharp crystals against my face. I moved clumsily away, seeing Brockway grin like a dried prune. Then with the dying hum of the furiously whirling drums, I heard the grains sifting lazily in the sudden stillness, sliding sand-like down the chute into the pot underneath.

I watched him go over and open a valve. A sharp new smell of oil arose.

"Now she's all set to cook down; all we got to do is put the fire to her," he said, pressing a button on something that looked like the burner of an oil furnace. There was an angry hum, followed by a slight explosion that caused something to rattle, and I could hear a low roaring begin.

"Know what that's going to be when it's cooked?"

"No, sir," I said.

"Well that's going to be the guts, what they call the *vee*-hicle of the paint. Least it will be by time I git through putting other stuff with it."

"But I thought the paint was made upstairs . . ."

"Naw, they just mixes in the color, make it look pretty. Right down here is where the real paint is made. Without what I do they couldn't do nothing, they be making bricks without straw. An' not only do I make up the base, I fixes the varnishes and lots of the oils too . . ."

"So that's it," I said. "I was wondering what you did down here."

"A whole lots of folks wonders about that without gitting anywhere. But as I was saying, caint a single doggone drop of paint move out of the factory lessen it comes through Lucius Brockway's hands."

"How long have you been doing this?"

"Long enough to know what I'm doing," he said. "And I learned it without all that education that them what's been sent down here is suppose to have. I learned it by doing it. Them personnel fellows don't want to face the facts, but Liberty Paints wouldn't be worth a plugged nickel if they didn't have me here to see that it got a good strong base. Old Man Sparland know it though. I caint stop laughing over the time when I was down with a touch of pneumonia and they put one of them so-called engineers to pooting around down here. Why, they started to having so much paint go bad they didn't know what to do. Paint was bleeding and wrinkling, wouldn't cover or nothing—you know, a man could make hisself all kinds of money if he found out what makes paint bleed. Anyway, everything was going bad. Then word got to me that they done put that fellow in my place and when I got well I wouldn't come back. Here I been with 'em so long and loyal and everything. Shucks, I just sent 'em word that Lucius Brockway was retiring!

"Next thing you know here come the Old Man. He so old hisself his chauffeur has to help him up them steep stairs at my place. Come in a-puffing and a-blowing, says, 'Lucius, what's this I hear 'bout you retiring?'

" 'Well, sir, Mr. Sparland, sir,' I says, 'I been pretty sick, as you well know, and I'm gitting kinder along in my years, as you well know, and I hear that this here Italian fellow you got in my place is doing so good I thought I'd might as well take it easy round the house.'

"Why, you'd a-thought I'd done cursed him or something. 'What kind of talk is that from you, Lucius Brockway,' he said, 'taking it easy round the house when we need you out to the plant? Don't you know the quickest way to die is to retire? Why, that fellow out at the plant don't know a thing about those furnaces. I'm so worried about what he's going to do, that he's liable to blow up the plant or something that I took out some extra insurance. He can't do your job,' he said. 'He don't have the touch. We haven't put out a first-class batch of paint since you been gone.' Now that was the Old Man hisself!" Lucius Brockway said.

"So what happened?" I said.

"What you mean, what happened?" he said, looking as though it were the most unreasonable question in the world. "Shucks, a few days later the Old Man had me back down here in full control. That engineer got so mad when he found out he had to take orders from me he quit the next day."

He spat on the floor and laughed. "Heh, heh, heh, he was a fool, that's what. A fool! He wanted to boss *me* and I know more about this basement than anybody, boilers and everything. I helped lay the pipes and everything, and what I mean is I knows the location of each and every pipe and switch and cable and wire and everything else—both in the floors and in the walls *and* out in the yard. Yes, sir! And what's more, I got it in my head so good I can trace it out on paper down to the last nut and bolt; and ain't never been to nobody's engineering school neither, ain't even passed by one, as far as I know. Now what you think about that?"

"I think it's remarkable," I said, thinking, I don't like this old man.

"Oh, I wouldn't call it that," he said. "It's just that I been round here so long. I been studying this machinery for over twenty-five years. Sho, and that fellow thinking 'cause he been to some school and learned how to read a blueprint and how to fire a boiler he knows more 'bout this plant than Lucius Brockway. That fool couldn't make no engineer 'cause he can't see what's staring him straight in the face . . . Say, you forgittin' to watch them gauges."

I hurried over, finding all the needles steady.

"They're okay," I called.

"All right, but I'm warning you to keep an eye on 'em. You cain't forgit down here, 'cause if you do, you liable to blow up something. They got all this machinery, but that ain't everything; *we are the machines inside the machine.*

"You know the best selling paint we got, the one that *made* this here business?" he asked as I helped him fill a vat with a smelly substance.

"No, I don't."

"Our white, Optic White."

"Why the white rather than the others?"

" 'Cause we started stressing it from the first. We make the best white paint in the world, I don't give a damn what nobody says. Our white is so white you can paint a chunka coal and you'd have to crack it open with a sledge hammer to prove it wasn't white clear through!"

His eyes glinted with humorless conviction and I had to drop my head to hide my grin.

"You notice that sign on top of the building?"

"Oh, you can't miss that," I said.

"You read the slogan?"

"I don't remember, I was in such a hurry."

"Well, you might not believe it, but I helped the Old Man make up that slogan. 'If It's Optic White, It's the Right White,' " he quoted with an upraised finger, like a preacher quoting holy writ. "I got me a three-hundred-dollar bonus for helping to think that up. These newfangled advertising folks is been tryin' to work up something about the other colors, talking about rainbows or something, but hell, *they* caint get nowhere."

" 'If It's Optic White, It's the Right White,' " I repeated and suddenly had to repress a laugh as a childhood jingle rang through my mind:

" 'If you're white, you're right,' " I said.

"That's it," he said. "And that's another reason why the Old Man ain't goin' to let nobody come down here messing with me. *He* knows what a lot of them new fellers don't; *he* knows that the reason our paint is so good is because of the way Lucius Brockway puts the pressure on them oils and resins before they even leaves the tanks." He laughed maliciously. "They thinks 'cause everything down here is done by machinery, that's all there is to it. They crazy! Ain't a continental thing that happens down here that ain't as iffen I done put my black hands into it! Them machines just do the cooking, these here hands right here do the sweeting. Yes sir! Lucius Brockway hit it square on the head! I dips my fingers in and sweets it! Come on, let's eat . . ."

"But what about the gauges?" I said, seeing him go over and take a thermos bottle from a shelf near one of the furnaces.

"Oh, we'll be here close enough to keep an eye on 'em. Don't you worry 'bout that."

"But I left my lunch in the locker room over at Building No. 1."

"Go on and git it and come back here and eat. Down here we have to always be on the job. A man don't need no more'n fifteen minutes to eat no-how; then I say let him git on back on the job."

* * *

QUESTIONS

1. What are the important values attributed to ascent and descent in traditional myth?

2. Describe the four levels which provide the images for traditional poetic symbolism. What is the romantic "topocosm"? How does it differ from the traditional order? What is the relationship of these changes in poetic practice to the discoveries of science? Given the direction of contemporary scientific interests, what further changes would you predict in poetic symbolism?

3. What uses of "up" and "down" images are current in popular culture and popular media? What groups or kinds of people value various directions?

4. What is the significance of the fact that in the twentieth century "images of descent are, so to speak, in the ascendant"?

5. In Arnold's poems, what general distinction applies to the differences between surface and subsurface, between land and sea? What value is placed upon water? Is it attractive, repulsive, ambiguous? Is the world beneath the surface a place one wishes to move toward, or to avoid?

6. The separations between land and sea seem to be used to illustrate separations of other kinds. What kinds of "alienations" from opposite qualities do these poems consider or express?

7. Myth and folklore often make associations between water and the female: the Mermaid, the Lorelei, the Sirens. What reasons can be given for this connection?

8. In addition to the voyage of the Ancient Mariner, a number of the most important works of imagination have used water voyages as central themes of narrative: Joseph Conrad's *Heart of Darkness*, Herman Melville's *Moby Dick*, and Mark Twain's *Huckleberry Finn*. See also James Dickey's *Deliverance* and Robert Penn Warren's *Flood*. Other important poems which contain specific use of this pattern are Arnold's *Dover Beach* and *The Buried Life*, T. S. Eliot's *The Love Song of J. Alfred Prufrock* (especially the final lines) and parts of *The Waste Land*, and Robert Frost's *Neither Out Far Nor In Deep*.

9. Death by drowning, especially of women, was a favorite theme of 19th century writers and painters. In George Eliot's *The Mill on the Floss,* there is a passionate flood; in Dickens's *David Copperfield,* there is the drowning in a storm at sea of Steerforth and Little Emily; and in Hardy's *The Return of the Native,* there is the drowning of Eustacia Vye, who started on top of a hill and ended in the raging flood waters of a mill pond. Stephen Dedalus, the protagonist of Joyce's *A Portrait of the Artist as a Young Man,* hates water, perhaps because of his name. The alert reader will undoubtedly be able to provide examples of his own of this prevalent myth.

10. Why is it more difficult to find air and sky poems in modern mythology than earth and water poems? In addition to *Leda and the Swan* and *The Wild Swans at Coole,* see also Yeats's *Vacillation, A Dialogue of Self and Soul, Among School Children,* and *The Magi* (see above). Wallace Stevens frequently uses height as an image for chilly, unearthly, "mythy" purity: see *Sunday Morning* and *A High Toned Old Christian Woman.*

11. Yeats's interest in image patterns is seen in the use of swans in *The Wild Swans at Coole.* What aspects of the swans' "character" is important to Yeats's meaning? Would another bird do as well: herons, seagulls, falcons, egrets?

12. Why is Yeats so specific in his account of the "rape" of Leda by the swan? What sympathies or questions does the poem suggest? What is Leda's state of mind? What are the consequences of this meeting? Consider the contrast between this meeting of God and Man and the Annunciation in Christian myth.

13. Gerard Manley Hopkins was a Roman Catholic, a Jesuit, and a mystic. What aspects of this poem fall within the outlines of modern mythology? What characteristics of the bird are important to the meaning of the poem? What is the effect of the sudden descent?

14. Consider the mythic imagery of space travel and rocketry, of scuba diving, of *Jonathan Livingston Seagull.*

15. Draw as many generalizations as possible which will apply to the common elements in the poems by Frost, Wilbur, Roethke, and Dickey, particularly with regard to the meaning of movement upward and downward and of the meeting between the two directions.

16. Dedalus was a creative person, an artist. Why should an inventor or artistic person be particularly liable to the dangers of high flying? What do James Dickey and Robert Frost see as the benefit of climbing away from earth? Why, in Wilbur's poem, do we admire the juggler?

17. Frost's poem, like many others of his, seems innocently literal, until one notices that climbing, going up in a certain way and coming down in a certain way—is the central concern of the poet, not woods or trees. What is the special aspect of sky which Frost refers to? What is the reason that

swinging birches is a solitary act, not a team sport? What implications about horizontal movements are there in this poem? For more horizontal mythology see *The Road Not Taken* and *Stopping By Woods on a Snowy Evening*; for more verticality, see *After Apple-Picking* and *The Silken Tent*.

18. Roethke's poem suggests with some humor that the edges of bodies of water, shores, beaches, and banks are themselves mediating locations; what does the location and particular nature of the Bear's activity add to the fatal charm he offers to the Lady?

19. There are three levels used in *Power and Light* to suggest relationships to power: the lineman's work at the tops of utility poles, the basement beneath his home, and the kitchen between. What takes place at each level; how are the levels connected? Locate and discuss all the allusions to connections and to electricity in the poem. Consider carefully the meaning of "It is all in how you are grounded."

PART VI

The Language of the Unconscious

The Language of the Unconscious

Long before Freud described the structure and effects of the unconscious, poets had been writing from and about the deeper levels of the psyche, and employing its symbolic forms for their own purposes, without benefit of scientific verification. Freud himself was entirely aware of the particular relationship between psychoanalysis and art, recognizing the connection between the processes of mind he was encountering in his work with mental illness and the ways in which painters, dramatists, and poets thought and created. Freud gave a more systematic and documented account of these operations of the mind; but he did not discover them. It is the poet or, more accurately, the creative forces of the human psyche that give rise to symbolism, and to Freudianism, not Freud or Freudian critics.

It is therefore important to notice the points of connection between psychoanalytic theory and literary criticism and to take the former as a means of helping to do the latter better. For although a measure of hostility still exists toward a psychoanalytic approach to literature, it is becoming possible for the study of literature to be as much benefited by psychoanalytic discoveries as Freud was benefited in his work by the study of art. This emphasis reminds us, however, that we are interested in better understanding the language of poetry and that our interest in psychoanalysis need extend only to the degree to which it assists this understanding. For the student of literature, the degree of truth which he attributes to psychoanalytic study as "pure" science, or as applied to the practice of curing mental illness, is quite secondary.

The connection between literature and psychoanalysis occurs because of a basic psychological event: the transformation of inner impulse or feeling to an outer object or form or act which represents or symbolizes it. This transformation occurs (see Susanne Langer in Part I) in all movements from thought or motive to action, whether the act is a word, sentence, gesture, or lyric poem. To this straightforward, daylight symbolism Freud adds a nocturnal aspect—the change of unconscious motives, feelings, and energies into the images and events of the dream. Moreover, the "devices" by which the dreamer makes these transformations are essentially literary ones: analogy, condensation, synecdoche (substitution of a part for the whole), narrative itself, and of course, symbolism.

This intimate connection between myth and dream is best illustrated or discussed by understanding that for Freud, both myth and dreams represent modes of expression in which the unconscious impulses of the psyche, hidden from the conscious, reasonable mind, are made manifest. In a fundamental sense, the "function" of an individual dream and a collective, archetypal myth are the same, arising from the conflict between conscious and unconscious, between, in a sense, two parts of the mind.

To Freud, the most important myth was the story of Oedipus which, he held, represented the most basic and profound psychic conflict: the passionate love by the child for the parent of the opposite sex and the accompanying jealous hatred of the parent of the same sex. The child's struggle to master the conflicts in his feelings caused by this situation requires that he banish to the unconscious (repress) the hatred of the rival parent and shift the passion from the loved parent to another loved person. In childhood, symptoms of the conflict inevitably occur, though awareness of the basic cause of the conflict remains unrecognized. The myth, then, was seen by Freud as an accurate account of this universal human condition, illustrating the basically sexual nature of human motivations, and the way in which ignorance of motives, of one's history, can lead to tragedy and error.

It is worth noting that some of Freud's students and followers have qualified or amended this view. Carl Jung, for example, was more interested in the collective aspects of myth and gave myth a more religious meaning, possessing a creative or life-giving force and energy, one which holds society together and gives liberation to human creativity. Other psychoanalysts, Erich Fromm, Karen Horney, Otto Rank, and Melanie Klein also have modified the emphasis which Freud gave to the Oedipus story, suggesting a less particular and literal view.

Such an outline only suggests the vast amount of interpretation, theory, argument and counter-argument that Freud's work has given rise to. The reader should bear in mind that Freud's work may be fairly thought of as perhaps the most significant scientific achievement of our century, one which has had large consequences in the study of anthropology, psychology, literary criticism, and one whose philosophical implications are still being developed.

To return to the question of symbolism, we should note that in considering Freud's ideas, we are neither asking any new questions, departing from an attention to literature, nor raising any more mysterious or difficult issues than are already present in any other theory of poetry or creativity. Evidence of this assertion may be found in the fact that Freud's account of dreams raises many of the same theoretical questions as would have been raised had he been talking about a poet instead of a dreamer: how do we know that the analyst (reader) is not "reading in" to the dreamer's (poet's) dream (narrative) meaning derived from his own prejudices and subjectivity, his own preoccupation with sexuality for example? How do we know that the dreamer's dream does not simply mean "itself," that is, that it is nothing more than a "simple" fantasy, whimsically and innocently constructed by the combined effects of sleep, chance, and an onion sandwich before retiring? Or, how do we resolve the matter of intention, which becomes, as a matter of fact, even more difficult in the case of the dreamer, whose denials of latent meaning are likely to be more vigorous and positive than those of the poet?

And what about this preoccupation with sexuality and sexual anatomy? It is interesting to note that Freud himself "apologizes" for the limited interests which the unconscious has, giving us as it does such an extensive repertoire of things to represent such an embarrassingly small number of objects. A penis is only a penis, but it may be represented by anything straight and elongated. Female anatomy, as reflected by the unconscious, is relatively simple in form, though the variety of objects capable of representing roundness, receptivity, and "inner space" is apparently very large.

Despite these questions, there are a number of reasons why we must confront the psychoanalytic view of literature, whether it be strictly Freudian or more recent accounts of the matter. In the first place, while Freud's theory has been modified, refined, and altered at various points, its basic insights and direction have not been very much changed. Indeed, such is the prevalence of Freud's basic view of the mind that (with the exception of the behaviorist school) even critics who dissent most strenuously from the Freudian approach often do so from premises derived from the theory itself. Secondly, the further implications of these particular parts of psychoanalytic theory for their contributions to the study of other forms of literature—linguistics, folklore, humor, mythology, and the like—are very great. Third, the importance of symbolic forms of expression (mostly Freudian) in modern art, a situation which both contributes to Freudian theory and grows from awareness of it on the part of artists, is such that one can hardly avoid dealing with Freud. This is particularly true in media which are more visual than verbal (painting, dance, drama, and film). While representational painting has always contained extended imagery, drawing upon traditional Classic and Christian mythology, the development of Symbolist and Surrealist schools of art has given additional strength to these forms of expression, and film makers have adapted them almost as a matter of course. The work of Bergman, Fellini, Buñuel, Losey, and numerous others can hardly be approached at all without some sense of the particular kind of symbolism which Freud has described.

*   *   *

The selection which follows is one of the many places in Freud's work where the symbolism of dreams is discussed. The major work on the subject is his *The Interpretation of Dreams,* which contains many examples of analysis of dream imagery.

SYMBOLISM IN DREAMS°

Sigmund Freud (1856–1939)

Ladies and Gentlemen,—We have found that the distortion in dreams, which interferes with our understanding of them, is the result of a censoring activity which is directed against unacceptable, unconscious, wishful impulses. We have not, of course, maintained that the censorship is the sole factor responsible for the distortion in dreams, and in fact when we study them further we can discover that other factors play a part in producing this result. This amounts to our saying that even if the dream-censorship was out of action we should still not be in a position to understand dreams, the manifest dream would still not be identical with the latent dream-thoughts.

We come upon this other factor which prevents dreams from being lucid, this new contribution to dream-distortion, by noticing a gap in our technique. I have already admitted to you that it does sometimes really happen that nothing occurs to a person under analysis in response to particular elements of his dreams. It is true that this does not happen as often as he asserts; in a great many cases, with perseverance, an idea is extracted from him. But nevertheless there remain cases in which an association fails to emerge or, if it *is* extracted, does not give us what we expected from it. If this happens during a psycho-analytic treatment, it has a peculiar significance with which we are not here concerned.° But

---

°[As Freud tells us in *The Interpretation of Dreams,* it was relatively late before he realized the full importance of dream-symbolism, largely under the influence of Wilhelm Stekel (1911). It was not until the fourth (1914) edition of *The Interpretation of Dreams* that a special section was devoted to the subject. That section (Chapter VI, Section E) represents, apart from the present lecture, Freud's main discussion of symbolism. The topic appears, of course, in many other places both in *The Interpretation of Dreams* and in other works throughout Freud's life, and references to these will be found at a few points below. It may be added, however, that the present lecture has claims to being regarded as the most important of all Freud's writings on symbolism.] All bracketed notes in this selection are by the translator, James Strachey.

°[The reference here is to the blocking of free associations by unconscious stirring-up of the transference.]

Selection reprinted from *The Complete Introductory Lectures on Psychoanalysis* by Sigmund Freud, translated and edited by James Strachey. © 1966 by W.W. Norton and Company, Inc. © 1965, 1964 by James Strachey.

it also happens in the interpretation of normal people's dreams or in that of our own. If we convince ourselves that in such cases no amount of pressure is of any use, we eventually discover that this unwished-for event regularly occurs in connection with particular dream-elements, and we begin to recognize that a fresh general principle is at work where we had begun by thinking we were only faced by an exceptional failure of technique.

In this way we are tempted to interpret these 'mute' dream-elements ourselves, to set about translating them with our own resources. We are then forced to recognize that whenever we venture on making a replacement of this sort we arrive at a satisfactory sense for the dream, whereas it remains senseless and the chain of thought is interrupted so long as we refrain from intervening in this way. An accumulation of many similar cases eventually gives the necessary certainty to what began as a timid experiment.

I am putting all this in a rather schematic way; but that is permissible, after all, for didactic purposes, nor has it been falsified, but merely simplified.

In this way we obtain constant translations for a number of dream-elements—just as popular 'dream-books' provide them for *everything* that appears in dreams. You will not have forgotten, of course, that when we use our *associative* technique° constant replacements of dream-elements never come to light.

You will object at once that this method of interpretation strikes you as far more insecure and open to attack than the earlier one by means of free association. There is, however, something further. For when, with experience, we have collected enough of these constant renderings, the time comes when we realize that we should in fact have been able to deal with these portions of dream-interpretation from our own knowledge, and that they could really be understood without the dreamer's associations. How it is that we must necessarily have known their meaning will become clear in the second half of our present discussion.

A constant relation of this kind between a dream-element and its translation is described by us as a 'symbolic' one, and the dream-element itself as a 'symbol' of the unconscious dream-thought. You will recall that earlier, when we were investigating the relations between dream-elements and the 'genuine' thing behind them, I distinguished three such relations—those of a part to a whole, of allusion and of plastic portrayal. I warned you at the time that there was a fourth, but I did not name it. This fourth relation is the symbolic one which I am now intro-

---

°*our associative technique:* the normal procedure of psychoanalysis, which asks the patient to associate freely one idea with another

ducing. It gives occasion for some most interesting discussions, and I will turn to them before laying before you the detailed results of our observations of symbolism.

Symbolism is perhaps the most remarkable chapter of the theory of dreams. In the first place, since symbols are stable translations, they realize to some extent the ideal of the ancient as well as of the popular interpretation of dreams, from which, with our technique, we had departed widely. They allow us in certain circumstances to interpret a dream without questioning the dreamer, who indeed would in any case have nothing to tell us about the symbol.° If we are acquainted with the ordinary dream-symbols, and in addition with the dreamer's personality, the circumstances in which he lives and the impressions which preceded the occurrence of the dream, we are often in a position to interpret a dream straightaway—to translate it at sight, as it were. A piece of virtuosity of this kind flatters the dream-interpreter and impresses the dreamer; it forms an agreeable contrast to the laborious work of questioning the dreamer. But do not allow yourselves to be led astray by this. It is not our business to perform acts of virtuosity. Interpretation based on a knowledge of symbols is not a technique which can replace or compete with the associative one. It forms a supplement to the latter and yields results which are only of use when introduced into it. And as regards acquaintance with the dreamer's psychical situation, you must bear in mind that the dreams of people you know well are not the only ones you have to analyse, that you are not as a rule familiar with the events of the previous day, which were the instigators of the dream, but that the associations of the person you are analysing will provide you precisely with a knowledge of what we call the psychical situation.

Moreover it is quite specially remarkable—having regard, too, to some considerations which we shall mention later—that the most violent resistances have been expressed once again to the existence of a symbolic relation between dreams and the unconscious. Even people of judgement and reputation, who, apart from this, have gone a long way in agreeing with psycho-analysis, have at this point withheld their support. This behaviour is all the stranger in view, first, of the fact that symbolism is not peculiar to dreams alone and is not characteristic of them, and, secondly, that symbolism in dreams is by no means a discovery of psychoanalysis, however many other surprising discoveries it has made. The philosopher K. A. Scherner (1861) must be described as the discoverer of dream-symbolism, if its beginning is to be placed in modern times at all. Psycho-analysis has confirmed Scherner's findings, though it has made material modifications in them.

°who . . . symbol: because the purpose of the dream is to transform unconscious meanings unacceptable to the conscious mind into acceptable terms

You will now want to hear something of the nature of dream-symbolism and to be given some examples of it. I will gladly tell you what I know, though I must confess that our understanding of it does not go as far as we should like.

The essence of this symbolic relation is that it is a comparison, though not a comparison of *any* sort. Special limitations seem to be attached to the comparison, but it is hard to say what these are. Not everything with which we can compare an object or a process appears in dreams as a symbol for it. And on the other hand a dream does not symbolize every possible element of the latent dream-thoughts but only certain definite ones. So there are restrictions here in both directions. We must admit, too, that the concept of a symbol cannot at present be sharply delimited: it shades off into such notions as those of a replacement or representation, and even approaches that of an allusion. With a number of symbols the comparison which underlies them is obvious. But again there are other symbols in regard to which we must ask ourselves where we are to look for the common element, the *tertium comparationis,*° of the supposed comparison. On further reflection we may afterwards discover it or it may definitely remain concealed. It is strange, moreover, that if a symbol is a comparison it should not be brought to light by an association, and that the dreamer should not be acquainted with it but should make use of it without knowing about it: more than that, indeed, that the dreamer feels no inclination to acknowledge the comparison even after it has been pointed out to him. You see, then, that a symbolic relation is a comparison of a quite special kind, of which we do not as yet clearly grasp the basis, though perhaps we may later arrive at some indication of it.

The range of things which are given symbolic representation in dreams is not wide: the human body as a whole, parents, children, brothers and sisters, birth, death, nakedness—and something else besides. The one typical—that is regular—representation of the human figure as a whole is a *house,* as was recognized by Scherner, who even wanted to give this symbol a transcendant importance which it does not possess. It may happen in a dream that one finds oneself climbing down the façade of a house, enjoying it at one moment, frightened at another. The houses with smooth walls are men, the ones with projections and balconies that one can hold on to are women. One's parents appear in dreams as the *Emperor* and *Empress,* the *King* and *Queen* or other honoured personages; so here dreams are displaying much filial piety. They treat children and brothers and sisters less tenderly: these are symbolized as *small ani-*

°*tertium comparationis:* the "third" or common element which relates the first two *mals* or *vermin.* Birth is almost invariably represented by something which has a connection with *water:* one either falls into the water or climbs out of it, one rescues someone from the water or is rescued by someone—that is to say, the relation is one of mother to child. Dying is replaced in dreams by *departure,* by a *train journey,* being dead by various obscure and, as it were, timid hints, nakedness by *clothes* and *uniforms.* You see how indistinct the boundaries are here between symbolic and allusive representation.

It is a striking fact that, compared with this scanty enumeration, there is another field in which the objects and topics are represented with an extraordinarily rich symbolism. This field is that of sexual life— the genitals, sexual processes, sexual intercourse. The very great majority of symbols in dreams are sexual symbols. And here a strange disproportion is revealed. The topics I have mentioned are few, but the symbols for them are extremely numerous, so that each of these things can be expressed by numbers of almost equivalent symbols. The outcome, when they are interpreted, gives rise to general objection. For, in contrast to the multiplicity of the representations in the dream, the interpretations of the symbols are very monotonous, and this displeases everyone who hears of it; but what is there that we can do about it?

Since this is the first time I have spoken of the subject-matter of sexual life in one of these lectures, I owe you some account of the way in which I propose to treat the topic. Psycho-analysis finds no occasion for concealments and hints, it does not think it necessary to be ashamed of dealing with this important material, it believes it is right and proper to call everything by its correct name, and it hopes that this will be the best way of keeping irrelevant thoughts of a disturbing kind at a distance. The fact that these lectures are being given before a mixed audience of both sexes can make no difference to this. Just as there can be no science *in usum Delphini,*° there can be none for schoolgirls; and the ladies among you have made it clear by their presence in this lecture-room that they wish to be treated on an equality with men.

The male genitals, then, are represented in dreams in a number of ways that must be called symbolic, where the common element in the comparison is mostly very obvious. To begin with, for the male genitals as a whole the sacred number 3 is of symbolic significance. The more striking and for both sexes the more interesting component of the genitals, the male organ, finds symbolic substitutes in the first instance in things that resemble it in shape—things, accordingly, that are long and

---

°*in . . . Delphini:* "for the use of the Dauphin"—an edition of the classics prepared for his son by order of Louis XIV: "bowdlerized," i.e., a text with objectional passages removed

up-standing, such as *sticks, umbrellas, posts, trees* and so on; further, in objects which share with the thing they represent the characteristic of penetrating into the body and injuring—thus, sharp *weapons* of every kind, *knives, daggers, spears, sabres,* but also fire-arms, *rifles, pistols* and *revolvers* (particularly suitable owing to their shape). In the anxiety dreams of girls, being followed by a man with a knife or a fire-arm plays a large part. This is perhaps the commonest instance of dream-symbolism and you will now be able to translate it easily. Nor is there any difficulty in understanding how it is that the male organ can be replaced by objects from which water flows—*water-taps, watering-cans,* or *fountains*—or again by other objects which are capable of being lengthened, such as *hanging-lamps, extensible pencils,* etc. A no less obvious aspect of the organ explains the fact that *pencils, pen-holders, nail-files, hammers,* and other *instruments* are undoubted male sexual symbols.

The remarkable characteristic of the male organ which enables it to rise up in defiance of the laws of gravity, one of the phenomena of erection, leads to its being represented symbolically by *balloons, flying-machines* and most recently by *Zeppelin airships.* But dreams can symbolize erection in yet another, far more expressive manner. They can treat the sexual organ as the essence of the dreamer's whole person and make him himself *fly.* Do not take it to heart if dreams of flying, so familiar and often so delightful, have to be interpreted as dreams of general sexual excitement, as erection-dreams. Among students of psychoanalysis, Paul Federn [1914] has placed this interpretation beyond any doubt; but the same conclusion was reached from his investigations by Mourly Vold [1910–12], who has been so much praised for his sobriety, who carried out the dream-experiments I have referred to with artifically arranged positions of the arms and legs and who was far removed from psycho-analysis and may have known nothing about it. And do not make an objection out of the fact that women can have the same flying dreams as men. Remember, rather, that our dreams aim at being the fulfilments of wishes and that the wish to be a man is found so frequently, consciously or unconsciously, in women. Nor will anyone with a knowledge of anatomy be bewildered by the fact that it is possible for women to realize this wish through the same sensations as men. Women possess as part of their genitals a small organ similar to the male one; and this small organ, the clitoris, actually plays the same part in childhood and during the years before sexual intercourse as the large organ in men.

Among the less easily understandable male sexual symbols are certain *reptiles* and *fishes,* and above all the famous symbol of the *snake.* It is certainly not easy to guess why *hats* and *overcoats* or *cloaks* are employed in the same way, but their symbolic significance is quite unquestionable. And finally we can ask ourselves whether the replacement of the male limb by another limb, the foot or the hand, should be described as symbolic. We are, I think, compelled to do so by the context and by counterparts in the case of women.

The female genitals are symbolically represented by all such objects as share their characteristic of enclosing a hollow space which can take something into itself: by *pits, cavities* and *hollows,* for instance, by *vessels* and *bottles,* by *receptacles, boxes, trunks, cases, chests, pockets,* and so on. *Ships,* too, fall into this category. Some symbols have more connection with the uterus than with the female genitals: thus, *cupboards, stoves* and, more especially, *rooms.* Here room-symbolism touches on house-symbolism. *Doors* and *gates,* again, are symbols of the genital orifice. Materials, too, are symbols for women: *wood, paper* and objects made of them, like *tables* and *books.* Among animals, *snails* and *mussels* at least are undeniably female symbols; among parts of the body, the *mouth* (as a substitute for the genital orifice); among buildings, *churches* and *chapels.* Not every symbol, as you will observe, is equally intelligible.

The breasts must be reckoned with the genitals, and these, like the larger hemispheres of the female body, are represented by *apples, peaches,* and *fruit* in general. The pubic hair of both sexes is depicted in dreams as *woods* and *bushes.* The complicated topography of the female genital parts makes one understand how it is that they are often represented as *landscapes,* with rocks, woods and water, while the imposing mechanism of the male sexual apparatus explains why all kinds of complicated machinery which is hard to describe serve as symbols for it.

Another symbol of the female genitals which deserves mention is a *jewel-case. Jewel* and *treasure* are used in dreams as well as in waking life to describe someone who is loved. *Sweets* frequently represent sexual enjoyment. Satisfaction obtained from a person's own genitals is indicated by all kinds of *playing,* including *piano-playing.* Symbolic representations *par excellence* of masturbation are *gliding* or *sliding* and *pulling off a branch.* The *falling out of a tooth* or the *pulling out of a tooth* is a particularly notable dream-symbol. Its first meaning is undoubtedly castration as a punishment for masturbating. We come across special representations of sexual intercourse less often than might be expected from what has been said so far. Rhythmical activities such as *dancing, riding* and *climbing* must be mentioned here, as well as violent experiences such as *being run over;* so, too, certain *manual crafts,* and, of course, *threatening with weapons.*

You must not picture the use or the translation of these symbols as something quite simple. In the course of them all kinds of things happen which are contrary to our expectations. It seems almost incredible, for instance, that in these symbolic representations the differences between the sexes are often not clearly observed. Some symbols signify genitals in general, irrespective of whether they are male or female: for instance, a *small* child, a *small* son or a *small* daughter.° Or again, a predominantly male symbol may be used for the female genitals or vice versa. We cannot understand this till we have obtained some insight into the development of sexual ideas in human beings. In some instances the ambiguity of the symbols may only be an apparent one; and the most marked symbols, such as *weapons, pockets* and *chests* are excluded from this bisexual use.

I will now go on to make a survey, starting not from the thing represented but from the symbol, of the fields from which sexual symbols are mostly derived, and I will make a few additional remarks, with special reference to the symbols where the common element in the comparison is not understood. The *hat* is an obscure symbol of this kind—perhaps, too, head-coverings in general—with a male significance as a rule, but also capable of a female one.° In the same way an *overcoat* or *cloak* means a man, perhaps not always with a genital reference; it is open to you to ask why.° Neckties, which hang down and are not worn by women, are a definitely male symbol. *Underclothing* and *linen* in general are female. *Clothes* and *uniforms,* as we have already seen, are a substitute for nakedness or bodily shapes. *Shoes* and *slippers* are female genitals. *Tables* and *wood* have already been mentioned as puzzling but certainly female symbols. *Ladders, steps* and *staircases,* or, more precisely, walking on them, are clear symbols of sexual intercourse. On reflection, it will occur to us that the common element here is the rhythm of walking up them—perhaps, too, the increasing excitement and breathlessness the higher one climbs.

We have earlier referred to *landscapes* as representing the female genitals. *Hills* and *rocks* are symbols of the male organ. *Gardens* are common symbols of the female genitals. *Fruit* stands, not for children, but for the breasts. *Wild animals* mean people in an excited sensual state, and further, evil instincts or passions. *Blossoms* and *flowers* indicate women's genitals, or, in particular, virginity. Do not forget that blossoms are actually the genitals of plants.°

°[That is, any one of these three may be used in a dream as a symbol for either the male or the female genitals.]

°[Hat-symbolism was discussed by Freud in his short paper 'A Connection between a Symbol and a Symptom' (1916c).]

°[In *I. of D.,* VI(E), Freud suggests that the explanation may be a verbal assonance between '*Mann*' and '*Mantel*' (the German for 'overcoat' or 'cloak'). A further discussion of this symbol occurs in Lecture XXIX of the *New Introductory Lectures* (1933a).] *I. of D.* = *Interpretation of Dreams*

°[A dream with a large amount of flower symbolism is reported in Section C of Chapter VI of *I. of D.* See also Section D of that chapter.]

We are acquainted already with *rooms* as a symbol. The representation can be carried further, for windows, and doors in and out of rooms, take over the meaning of orifices in the body. And the question of the room being *open* or *locked* fits in with this symbolism, and the *key* that opens it is a decidedly male symbol.

Here, then, is material used for symbolism in dreams. It is not complete and could be carried deeper as well as further. But I fancy it will seem to you more than enough and may even have exasperated you. 'Do I really live in the thick of sexual symbols?' you may ask. 'Are all the objects around me, all the clothes I put on, all the things I pick up, all of them sexual symbols and nothing else?' There is really ground enough for raising astonished questions, and, as a first one, we may enquire how we in fact come to know the meaning of these dream-symbols, upon which the dreamer himself gives us insufficient information or none at all.

My reply is that we learn it from very different sources—from fairy tales and myths, from buffoonery and jokes, from folklore (that is, from knowledge about popular manners and customs, sayings and songs) and from poetic and colloquial linguistic usage. In all these directions we come upon the same symbolism, and in some of them we can understand it without further instruction. If we go into these sources in detail, we shall find so many parallels to dream-symbolism that we cannot fail to be convinced of our interpretations.

According to Scherner, as we have said, the human body is often represented in dreams by the symbol of a house. Carrying this representation further, we found that windows, doors and gates stood for openings in the body and that façades of houses were either smooth or provided with balconies and projections to hold on to. But the same symbolism is found in our linguistic usage—when we greet an acquaintance familiarly as an *'altes Haus'* ['old house'], when we speak of giving someone *'eins aufs Dachl'* [a knock on the head, literally, 'one on the roof'], or when we say of someone else that 'he's not quite right in the upper storey'. In anatomy the orifices of the body are in so many words termed *'Leibespforten'* [literally, 'portals of the body'].

It seems surprising at first to find one's parents in dreams as an imperial or royal couple. But it has its parallel in fairy tales. It begins to dawn on us that the many fairy tales which begin 'Once upon a time there were a King and Queen' only mean to say that there were once a father and mother. In a family the children are jokingly called 'princes' and the eldest 'crown prince'. The King himself calls himself the father of his country. We speak of small children jokingly as *'Würmer'* ['worms'] and speak sympathetically of a child as *'der arme Wurm'* ['the poor worm'].

Let us go back to house-symbolism. When in a dream we make use of the projections on houses for catching hold of, we may be reminded of a common vulgar expression for well-developed breasts: 'She's got something to catch hold of.' There is another popular expression in such cases: 'She's got plenty of wood in front of the house', which seems to confirm our interpretation of wood as a female, maternal symbol.°

And, speaking of wood, it is hard to understand how that material came to represent what is maternal and female. But here comparative philology may come to our help. Our German word 'Holz' seems to come from the same root as the Greek 'ὕλη [hulē]', meaning 'stuff', 'raw material'. This seems to be an instance of the not uncommon event of the general name of a material eventually coming to be reserved for some particular material. Now there is an island in the Atlantic named 'Madeira'. This name was given to it by the Portuguese when they discovered it, because at that time it was covered all over with woods. For in the Portuguese language 'madeira' means 'wood'. You will notice, however, that 'madeira' is only a slightly modified form of the Latin word 'materia', which once more means 'material' in general. But 'materia' is derived from 'mater', 'mother': the material out of which anything is made is, as it were, a mother to it. This ancient view of the thing survives, therefore, in the symbolic use of wood for 'woman' or 'mother'.

Birth is regularly expressed in dreams by some connection with water: one falls into the water or one comes out of the water—one gives birth or one is born. We must not forget that this symbol is able to appeal in two ways to evolutionary truth. Not only are all terrestrial mammals, including man's ancestors, descended from aquatic creatures (this is the more remote of the two facts), but every individual mammal, every human being, spent the first phase of its existence in water—namely as an embryo in the amniotic fluid in its mother's uterus, and came out of that water when it was born. I do not say that the dreamer knows this; on the other hand, I maintain that he need not know it. There is something else that the dreamer probably knows from having been told it in his childhood; and I even maintain of that too that his knowledge of it contributed nothing to the construction of the symbol. He was told in his nursery that the stork brings the babies. But where does it fetch them from? From the pond, or from the stream—once again, then, from the water. One of my patients after he had been given this information—he was a little Count at the time—disappeared for a whole afternoon. He was found at last lying by the edge of the castle pool, with his little face bending over the surface of the water eagerly peering down to try and see the babies at the bottom.

°wood . . . symbol: The common American colloquialisms describing such a woman as "stacked" or perhaps "built" may confirm the allusion to wood.

In myths about the birth of heroes—to which Otto Rank [1909] has devoted a comparative study, the oldest being that of King Sargon of Agade (about 2800 B.C.)—a predominant part is played by exposure in the water and rescue from the water. Rank has perceived that these are representations of birth, analogous to those that are usual in dreams. If one rescues someone from the water in a dream, one is making oneself into his mother, or simply into *a* mother. In myths a person who rescues a baby from the water is admitting that she is the baby's true mother. There is a well-known comic anecdote according to which an intelligent Jewish boy was asked who the mother of Moses was. He replied without hesitation: 'The Princess.' 'No,' he was told, 'she only took him out of the water.' 'That what *she* says,' he replied, and so proved that he had found the correct interpretation of the myth.°

Departure in dreams means dying. So, too, if a child asks where someone is who has died and whom he misses, it is common nursery usage to reply that he has gone on a journey. Once more I should like to contradict the belief that the dream-symbol is derived from this evasion. The dramatist is using the same symbolic connection when he speaks of the after-life as 'the undiscovered country from whose bourn no *traveller* returns'. Even in ordinary life it is common to speak of 'the last journey'. Every one acquainted with ancient rituals is aware of how seriously (in the religion of Ancient Egypt, for instance) the idea is taken of a journey to the land of the dead. Many copies have survived of *The Book of the Dead*, which was supplied to the mummy like a Baedeker to take with him on the journey. Ever since burial-places have been separated from dwelling-places the dead person's last journey has indeed become a reality.

It is just as little the case that genital symbolism is something that is found only in dreams. Every one of you has probably at one time or another spoken impolitely of a woman as an '*alte Schachtel*' ['old box'], perhaps without knowing that you were using a genital symbol. In the New Testament we find women referred to as 'the weaker vessel'. The Hebrew scriptures, written in a style that comes close to poetry, are full of sexually symbolic expressions, which have not always been correctly understood and whose exegesis (for instance, in the case of the Song of Solomon°) has led to some misunderstandings. In later Hebrew literature it is very common to find a woman represented by a house, whose door stands for the sexual orifice. A man complains, for instance, in a case of lost virginity, that he has 'found the door open'. So, too, the symbol of a table for a woman in these writings. Thus, a woman says of her hus-

---

°[Freud used this 'correct interpretation of the myth' as the basis of his last work, *Moses and Monotheism* (1939a).]

°[Some examples are given in Section D of Chapter VI of *I. of D.*]

band: 'I laid the table for him, but he turned it round.' Lame children are said to come about through the man's 'turning the table round'. I take these examples from a paper by Dr. L. Levy of Brünn [1914].

The fact that ships, too, in dreams stand for women is made credible by the etymologists, who tell us that 'Schiff [ship]' was originally the name of an earthenware vessel and is the same word as 'Schaff' [a dialect word meaning 'tub']. That ovens represent women and the uterus is confirmed by the Greek legend of Periander of Corinth and his wife Melissa. The tyrant, according to Herodotus, conjured up the shade of his wife, whom he had loved passionately but had murdered out of jealousy, to obtain some information from her. The dead woman proved her identity by saying that he (Periander) had *pushed his bread into a cold oven'*, as a disguise for an event which no one else could know of. In the periodical *Anthropophyteia*, edited by F. S. Krauss, an invaluable source of knowledge of sexual anthropology, we learn that in a particular part of Germany they say of a woman who has given birth to a child that *'her oven has come to pieces'*. Kindling the fire, and everything to do with it, is intimately interwoven with sexual symbolism. Flame is always a male genital, and the hearth is its female counterpart.

If you have felt surprised at the frequency with which landscapes are used in dreams to represent the female genitals, you can learn from mythology the part played by *Mother Earth* in the concepts and cults of the peoples of antiquity and how their view of agriculture was determined by this symbolism. You will perhaps be inclined to trace the fact that in dreams a room represents a woman to the common usage in our language by which *'Frau'* is replaced by *'Frauenzimmer'*°—the human being is replaced by the apartment allotted to her. Similarly we speak of the 'Sublime Porte'°, meaning the Sultan and his government. So too the title of the Ancient Egyptian ruler, 'Pharaoh', means simply 'Great Courtyard'. (In the Ancient East the courts between the double gateways of a city were public meeting-places like the market-places of the classical world.) This derivation, however, appears to be too superficial. It seems to me more likely that a room became the symbol of a woman as being the space which encloses human beings. We have already found 'house' used in a similar sense; and mythology and poetical language enable us to add 'city', 'citadel', 'castle' and 'fortress' as further symbols for 'woman'. The question could be easily settled from the dreams of people who do not speak or understand German. During the last few years I have mainly treated foreign-speaking patients, and I seem to remember that in their dreams too *'Zimmer'* ['room'] meant *'Frauen-*

°[Literally 'woman's apartment'. The word is very often used in German as a slightly derogatory synonym for 'woman'.]

°[Literally, 'Gateway', the old diplomatic term for the Ottoman Court at Constantinople before 1923, derived *via* the French from the Turkish title.]

zimmer', though they had no similar usage in their languages. There are other indications that the symbolic relation can go beyond the limits of language—which, incidentally was asserted long ago by an old investigator of dreams, Schubert [1814]. However, none of my dreamers were completely ignorant of German, so the decision must be left to psychoanalysts who can collect data from unilingual people in other countries.

There is scarcely one of the symbolic representations of the male genitals which does not recur in joking, vulgar or poetic usage, especially in the ancient classical dramatists. But here we meet not only the symbols which appear in dreams, but others besides—for instance tools employed in various operations, and particularly the plough. Moreover, the symbolic representation of masculinity leads us to a very extensive and much disputed region, which, on grounds of economy, we shall avoid. I should like, however, to devote a few words to one symbol, which, as it were, falls outside this class—the number 3. Whether this number owes its sacred character to this symbolic connection remains undecided. But what seems certain is that a number of tripartite things that occur in nature—the clover leaf, for instance—owe their use for coats of arms and emblems to this symbolic meaning. Similarly, the tripartite lily—the so-called *fleur-de-lis*—and the remarkable heraldic device of two islands so far apart as Sicily and the Isle of Man—the *triskeles* (three bent legs radiating from a centre)—seem to be stylized versions of the male genitals. Likenesses of the male organ were regarded in antiquity as the most powerful *apotropaic* (means of defence) against evil influences, and, in conformity with this, the lucky charms of our own day can all be easily recognized as genital or sexual symbols. Let us consider a collection of such things—as they are worn, for instance, in the form of small silver hanging trinkets: a four-leaved clover, a pig, a mushroom, a horse-shoe, a ladder, a chimney-sweep. The four-leaved clover has taken the place of the three-leaved one which is really suited to be a symbol. The pig is an ancient fertility symbol. The mushroom is an undoubted penis-symbol: there are mushrooms [fungi] which owe their systematic name (*Phallus impudicus*) to their unmistakable resemblance to the male organ. The horseshoe copies the outline of the female genital orifice, while the chimney-sweep, who carries the ladder, appears in this company on account of his activities, with which sexual intercourse is vulgarly compared. We have made the acquaintance of his ladder in dreams as a sexual symbol; here German linguistic usage comes to our help and shows us how the word 'steigen' ['to climb,' or 'to mount'] is used in what is *par excellence* a sexual sense. We say 'den Frauen nachsteigen' ['to run' (literally 'climb') 'after women'], and 'ein alter Steiger' ['an old rake' (literally 'climber')]. In French, in which the word for steps on a staircase is 'marches', we find a precisely analogous term 'un vieux marcheur'. The fact that in many large animals climbing or 'mounting' on the female is a necessary preliminary to sexual intercourse probably fits into this context.

'Pulling off a branch' as a symbolic representation of masturbation is not merely in harmony with vulgar descriptions of the act° but has far-reaching mythological parallels. But that masturbation, or rather the punishment for it—castration—, should be represented by the falling out or pulling out of teeth is especially remarkable, since there is a counterpart to it in anthropology which can be known to only a very small number of dreamers. There seems to me no doubt that the circumcision practised by so many peoples is an equivalent and substitute for castration. And we now learn that certain primitive tribes in Australia carry out circumcision as a puberty rite (at the festival to celebrate a boy's attaining sexual maturity), while other tribes, their near neighbours, have replaced this act by the knocking out of a tooth.

Here I bring my account of these specimens to an end. They are only specimens. We know more on the subject; but you may imagine how much richer and more interesting a collection like this would be if it were brought together, not by amateurs like us, but by real professionals in mythology, anthropology, philology and folklore.

A few consequences force themselves on our notice; they cannot be exhaustive, but they offer us food for reflection.

In the first place we are faced by the fact that the dreamer has a symbolic mode of expression at his disposal which he does not know in waking life and does not recognize. This is as extraordinary as if you were to discover that your housemaid understood Sanskrit, though you know that she was born in a Bohemian village and never learnt it. It is not easy to account for this fact by the help of our psychological views. We can only say that the knowledge of symbolism is unconscious to the dreamer, that it belongs to his unconscious mental life. But even with this assumption we do not meet the point. Hitherto it has only been necessary for us to assume the existence of unconscious endeavours— endeavours, that is, of which, temporarily or permanently, we know nothing. Now, however, it is a question of more than this, of unconscious pieces of knowledge, of connections of thought, of comparisons between different objects which result in its being possible for one of them to be regularly put in place of the other. These comparisons are not freshly made on each occasion; they lie ready to hand and are complete, once and for all. This is implied by the fact of their agreeing in the case of different individuals—possibly, indeed, agreeing in spite of differences of language. What can be the origin of these symbolic relations? Linguistic usage covers only a small part of them. The multiplicity of parallels in

---

°[Cf. the English 'tossing off'.]—or the American "jerking off."

other spheres of knowledge are mostly unknown to the dreamer; we ourselves have been obliged to collect them laboriously.

Secondly, these symbolic relations are not something peculiar to dreamers or to the dream-work° through which they come to expression. This same symbolism, as we have seen, is employed by myths and fairy tales, by the people in their sayings and songs, by colloquial linguistic usage and by the poetic imagination. The field of symbolism is immensely wide, and dream-symbolism is only a small part of it; indeed, it serves no useful purpose to attack the whole problem from the direction of dreams. Many symbols which are commonly used elsewhere appear in dreams very seldom or not at all. Some dream-symbols are not to be found in all other fields but only, as you have seen, here and there. One gets an impression that what we are faced with here is an ancient but extinct mode of expression, of which different pieces have survived in different fields, one piece only here, another only there, a third, perhaps, in slightly modified forms in several fields. And here I recall the phantasy of an interesting psychotic patient, who imagined a 'basic language' of which all these symbolic relations would be residues.

Thirdly, it must strike you that the symbolism in the other fields I have mentioned is by no means solely sexual symbolism, whereas in dreams symbols are used almost exclusively for the expression of sexual objects and relations. This is not easily explained either. Are we to suppose that symbols which originally had a sexual significance later acquired another application and that, furthermore, the toning-down of representation by symbols into other kinds of representation may be connected with this? These questions can evidently not be answered so long as we have considered dream-symbolism alone. We can only hold firmly to the suspicion that there is a specially intimate relation between true symbols and sexuality.

In this connection we have been given an important hint during the last few years. A philologist, Hans Sperber [1912], of Uppsala, who works independently of psycho-analysis, has put forward the argument that sexual needs have played the biggest part in the origin and development of speech. According to him, the original sounds of speech served for communication, and summoned the speaker's sexual partner; the further development of linguistic roots accompanied the working activities of primal man. These activities, he goes on, were performed in common and were accompanied by rhythmically repeated utterances. In this way a sexual interest became attached to work. Primal man made work acceptable, as it were, by treating it as an equivalent and substitute for sexual activity. The words enunciated during work in common thus had two meanings; they denoted sexual acts as well as the working activity

---

°*dream-work*":   the construction or thing that the dreamer "makes"

equated with them. As time went on, the words became detached from the sexual meaning and fixed to the work. In later generations the same thing happened with new words, which had a sexual meaning and were applied to new forms of work. In this way a number of verbal roots would have been formed, all of which were of sexual origin and had subsequently lost their sexual meaning. If the hypothesis I have here sketched out is correct, it would give us a possibility of understanding dream-symbolism. We should understand why dreams, which preserve something of the earliest conditions, have such an extraordinarily large number of sexual symbols, and why, in general, weapons and tools always stand for what is male, while materials and things that are worked upon stand for what is female. The symbolic relation would be the residue of an ancient verbal identity; things which were once called by the same name as the genitals could now serve as symbols for them in dreams.

The parallels we have found to dream-symbolism also allow us to form an estimate of the characteristic of psycho-analysis which enables it to attract general interest in a way in which neither psychology nor psychiatry has succeeded in doing. In the work of psycho-analysis, links are formed with numbers of other mental sciences, the investigation of which promises results of the greatest value: links with mythology and philology, with folklore, with social psychology and the theory of religion. You will not be surprised to hear that a periodical has grown up on psycho-analytic soil whose sole aim is to foster these links. This periodical is known as *Imago*, founded in 1912 and edited by Hanns Sachs and Otto Rank.° In all these links the share of psycho-analysis is in the first instance that of giver and only to a less extent that of receiver. It is true that this brings it an advantage in the fact that its strange findings become more familiar when they are met with again in other fields; but on the whole it is psycho-analysis which provides the technical methods and the points of view whose application in these other fields should prove fruitful. The mental life of human individuals, when subjected to psycho-analytic investigation, offers us the explanations with the help of which we are able to solve a number of riddles in the life of human communities or at least to set them in a true light.

Incidentally, I have said nothing at all to you yet as to the circumstances in which we can obtain our deepest insight into the hypothetical 'primal language' and as to the field in which most of it has survived. Until you know this you cannot form an opinion of its whole significance. For this field is that of the neuroses and its material is the symptoms and other manifestations of neurotic patients, for the explanation and treatment of which psycho-analysis was, indeed, created.

°[It ceased publication in 1941. A journal with a similar aim, *The American Imago*, was founded by Hanns Sachs in Boston in 1939.]

The fourth of my reflections takes us back to the beginning and directs us along our prescribed path. I have said that even if there were no dream-censorship, dreams would still not be easily intelligible to us, for we should still be faced with the task of translating the symbolic language of dreams into that of our waking thought. Thus symbolism is a second and independent factor in the distortion of dreams, alongside of the dream-censorship. It is plausible to suppose, however, that the dream-censorship finds it convenient to make use of symbolism, since it leads towards the same end—the strangeness and incomprehensibility of dreams.

It will shortly become clear whether a further study of dreams may not bring us up against yet another factor that contributes to the distortion of dreams. But I should not like to leave the subject of dream-symbolism without once more touching on the problem of how it can meet with such violent resistance in educated people when the wide diffusion of symbolism in myths, religion, art and language is so unquestionable. May it not be that what is responsible is once again its connection with sexuality?

*   *   *

The Unconscious in Poetry

The following poems are among the odd works of poetry that seem in some way drawn straight out of the unconscious. They assert their images simply and directly without transforming them into conventional, daylight discourse. Poems of this kind often receive elaborate and sometimes silly interpretations, yet have remained intensely popular and appealing to many readers.

KUBLA KHAN: OR, A VISION IN A DREAM. A FRAGMENT

Samuel Taylor Coleridge (1772–1834)

In Xanadu did Kubla Khan
A stately pleasure dome decree:
Where Alph, the sacred river, ran
Through caverns measureless to man
   Down to a sunless sea.   5
So twice five miles of fertile ground
With walls and towers were girdled round:
And there were gardens bright with sinuous rills,

Where blossomed many an incense-bearing tree;
And here were forests ancient as the hills,   10
Enfolding sunny spots of greenery.

But oh! that deep romantic chasm which slanted
Down the green hill athwart a cedarn cover!
A savage place! as holy and enchanted
As e'er beneath a waning moon was haunted   15
By woman wailing for her demon-lover!
And from this chasm, with ceaseless turmoil seething,
As if this earth in fast thick pants were breathing,
A mighty fountain momently was forced;
Amid whose swift half-intermitted burst   20
Huge fragments vaulted like rebounding hail,
Or chaffy grain beneath the thresher's flail:
And 'mid these dancing rocks at once and ever
It flung up momently the sacred river.
Five miles meandering with a mazy motion   25
Through wood and dale the sacred river ran,
Then reached the caverns measureless to man,
And sank in tumult to a lifeless ocean;
And 'mid this tumult Kubla heard from far
Ancestral voices prophesying war!   30
    The shadow of the dome of pleasure
    Floated midway on the waves;
    Where was heard the mingled measure
    From the fountain and the caves.
It was a miracle of rare device,   35
A sunny pleasure-dome with caves of ice!

A damsel with a dulcimer
In a vision once I saw:
It was an Abyssinian maid,
And on her dulcimer she played,   40
Singing of Mount Abora.
Could I revive within me
Her symphony and song,
    To such a deep delight 'twould win me,
That with music loud and long,   45
I would build that dome in air,
That sunny dome! those caves of ice!
And all who heard should see them there,
And all should cry, Beware! Beware!
His flashing eyes, his floating hair!   50

Weave a circle round him thrice,
And close your eyes with holy dread,
For he on honey-dew hath fed,
And drunk the milk of Paradise.

[handwritten: opium]
[handwritten: He lost it & can't recreate its]
[handwritten: Virginity is part of life.]
[handwritten: phallic symbol.]

THE SICK ROSE

William Blake (1757–1827)

O Rose, thou art sick!
The invisible worm,
That flies in the night,
In the howling storm,

Has found out thy bed   *[handwritten: virginity]*   5
Of crimson joy,
And his dark secret love
Does thy life destroy.

*   *   *

Since under certain conditions (as Freud has suggested) practically anything can take on a sexual connotation, it is very easy to overdo implications of this kind. Nonetheless, double meanings of a simple sort are a staple of bawdy humor, folk music and even of nursery rhymes. The usual case is one in which a simple statement contains an overtone of sexual substance, or the tone of the statement contains an invitation to see it as containing such reference. A few simple examples appear below.

1. Little Tommy Tittlemouse
    Lived in a little house;
    He caught fishes
    In other men's ditches.

2. If you don't like my apples,
    Then don't shake my tree;
    I'm not after your boy friend,
    He's after me.

3. Eaper Weaper, chimbley-sweeper,
   Had a wife but couldn't keep her,
   Had anovver, didn't love her.
   Up the chimbley he did shove her.

*   *   *

The Symbolism of Neurosis

Peter Taylor's short story, *A Spinster's Tale,* is an example of conscious, post-Freudian use of symbols drawn from psychoanalytic theory.
These symbols are products of the unhappy and distorted consciousness
of the narrator, and they represent the dramatic conflict in her mind
between her fear of Mr. Speed and her attraction to him. As she grows
up, the images of dreams become indistinguishable from her daylight
reality. Tennyson's poem, *The Lady of Shalott,* is another kind of spinster's tale.

A SPINSTER'S TALE

Peter Taylor (1919–   )

My brother would often get drunk when I was a little girl, but that
put a different sort of fear into me from what Mr. Speed did. With Brother
it was a spiritual thing. And though it was frightening to know that he
would have to burn for all that giggling and bouncing around on the stair
at night, the truth was that he only seemed jollier to me when I would
stick my head out of the hall door. It made him seem almost my age for
him to act so silly, putting his white forefinger all over his flushed face
and finally over his lips to say, "Sh-sh-sh-sh!" But the really frightening
thing about seeing Brother drunk was what I always heard when I had
slid back into bed. I could always recall my mother's words to him when
he was sixteen, the year before she died, spoken in her greatest sincerity,
in her most religious tone:

"Son, I'd rather see you in your grave."

Yet those nights put a scaredness into me that was clearly distinguish-
able from the terror that Mr. Speed instilled by stumbling past our
house two or three afternoons a week. The most that I knew about Mr.
Speed was his name. And this I considered that I had somewhat fabri-

cated—by allowing him the "Mr."—in my effort to humanize and soften the monster that was forever passing our house on Church Street. My father would point him out through the wide parlor window in soberness and severity to my brother with: "There goes Old Speed, again." Or on Saturdays when Brother was with the Benton boys and my two uncles were over having toddies with Father in the parlor, Father would refer to Mr. Speed's passing with a similar speech, but in a blustering tone of merry tolerance: "There goes Old Speed, again. The rascal!" These designations were equally awful, both spoken in tones that were foreign to my father's manner of addressing me; and not unconsciously I prepared the euphemism, Mister Speed, against the inevitable day when I should have to speak of him to someone.

I was named Elizabeth, for my mother. My mother had died in the spring before Mr. Speed first came to my notice on that late afternoon in October. I had bathed at four with the aid of Lucy, who had been my nurse and who was now the upstairs maid; and Lucy was upstairs turning back the covers of the beds in the rooms with their color schemes of blue and green and rose. I wandered into the shadowy parlor and sat first on one chair, then on another. I tried lying down on the settee that went with the parlor set, but my legs had got too long this summer to stretch out straight on the settee. And my feet looked long in their pumps against the wicker arm. I looked at the pictures around the room blankly and at the stained-glass windows on either side of the fireplace; and the winter light coming through them was hardly bright enough to show the colors. I struck a match on the mosaic hearth and lit the gas-logs.

Kneeling on the hearth I watched the flames till my face felt hot. I stood up then and turned directly to one of the full-length mirror-panels that were on each side of the front window. This one was just to the right of the broad window and my reflection in it stood out strangely from the rest of the room in the dull light that did not penetrate beyond my figure. I leaned closer to the mirror trying to discover a resemblance between myself and the wondrous Alice who walked through a looking-glass. But that resemblance I was seeking I could not find in my sharp features, or in my heavy, dark curls hanging like fragments of hosepipe to my shoulders.

I propped my hands on the borders of the narrow mirror and put my face close to watch my lips say, "Away." I would hardly open them for the "a"; and then I would contort my face by the great opening I made for the "way." I whispered, "Away, away." I whispered it over and over, faster and faster, watching myself in the mirror: "A-way—a-way—a-way-away-awayaway." Suddenly I burst into tears and turned from the gloomy mirror to the daylight at the wide parlor window. Gazing tearfully through the expanse of plate glass there, I beheld Mr. Speed walking like a cripple with one foot on the curb and one in the street. And faintly I could hear him cursing the trees as he passed them, giving each a lick with his heavy walking cane.

Presently I was dry-eyed in my fright. My breath came short, and I clasped the black bow at the neck of my middy blouse.

When he had passed from view, I stumbled back from the window. I hadn't heard the houseboy enter the parlor, and he must not have noticed me there. I made no move of recognition as he drew the draperies across the wide front window for the night. I stood cold and silent before the gas-logs with a sudden inexplicable memory of my mother's cheek and a vision of her in her bedroom on a spring day.

That April day when spring had seemed to crowd itself through the windows into the bright upstairs rooms, the old-fashioned mahogany sick-chair had been brought down from the attic to my mother's room. Three days before, a quiet service had been held there for the stillborn baby, and I had accompanied my father and brother to our lot in the gray cemetery to see the box (large for so tiny a parcel) lowered and covered with mud. But in the parlor now by the gas-logs I remembered the day that my mother had sent for the sick-chair and for me.

The practical nurse, sitting in a straight chair busy at her needlework, looked over her glasses to give me some little instruction in the arrangement of my mother's pillows in the chair. A few minutes before, this practical nurse had lifted my sick mother bodily from the bed, and I had had the privilege of rolling my mother to the big bay window that looked out ideally over the new foliage of small trees in our side yard.

I stood self-consciously straight, close by my mother, a maturing little girl awkward in my curls and long-waisted dress. My pale mother, in her silk bed-jacket, with a smile leaned her cheek against the cheek of her daughter. Outside it was spring. The furnishings of the great blue room seemed to partake for that one moment of nature's life. And my mother's cheek was warm on mine. This I remembered when I sat before the gas-logs trying to put Mr. Speed out of my mind; but that a few moments later my mother beckoned to the practical nurse and sent me suddenly from the room, my memory did not dwell upon. I remembered only the warmth of the cheek and the comfort of that other moment.

I sat near the blue burning logs and waited for my father and my brother to come in. When they came saying the same things about office and school that they said every day, turning on lights beside chairs that they liked to flop into, I realized not that I was ready or unready for them but that there had been, within me, an attempt at a preparation for such readiness.

They sat so customarily in their chairs at first and the talk ran so easily that I thought that Mr. Speed could be forgotten as quickly and painlessly as a doubting of Jesus or a fear of death from the measles.

But the conversation took insinuating and malicious twists this afternoon. My father talked about the possibilities of a general war and recalled opinions that people had had just before the Spanish-American. He talked about the hundreds of men in the Union Depot. Thinking of all those men there, that close together, was something like meeting Mr. Speed in the front hall. I asked my father not to talk about war, which seemed to him a natural enough request for a young lady to make.

"How is your school, my dear?" he asked me. "How are Miss Hood and Miss Herron? Have they found who's stealing the boarders' things, my dear?"

All of those little girls safely in Belmont School being called for by gentle ladies or warm-breasted Negro women were a pitiable sight beside the beastly vision of Mr. Speed which even they somehow conjured.

At dinner, with Lucy serving and sometimes helping my plate (because she had done so for so many years), Brother teased me first one way and then another. My father joined in on each point until I began to take the teasing very seriously, and then he told Brother that he was forever carrying things too far.

Once at dinner I was convinced that my preposterous fears that Brother knew what had happened to me by the window in the afternoon were not at all preposterous. He had been talking quietly. It was something about the meeting that he and the Benton boys were going to attend after dinner. But quickly, without reason, he turned his eyes on me across the table and fairly shouted in his new deep voice: "I saw three horses running away out on Harding Road today! They were just like the mules we saw at the mines in the mountains! They were running to beat hell and with little girls riding them!"

The first week after I had the glimpse of Mr. Speed through the parlor window, I spent the afternoons dusting the bureau and mantel and bedside table in my room, arranging on the chaise longue the dolls which at this age I never played with and rarely even talked to; or I would absent-mindedly assist Lucy in turning down the beds and maybe watch the houseboy set the dinner table. I went to the parlor only when Father came or when Brother came earlier and called me in to show me a shin bruise or a box of cigarettes which a girl had given him.

Finally I put my hand on the parlor doorknob just at four one afternoon and entered the parlor, walking stiffly as I might have done with my hands in a muff going into church. The big room with its heavy furniture and pictures showed no change since the last afternoon that I had spent there, unless possibly there were fresh antimacassars on the chairs. I confidently pushed an odd chair over to the window and took my seat and sat erect and waited.

My heart would beat hard when, from the corner of my eye, I caught sight of some figure moving up Church Street. And as it drew nearer, showing the form of some Negro or neighbor or drummer,° I would sigh from relief and from regret. I was ready for Mr. Speed. And I knew that he would come again and again, that he had been passing our house for inconceivable numbers of years. I knew that if he did not appear today, he would pass tomorrow. Not because I had had accidental, unavoidable glimpses of him from upstairs windows during the past week, nor because there were indistinct memories of such a figure, hardly noticed, seen on afternoons that preceded that day when I had seen him stumbling like a cripple along the curb and beating and cursing the trees did I know that Mr. Speed was a permanent and formidable figure in my life which I would be called upon to deal with; my knowledge, I was certain, was purely intuitive.

I was ready now not to face him with his drunken rage directed at me, but to look at him far off in the street and to appraise him. He didn't come that afternoon, but he came the next. I sat prim and straight before the window. I turned my head neither to the right to anticipate the sight of him nor to the left to follow his figure when it had passed. But when he was passing before my window, I put my eyes full on him and looked though my teeth chattered in my head. And now I saw his face heavy, red, fierce like his body. He walked with an awkward, stomping sort of stagger, carrying his gray top coat over one arm; and with his other hand he kept poking his walnut cane into the soft sod along the sidewalk. When he was gone, I recalled my mother's cheek again, but the recollection this time, though more deliberate, was dwelt less upon; and I could only think of watching Mr. Speed again and again.

There was snow on the ground the third time that I watched Mr. Speed pass our house. Mr. Speed spat on the snow, and with his cane he aimed at the brown spot that his tobacco made there. And I could see that he missed his aim. The fourth time that I sat watching for him from the window, snow was actually falling outside; and I felt a sort of anxiety to know what would ever drive him into my own house. For a moment I doubted that he would really come to my door; but I prodded myself with the thought of his coming and finding me unprepared. And I continued to keep my secret watch for him two or three times a week during the rest of the winter.

Meanwhile my life with my father and brother and the servants in the shadowy house went on from day to day. On week nights the evening meal usually ended with petulant arguing between the two men, the atlas or the encyclopedia usually drawing them from the table to read out the statistics. Often Brother was accused of having looked-them-

---

°*drummer:* a door to door salesman

up-previously and of maneuvering the conversation toward the particular subject, for topics were very easily introduced and dismissed by the two. Once I, sent to the library to fetch a cigar, returned to find the discourse shifted in two minutes' time from the Kentucky Derby winners to the languages in which the Bible was first written. Once I actually heard the conversation slip, in the course of a small dessert, from the comparative advantages of urban and agrarian life for boys between the ages of fifteen and twenty to the probable origin and age of the Icelandic parliament and then to the doctrines of the Campbellite church.

That night I followed them to the library and beheld them fingering the pages of the flimsy old atlas in the light from the beaded lampshade. They paid no attention to me and little to one another, each trying to turn the pages of the book and mumbling references to newspaper articles and to statements of persons of responsibility. I slipped from the library to the front parlor across the hall where I could hear the contentious hum. And I lit the gas-logs, trying to warm my long legs before them as I examined my own response to the unguided and remorseless bickering of the masculine voices.

It was, I thought, their indifferent shifting from topic to topic that most disturbed me. Then I decided that it was the tremendous gaps that there seemed to be between the subjects that was bewildering to me. Still again I thought that it was the equal interest which they displayed for each subject that was dismaying. All things in the world were equally at home in their arguments. They exhibited equal indifference to the horrors that each topic might suggest; and I wondered whether or not their imperturbability was a thing that they had achieved.

I knew that I had got myself so accustomed to the sight of Mr. Speed's peregrinations, persistent, yet, withal, seemingly without destination, that I could view his passing with perfect equanimity. And from this I knew that I must extend my preparation for the day when I should have to view him at closer range. When the day would come, I knew that it must involve my father and my brother and that his existence therefore must not remain an unmentionable thing, the secrecy of which to explode at the moment of crisis, only adding to its confusion.

Now, the door to my room was the first at the top of the long red-carpeted stairway. A wall light beside it was left burning on nights when Brother was out, and, when he came in, he turned it off. The light shining through my transom was a comforting sight when I had gone to bed in the big room; and in the summertime I could see the reflection of light bugs on it, and often one would plop against it. Sometimes I would wake up in the night with a start and would be frightened in the dark, not knowing what had awakened me until I realized that Brother had just turned out the light. On other nights, however, I would hear him close the front door and hear him bouncing up the steps. When I then stuck my head out the door, usually he would toss me a piece of candy and he always signaled to me to be quiet.

I had never intentionally stayed awake till he came in until one night toward the end of February of that year, and I hadn't been certain then that I should be able to do it. Indeed, when finally the front door closed, I had dozed several times sitting up in the dark bed. But I was standing with my door half open before he had come a third of the way up the stair. When he saw me, he stopped still on the stairway resting his hand on the banister. I realized that purposefulness must be showing on my face, and so I smiled at him and beckoned. His red face broke into a fine grin, and he took the next few steps two at a time. But he stumbled on the carpeted steps. He was on his knees, yet with his hand still on the banister. He was motionless there for a moment with his head cocked to one side, listening. The house was quiet and still. He smiled again, sheepishly this time, and kept putting his white forefinger to his red face as he ascended on tiptoe the last third of the flight of steps.

At the head of the stair he paused, breathing hard. He reached his hand into his coat pocket and smiled confidently as he shook his head at me. I stepped backward into my room.

"Oh," he whispered. "Your candy."

I stood straight in my white nightgown with my black hair hanging over my shoulders, knowing that he could see me only indistinctly. I beckoned to him again. He looked suspiciously about the hall, then stepped into the room and closed the door behind him.

"What's the matter, Betsy?" he said.

I turned and ran and climbed between the covers of my bed.

"What's the matter, Betsy?" he said. He crossed to my bed and sat down beside me on it.

I told him that I didn't know what was the matter.

"Have you been reading something you shouldn't, Betsy?" he asked.

I was silent.

"Are you lonely, Betsy?" he said. "Are you a lonely little girl?"

I sat up on the bed and threw my arms about his neck. And as I sobbed on his shoulder I smelled for the first time the fierce odor of his cheap whisky.

"Yes, I'm always lonely," I said with directness, and I was then silent with my eyes open and my cheek on the shoulder of his overcoat which was yet cold from the February night air.

He kept his face turned away from me and finally spoke out of the other corner of his mouth, I thought, "I'll come home earlier some afternoons and we'll talk and play."

"Tomorrow."

When I had said this distinctly, I fell away from him back on the bed. He stood up and looked at me curiously, as though in some way repelled by my settling so comfortably in the covers. And I could see his eighteen-year-old head cocked to one side as though trying to see my face in the dark. He leaned over me, and I smelled his whisky breath. It was not repugnant to me. It was blended with the odor that he always had. I thought that he was going to strike me. He didn't, however, and in a moment was opening the door to the lighted hall. Before he went out, again I said:

"Tomorrow."

The hall light dark and the sound of Brother's footsteps gone, I naturally repeated the whole scene in my mind and upon examination found strange elements present. One was something like a longing for my brother to strike me when he was leaning over me. Another was his bewilderment at my procedure. On the whole I was amazed at the way I had carried the thing off. Now I only wished that in the darkness when he was leaning over me I had said languidly, "Oh, Brother," had said it in a tone indicating that we had in common some unmentionable trouble. Then I should have been certain of his presence next day. As it was, though, I had little doubt of his coming home early.

I would not let myself reflect further on my feelings for my brother —my desire for him to strike me and my delight in his natural odor. I had got myself in the habit of postponing such elucidations until after I had completely settled with Mr. Speed. But, as after all such meetings with my brother, I reflected upon the posthumous punishments in store for him for his carousing and drinking and remembered my mother's saying that she had rather see him in his grave.

The next afternoon at four I had the chessboard on the tea table before the front parlor window. I waited for my brother, knowing pretty well that he would come and feeling certain that Mr. Speed would pass. (For this was a Thursday afternoon; and during the winter months I had found that there were two days of the week on which Mr. Speed never failed to pass our house. These were Thursday and Saturday.) I led my brother into that dismal parlor chattering about the places where I had found the chessmen long in disuse. When I paused a minute, slipping into my seat by the chessboard, he picked up with talk of the senior class play and his chances for being chosen valedictorian. Apparently I no longer seemed an enigma to him. I thought that he must have concluded that I was just a lonely little girl named Besty. But I doubted that his nature was so different from my own that he could sustain objective sympathy for another child, particularly a younger sister, from one day to another. And since I saw no favors that he could ask from me at this time, my conclusion was that he believed that he had never exhibited his drunkenness to me with all his bouncing about on the stair at night; but that he was not certain that talking from the other corner of his mouth had been precaution enough against his whisky breath.

We faced each other over the chessboard and set the men in order. There were only a few days before it would be March, and the light through the window was first bright and then dull. During my brother's moves I stared out the window at the clouds that passed before the sun and watched pieces of newspaper that blew about the yard. I was calm beyond my own credulity. I found myself responding to my brother's little jokes and showing real interest in the game. I tried to terrorize myself by imagining Mr. Speed's coming up to the very window this day. I even had him shaking his cane and his derby hat at us. But the frenzy which I expected at this step of my preparation did not come. And some part of Mr. Speed's formidability seemed to have vanished. I realized that by not hiding my face in my mother's bosom and by looking at him so regularly for so many months, I had come to accept his existence as a natural part of my life on Church Street, though something to be guarded against, or, as I had put it before, to be thoroughly prepared for when it came to my door.

The problem then, in relation to my brother, had suddenly resolved itself in something much simpler than the conquest of my fear of looking upon Mr. Speed alone had been. This would be only a matter of how I should act and of what words I should use. And from the incident of the night before, I had some notion that I'd find a suitable way of procedure in our household.

Mr. Speed appeared in the street without his overcoat but with one hand holding the turned-up lapels and collar of his gray suit coat. He followed his cane, stomping like an enraged blind man with his head bowed against the March wind. I squeezed from between my chair and the table and stood right at the great plate glass window, looking out. From the corner of my eye I saw that Brother was intent upon his play. Presently, in the wind, Mr. Speed's derby went back on his head, and his hand grabbed at it, pulled it back in place, then returned to hold his lapels. I took a sharp breath, and Brother looked up. And just as he looked out the window, Mr. Speed's derby did blow off and across the sidewalk, over the lawn. Mr. Speed turned, holding his lapels with his tremendous hand, shouting oaths that I could hear ever so faintly, and tried to stumble after his hat.

Then I realized that my brother was gone from the room; and he was outside the window with Mr. Speed chasing Mr. Speed's hat in the wind.

I sat back in my chair, breathless; one elbow went down on the chessboard disordering the black and white pawns and kings and castles.

And through the window I watched Brother handing Mr. Speed his derby. I saw his apparent indifference to the drunk man's oaths and curses. I saw him coming back to the house while the old man yet stood railing at him. I pushed the table aside and ran to the front door lest Brother be locked outside. He met me in the hall smiling blandly.

I said, "That's Mr. Speed."

He sat down on the bottom step of the stairway, leaning backward and looking at me inquisitively.

"He's drunk, Brother," I said. "Always."

My brother looked frankly into the eyes of this half-grown sister of his but said nothing for a while.

I pushed myself up on the console table and sat swinging my legs and looking seriously about the walls of the cavernous hallway at the expanse of oak paneling, at the inset canvas of the sixteenth-century Frenchman making love to his lady, at the hat rack, and at the grandfather's clock in the darkest corner. I waited for Brother to speak.

"You don't like people who get drunk?" he said.

I saw that he was taking the whole thing as a thrust at his own behavior.

"I just think Mr. Speed is very ugly, Brother."

From the detached expression of his eyes I knew that he was not convinced.

"I wouldn't mind him less if he were sober," I said. "Mr. Speed's like—a loose horse."

This analogy convinced him. He knew then what I meant.

"You mustn't waste your time being afraid of such things," he said in great earnestness. "In two or three years there'll be things that you'll have to be afraid of. Things you really can't avoid."

"What did he say to you?" I asked.

"He cussed and threatened to hit me with that stick."

"For no reason?"

"Old Mr. Speed's burnt out his reason with whisky."

"Tell me about him." I was almost imploring him.

"Everybody knows about him. He just wanders around town, drunk. Sometimes downtown they take him off in the Black Maria."°

I pictured him on the main streets that I knew downtown and in the big department stores. I could see him in that formal neighborhood where my grandmother used to live. In the neighborhood of Miss Hood and Miss Herron's school. Around the little houses out where my father's secretary lived. Even in nigger town.

"You'll get used to him, for all his ugliness," Brother said. Then we sat there till my father came in, talking almost gaily about things that

---

°*Black Maria:* a police patrol wagon

were particularly ugly in Mr. Speed's clothes and face and in his way of walking.

Since the day that I watched myself say "away" in the mirror, I had spent painful hours trying to know once more that experience which I now regarded as something like mystical. But the stringent course that I, motherless and lonely in our big house, had brought myself to follow while only thirteen had given me certain mature habits of thought. Idle and unrestrained daydreaming I eliminated almost entirely from my experience, though I delighted myself with fantasies that I quite consciously worked out and which, when concluded, I usually considered carefully, trying to fix them with some sort of childish symbolism.

Even idleness in my nightly dreams disturbed me. And sometimes as I tossed half awake in my big bed I would try to piece together my dreams into at least a form of logic. Sometimes I would complete an unfinished dream and wouldn't know in the morning what part I had dreamed and what part pieced out. I would often smile over the ends that I had plotted in half wakeful moments but found pride in dreams that were complete in themselves and easy to fix with allegory, which I called "meaning." I found that a dream could start for no discoverable reason, with the sight of a printed page on which the first line was, "Once upon a time"; and soon could have me a character in a strange story. Once upon a time there was a little girl whose hands began to get very large. Grown men came for miles around to look at the giant hands and to shake them, but the little girl was ashamed of them and hid them under her skirt. It seemed that the little girl lived in the stable behind my grandmother's old house, and I watched her from the top of the loft ladder. Whenever there was the sound of footsteps, she trembled and wept; so I would beat on the floor above her and laugh uproariously at her fear. But presently I was the little girl listening to the noise. At first I trembled and called out for my father, but then I recollected that it was I who had made the noises and I felt that I had made a very considerable discovery for myself.

I awoke one Saturday morning in early March at the sound of my father's voice in the downstairs hall. He was talking to the servants, ordering the carriage I think. I believe that I awoke at the sound of the carriage horses' names. I went to my door and called "good-bye" to him. He was twisting his mustache before the hall mirror, and he looked up the stairway at me and smiled. He was always abashed to be caught before a looking-glass, and he called out self-consciously and affectionately that he would be home at noon.

I closed my door and went to the little dressing table that he had had put in my room on my birthday. The card with his handwriting on it was still stuck in the corner of the mirror: "For my young lady daughter." I was so thoroughly aware of the gentleness in his nature this morning that any childish timidity before him would, I thought, seem an injustice, and I determined that I should sit with him and my uncles in the parlor that afternoon and perhaps tell them all of my fear of the habitually drunken Mr. Speed and with them watch him pass before the parlor window. That morning I sat before the mirror of my dressing table and put up my hair in a knot on the back of my head for the first time.

Before Father came home at noon, however, I had taken my hair down, and I was not now certain that he would be unoffended by my mention of the neighborhood drunkard. But I was resolute in my purpose, and when my two uncles came after lunch, and the three men shut themselves up in the parlor for the afternoon, I took my seat across the hall in the little library, or den, as my mother had called it, and spent the first of the afternoon skimming over the familiar pages of *Tales of Ol' Virginny*, by Thomas Nelson Page.

My father had seemed tired at lunch. He talked very little and drank only half his cup of coffee. He asked Brother matter-of-fact questions about his plans for college in the fall and told me once to try cutting my meat instead of pulling it to pieces. And as I sat in the library afterward, I wondered if he had been thinking of my mother. Indeed, I wondered whether or not he ever thought of her. He never mentioned her to us; and in a year I had forgotten exactly how he treated her when she had been alive.

It was not only the fate of my brother's soul that I had given thought to since my mother's death. Father had always had his toddy on Saturday afternoon with his two bachelor brothers. But there was more than one round of toddies served in the parlor on Saturday now. Throughout the early part of this afternoon I could hear the tinkle of the bell in the kitchen, and presently the houseboy would appear at the door of the parlor with a tray of ice-filled glasses.

As he entered the parlor each time, I would catch a glimpse over my book of the three men. One was usually standing, whichever one was leading the conversation. Once they were laughing heartily; and as the Negro boy came out with the tray of empty glasses, there was a smile on his face.

As their voices grew louder and merrier, my courage slackened. It was then I first put into words the thought that in my brother and father I saw something of Mr. Speed. And I knew that it was more than a taste of whisky they had in common.

At four o'clock I heard Brother's voice mixed with those of the Benton boys outside the front door. They came into the hall, and their voices were high and excited. First one, then another would demand to be heard with: "No, listen now; let me tell you what." In a moment I heard Brother on the stairs. Then two of the Benton brothers appeared in the doorway of the library. Even the youngest, who was not a year older than I and whose name was Henry, wore long pants, and each carried a cap in hand and a linen duster° over his arm. I stood up and smiled at them, and with my right forefinger I pushed the black locks which hung loosely about my shoulders behind my ears.

"We're going motoring in the Carltons' machine," Henry said.

I stammered my surprise and asked if Brother were going to ride in it. One of them said that he was upstairs getting his hunting cap, since he had no motoring cap. The older brother, Gary Benton, went back into the hall. I walked toward Henry, who was standing in the doorway.

"But does Father know you're going?" I asked.

As I tried to go through the doorway, Henry stretched his arm across it and looked at me with a critical frown on his face.

"Why don't you put up your hair?" he said.

I looked at him seriously, and I felt the heat of the blush that came over my face. I felt it on the back of my neck. I stooped with what I thought considerable grace and slid under his arm and passed into the hall. There were the other two Benton boys listening to the voices of my uncles and my father through the parlor door. I stepped between them and threw open the door. Just as I did so, Henry Benton commanded, "Elizabeth, don't do that!" And I, swinging the door open, turned and smiled at him.

I stood for a moment looking blandly at my father and my uncles. I was considering what had made me burst in upon them in this manner. It was not merely that I had perceived the opportunity of creating this little disturbance and slipping in under its noise, though I was not unaware of the advantage. I was frightened by the boys' impending adventure in the horseless carriage but surely not so much as I normally should have been at breaking into the parlor at this forbidden hour. The immediate cause could only be the attention which Henry Benton had shown me. His insinuation had been that I remained too much a little girl, and I had shown him that at any rate I was a bold, or at least a naughty, little girl.

My father was on his feet. He put his glass on the mantelpiece. And it seemed to me that from the three men came in rapid succession all possible arrangements of the words, Boys-come-in. Come-in-boys. Well-boys-come-in. Come-on-in. Boys-come-in-the-parlor. The boys went in, rather showing off their breeding and poise, I thought. The three men moved and talked clumsily before them, as the three Benton brothers went each to each of the men carefully distinguishing between my uncles' titles: doctor and colonel. I thought how awkward all of the members of my own family appeared on occasions that called for grace.

°*duster:* a smock worn to keep clothes from road dust

Brother strode into the room with his hunting cap sideways on his head, and he announced their plans, which the tactful Bentons, uncertain of our family's prejudices regarding machines, had not mentioned. Father and my uncles had a great deal to say about who was going-to-do-the-driving, and Henry Benton without giving an answer gave a polite invitation to the men to join them. To my chagrin both my uncles accepted with-the-greatest-of-pleasure what really had not been an invitation at all. And they persisted in accepting it even after Brother in his rudeness raised the question of room in the five-passenger vehicle.

Father said, "Sure. The more, the merrier." But he declined to go himself and declined for me Henry's invitation.

The plan was, then, as finally outlined by the oldest of the Benton brothers, that the boys should proceed to the Carltons' and that Brother should return with the driver to take our uncles out to the Carltons' house which was one of the new residences across from Centennial Park, where the excursions in the machine were to be made.

The four slender youths took their leave from the heavy men with the gold watch chains across their stomachs, and I had to shake hands with each of the Benton brothers. To each I expressed my regret that Father would not let me ride with them, emulating their poise with all my art. Henry Benton was the last, and he smiled as though he knew what I was up to. In answer to his smile I said, "Games are *so* much fun."

I stood by the window watching the four boys in the street until they were out of sight. My father and his brothers had taken their seats in silence, and I was aware of just how unwelcome I was in the room. Finally my uncle who had been a colonel in the Spanish War and who wore bushy blond sideburns whistled under his breath and said, "Well, there's no doubt about it, no doubt about it."

He winked at my father, and my father looked at me and then at my uncle. Then quickly in a ridiculously over-serious tone he asked, "What, sir? No doubt about what, sir?"

"Why, there's no doubt that this daughter of yours was flirting with the youngest of the Messrs. Benton."

My father looked at me and twisted his mustache and said with the same pomp that he didn't know what he'd do with me if I started that sort of thing. My two uncles threw back their heads, each giving a short laugh. My uncle the doctor took off his pince-nez and shook them at me and spoke in the same mock-serious tone of his brothers:

"Young lady, if you spend your time in such pursuits you'll only bring upon yourself and upon the young men about Nashville the greatest unhappiness. I, as a bachelor, must plead the cause of the young Bentons!"

I turned to my father in indignation that approached rage.

"Father," I shouted, "there's Mr. Speed out there!"

Father sprang from his chair and quickly stepped up beside me at the window. Then, seeing the old man staggering harmlessly along the sidewalk, he said in, I thought, affected easiness:

"Yes. Yes, dear."

"He's drunk," I said. My lips quivered, and I think I must have blushed at this first mention of the unmentionable to my father.

"Poor Old Speed," he said. I looked at my uncles, and they were shaking their heads, echoing my father's tone.

"What ever did happen to Speed's old maid sister?" my uncle the doctor said.

"She's still with him," Father said.

Mr. Speed appeared soberer today than I had ever seen him. He carried no overcoat to drag on the ground, and his stagger was barely noticeable. The movement of his lips and an occasional gesture were the only evidence of intoxication. I was enraged by the irony that his good behavior on this of all days presented. Had I been a little younger I might have suspected conspiracy on the part of all men against me, but I was old enough to suspect no person's being even interested enough in me to plot against my understanding, unless it be some vague personification of life itself.

The course which I took, I thought afterward, was the proper one. I do not think that it was because I was then really conscious that when one is determined to follow some course rigidly and is blockaded one must fire furiously, if blindly, into the blockade, but rather because I was frightened and in my fear forgot all logic of attack. At any rate, I fired furiously at the three immutable creatures.

"I'm afraid of him," I broke out tearfully. I shouted at them. "He's always drunk! He's always going by our house drunk!"

My father put his arms about me, but I continued talking as I wept on his shirt front, and I felt my father move one hand from my back to motion my uncles to go. And as they shut the parlor door after them, I felt that I had let them escape me.

I heard the sound of the motor fading out up Church Street, and Father led me to the settee. We sat there together for a long while, and neither of us spoke until my tears had dried.

I was eager to tell him just exactly how fearful I was of Mr. Speed's coming into our house. But he only allowed me to tell him that I *was* afraid; for when I had barely suggested that much, he said that I had no business watching Mr. Speed, that I must shut my eyes to some things. "After all," he said, nonsensically I thought, "you're a young lady now." And in several curiously twisted sentences he told me that I mustn't seek things to fear in this world. He said that it was most unlikely, besides, that Speed would ever have business at our house. He punched at his left side several times, gave a prolonged belch, settled a pillow behind his head, and soon was sprawled beside me on the settee, snoring.

But Mr. Speed did come to our house, and it was in less than two months after this dreary twilight. And he came as I had feared he might come, in his most extreme state of drunkenness and at a time when I was alone in the house with the maid Lucy. But I had done everything that a little girl, now fourteen, could do in preparation for such an eventuality. And the sort of preparation that I had been able to make, the clearance of all restraints and inhibitions regarding Mr. Speed in my own mind and in my relationship with my world, had necessarily, I think, given me a maturer view of my own limited experiences; though, too, my very age must be held to account for a natural step toward maturity.

In the two months following the day that I first faced Mr. Speed's existence with my father, I came to look at every phase of our household life with a more direct and more discerning eye. As I wandered about that shadowy and somehow brutally elegant house, sometimes now with a knot of hair on the back of my head, events and customs there that had repelled or frightened me I gave the closest scrutiny. In the daytime I ventured into such forbidden spots as the servants' and the men's bathrooms. The filth of the former became a matter of interest in the study of the servants' natures, instead of the object of ineffable disgust. The other became a fascinating place of wet shaving brushes and leather straps and red rubber bags.

There was an anonymous little Negro boy that I had seen many mornings hurrying away from our back door with a pail. I discovered that he was toting buttermilk from our icebox with the permission of our cook. And I sprang at him from behind a corner of the house one morning and scared him so that he spilled the buttermilk and never returned for more.

Another morning I heard the cook threatening to slash the houseboy with her butcher knife, and I made myself burst in upon them; and before Lucy and the houseboy I told her that if she didn't leave our house that day, I'd call my father and, hardly knowing what I was saying, I added, "And the police." She was gone, and Lucy had got a new cook before dinner time. In this way, from day to day, I began to take my place as mistress in our motherless household.

I could no longer be frightened by my brother with a mention of runaway horses. And instead of terrorized I felt only depressed by his long and curious arguments with my father. I was depressed by the number of the subjects to and from which they oscillated. The world as a whole still seemed unconscionably larger than anything I could comprehend.

But I had learned not to concern myself with so general and so unreal a problem until I had cleared up more particular and real ones.

It was during these two months that I noticed the difference between the manner in which my father spoke before my uncles of Mr. Speed when he passed and that in which he spoke of him before my brother. To my brother it was the condemning, "There goes Old Speed again." But to my uncles it was, "There goes Old Speed," with the sympathetic addition, "the rascal." Though my father and his brothers obviously found me more agreeable because a pleasant spirit had replaced my old timidity, they yet considered me a child; and my father little dreamed that I discerned such traits in his character, or that I understood, if I even listened to, their anecdotes and their long funny stories, and it was an interest in the peculiar choice of subject and in the way that the men told their stories.

When Mr. Speed came, I was accustomed to thinking that there was something in my brother's and in my father's natures that was fully in sympathy with the very brutality of his drunkenness. And I knew that they would not consider my hatred for him and for that part of him which I saw in them. For that alone I was glad that it was on a Thursday afternoon, when I was in the house alone with Lucy, that one of the heavy sort of rains that come toward the end of May drove Mr. Speed onto our porch for shelter.

Otherwise I wished for nothing more than the sound of my father's strong voice when I stood trembling before the parlor window and watched Mr. Speed stumbling across our lawn in the flaying rain. I only knew to keep at the window and make sure that he was actually coming into our house. I believe that he was drunker than I had ever before seen him, and his usual ire seemed to be doubled by the raging weather.

Despite the aid of his cane, Mr. Speed fell to his knees once in the muddy sod. He remained kneeling there for a time with his face cast in resignation. Then once more he struggled to his feet in the rain. Though I was ever conscious that I was entering into young-womanhood at that age, I can only think of myself as a child at that moment; for it was the helpless fear of a child that I felt as I watched Mr. Speed approaching our door. Perhaps it was the last time I ever experienced the inconsolable desperation of childhood.

Next I could hear his cane beating on the boarding of the little porch before our door. I knew that he must be walking up and down in that little shelter. Then I heard Lucy's exasperated voice as she came down the steps. I knew immediately, what she confirmed afterward, that she thought it Brother, eager to get into the house, beating on the door.

I, aghast, opened the parlor door just as she pulled open the great front door. Her black skin ashened as she beheld Mr. Speed, his face crimson, his eyes bleary, and his gray clothes dripping water. He shuffled through the doorway and threw his stick on the hall floor. Between his oaths and profanities he shouted over and over in his broken, old man's voice, "Nigger, nigger." I could understand little of his rapid and slurred speech, but I knew his rage went round and round a man in the rain and the shelter of a neighbor's house.

Lucy fled up the long flight of steps and was on her knees at the head of the stair, in the dark upstairs hall, begging me to come up to her. I only stared, as though paralyzed and dumb, at him and then up the steps at her. The front door was still open; the hall was half in light; and I could hear the rain on the roof of the porch and the wind blowing the trees which were in full green foliage.

At last I moved. I acted. I slid along the wall past the hat rack and the console table, my eyes on the drunken old man who was swearing up the steps at Lucy. I reached for the telephone; and when I had rung for central, I called for the police station. I knew what they did with Mr. Speed downtown, and I knew with what I had threatened the cook. There was a part of me that was crouching on the top step with Lucy, vaguely longing to hide my face from this in my own mother's bosom. But there was another part which was making me deal with Mr. Speed, however wrongly, myself. Innocently I asked the voice to send "the Black Maria" to our house number on Church Street.

Mr. Speed had heard me make the call. He was still and silent for just one moment. Then he broke into tears, and he seemed to be chanting his words. He repeated the word "child" so many times that I felt I had acted wrongly, with courage but without wisdom. I saw myself as a little beast adding to the injury that what was bestial in man had already done him. He picked up his cane and didn't seem to be talking either to Lucy or to me, but to the cane. He started out the doorway, and I heard Lucy come running down the stairs. She fairly glided around the newel post and past me to the telephone. She wasn't certain that I had made the call. She asked if I had called my father. I simply told her that I had not.

As she rang the telephone, I watched Mr. Speed cross the porch. He turned to us at the edge of the porch and shouted one more oath. But his foot touched the wet porch step, and he slid and fell unconscious on the steps.

He lay there with the rain beating upon him and with Lucy and myself watching him, motionless from our place by the telephone. I was frightened by the thought of the cruelty which I found I was capable of, a cruelty which seemed inextricably mixed with what I had called courage. I looked at him lying out there in the rain and despised and pitied him at the same time, and I was afraid to go minister to the helpless old Mr. Speed.

Lucy had her arms about me and kept them there until two gray horses pulling their black coach had galloped up in front of the house and two policemen had carried the limp body through the rain to the dreadful vehicle.

Just as the policemen closed the doors in the back of the coach, my father rode up in a closed cab. He jumped out and stood in the rain for several minutes arguing with the policemen. Lucy and I went to the door and waited for him to come in. When he came, he looked at neither of us. He walked past us saying only, "I regret that the bluecoats were called." And he went into the parlor and closed the door.

I never discussed the events of that day with my father, and I never saw Mr. Speed again. But, despite the surge of pity I felt for the old man on our porch that afternoon, my hatred and fear of what he had stood for in my eyes has never left me. And since the day that I watched myself say "away" in the mirror, not a week has passed but that he has been brought to my mind by one thing or another. It was only the other night that I dreamed I was a little girl on Church Street again and that there was a drunk horse in our yard.

* * *

THE LADY OF SHALOTT

Alfred, Lord Tennyson (1809–1892)

I

On either side the river lie
Long fields of barley and of rye,
That clothe the wold° and meet the sky;
And through the field the road runs by
    To many-towered Camelot;   5
And up and down the people go,
Gazing where the lilies blow
Round an island there below,
    The island of Shalott.

Willows whiten, aspens quiver,   10
Little breezes dusk and shiver
Through the wave that runs for ever
By the island in the river

°*wold:* plain °*shallop:* small boat °*pad:* a horse that moves at a gentle pace

Flowing down to Camelot.
Four gray walls, and four gray towers,   15
Overlook a space of flowers,
And the silent isle imbowers
   The Lady of Shalott.

By the margin, willow-veiled,
Slide the heavy barges trailed   20
By slow horses; and unnailed
The shallop° flitteth silken-sailed
   Skimming down to Camelot:
But who hath seen her wave her hand?
Or at the casement seen her stand?   25
Or is she known in all the land,
   The Lady of Shalott?

Only reapers, reaping early
In among the bearded barley,
Hear a song that echoes cheerly   30
From the river winding clearly,
   Down to towered Camelot;
And by the moon the reaper weary,
Piling sheaves in uplands airy,
Listening, whispers " 'Tis the fairy   35
   Lady of Shalott."

II

There she weaves by night and day
A magic web with colors gay.
She has heard a whisper say,
A curse is on her if she stay   40
   To look down to Camelot.
She knows not what the curse may be,
And so she weaveth steadily,
And little other care hath she,
   The Lady of Shalott.   45

And moving through a mirror clear
That hangs before her all the year,
Shadows of the world appear.
There she sees the highway near
   Winding down to Camelot;   50

There the river eddy whirls,
And there the surly village-churls,
And the red cloaks of market girls,
　　Pass onward from Shalott.

Sometimes a troop of damsels glad, 55
An abbott on an ambling pad,°
Sometimes a curly shepherd-lad,
Or long-haired page in crimson clad,
　　Goes by to towered Camelot;
And sometimes through the mirror blue 60
The knights come riding two and two:
She hath no loyal knight and true,
　　The Lady of Shalott.

But in her web she still delights
To weave the mirror's magic sights, 65
For often through the silent nights
A funeral, with plumes and lights
　　And music, went to Camelot;
Or when the moon was overhead,
Came two young lovers lately wed: 70
"I am half sick of shadows," said
　　The Lady of Shalott.

III

A bow-shot from her bower-eaves,
He rode between the barley-sheaves,
The sun came dazzling through the leaves, 75
And flamed upon the brazen greaves°
　　Of bold Sir Lancelot.
A red-cross knight for ever kneeled
To a lady in his shield,
That sparkled on the yellow field, 80
　　Beside remote Shalott.

The gemmy bridle glittered free,
Like to some branch of stars we see
Hung in the golden Galaxy°
The bridle bells rang merrily 85
　　As he rode down to Camelot;

°*greaves:* lower leg armor　°*golden Galaxy:* Milky Way

And from his blazoned baldric slung
A mighty silver bugle hung,
And as he rode his armor rung,
   Beside remote Shalott.   90

All in the blue unclouded weather
Thick-jewelled shone the saddle-leather,
The helmet and the helmet-feather
Burned like one burning flame together,
   As he rode down to Camelot;   95
As often through the purple night,
Below the starry clusters bright,
Some bearded meteor, trailing light,
   Moves over still Shalott.

His broad clear brow in sunlight glowed;   100
On burnished hooves his war-horse trode;
From underneath his helmet flowed
His coal-black curls as on he rode,
   As he rode down to Camelot.
From the bank and from the river   105
He flashed into the crystal mirror,
"Tirra lirra," by the river
   Sang Sir Lancelot.

She left the web, she left the loom,
She made three paces through the room,   110
She saw the water lily bloom,
She saw the helmet and the plume,
   She looked down to Camelot.
Out flew the web and floated wide;
The mirror cracked from side to side;   115
"The curse is come upon me," cried
   The Lady of Shalott.

IV

In the stormy east-wind straining,
The pale yellow woods were waning,
The broad stream in his banks complaining,   120
Heavily the low sky raining
   Over towered Camelot;
Down she came and found a boat
Beneath a willow left afloat,

And round about the prow she wrote   125
   The Lady of Shalott.

And down the river's dim expanse
Like some bold seër in a trance,
Seeing all his own mischance—
With a glassy countenance   130
   Did she look to Camelot.
And at the closing of the day
She loosed the chain, and down she lay;
The broad stream bore her far away,
   The Lady of Shalott.   135

Lying, robed in snowy white
That loosely flew to left and right—
The leaves upon her falling light—
Through the noises of the night
   She floated down to Camelot;   140
And as the boat-head wound along
The willowy hills and fields among,
They heard her singing her last song,
   The Lady of Shalott.

Heard a carol, mournful, holy,   145
Chanted loudly, chanted lowly,
Till her blood was frozen slowly,
And her eyes were darkened wholly,
   Turned to towered Camelot.
For ere she reached upon the tide   150
The first house by the water-side,
Singing in her song she died,
   The Lady of Shalott.

Under tower and balcony,
By garden-wall and gallery,   155
A gleaming shape she floated by,
Dead-pale between the houses high,
   Silent into Camelot.
Out upon the wharfs they came,
Knight and burgher, lord and dame,   160
And round the prow they read her name,
   The Lady of Shalott.

Who is this? and what is here?
And in the lighted palace near
Died the sound of royal cheer;   165
And they crossed themselves for fear,
    All the knights at Camelot.
But Lancelot mused a little space;
He said, "She has a lovely face;
God in his mercy lend her grace,   170
    The Lady of Shalott."

*   *   *

QUESTIONS

1. Give a brief account in Freudian terms of why we dream.
2. Freud notices that the use of symbolism in dreams was not a "discovery" of psychoanalysis. What evidence can be cited of earlier awareness by poets of the connection between dreams and hidden aspects of behavior?
3. Make an additional list of objects which could be used to symbolize male and female sexuality.
4. What are the sources of evidence Freud gives to make his "interpretations" of the images recounted by the dreamer? Where else does one encounter similar symbolic meaning? What kinds of evidence seem most convincing?
5. Answer Freud's rhetorical questions: "Do I really live in the thick of sexual symbols? Are all the objects around me, all the clothes I put on, all the things I pick up, all of them sexual symbols and nothing else?"
6. Think of some fairy tales, folk tales, or nursery rhymes which can be given a symbolic reading by Freud's method of analysis. Look particularly for cases where the literal details make no sense. What implications can be drawn from the fact that the psychological mechanisms of dreaming are also found in these other situations?
7. The predominance of sexual meanings in dreams is a point which many of Freud's critics have raised. How would his account be easier or harder to accept if he argued that other subjects are on the dreamer's mind?
8. What modifications of the vertical and horizontal movements described by Frye and considered in Parts III and IV do *Kubla Khan* and *The Sick Rose* make?
9. Neither Blake nor Coleridge had read Freud. To what extent do you find that these poems support or illustrate his later discussion of symbolism?

10. Make an interpretation of these two poems which does *not* contain references to sexuality.
11. What does Mr. Speed represent in Taylor's story? Explain why Betsy is ambivalent toward him? Give evidence of this ambivalence. What is her brother's and father's attitude toward Mr. Speed? What Freudian "trademarks" does Mr. Speed use?
12. What circumstances of the household make difficulties for the young girl? What is the effect and importance of the memories of her mother? What aspects of her father's and brother's behavior are most distressing to her?
13. Relate her attitude toward Mr. Speed to the title of the story.
14. What attitude toward Mr. Speed would have better results? What prevents her from assuming it?
15. Give an interpretation of her dreams. What is the significance of her dream of "a drunk horse in our yard"?
16. What aspects of the Lady of Shalott's "problem" are similar to those of the narrator in *A Spinster's Tale?* What are the Freudian aspects of the poem? Discuss the vertical and horizontal motions used.
17. For an elaborate Freudian story about repression and the neurosis of a proper Victorian woman see the novel by Henry James, *The Turn of the Screw.*

PART VII

Back to Theory: Some Final Assertions

Back to Theory: Some Final Assertions

Because symbolism has implications about the nature of reality; it raises important philosophic as well as literary questions. How we read a poem, insofar as it requires us to decide on the question of literal vs. figurative modes of communication, determines or depends upon how we assess and value nonempirical matters: is it love or chemistry, patriotism or economic determinism, morality or self-interest? It is not surprising, therefore, that the argument has strong antagonists, that intensity of expression on the question, hostility, and ardent passions are common.

Doubts and Satires

By now the reader will probably have a good sense of the degree to which he is convinced by the arguments made for nonliterality, but it may nonetheless be helpful if the concluding section of this book provides less analytic, more intense expressions of opinion on both sides of the matter. The first sampling offers doubts and satire.

A COAT

William Butler Yeats (1865–1939)

I made my song a coat
Covered with embroideries
Out of old mythologies
From heel to throat;
But the fools caught it,   5
Wore it in the world's eyes
As though they'd wrought it.
Song, let them take it,
For there's more enterprise
In walking naked.   10

*   *   *

From GULLIVER'S TRAVELS

Jonathan Swift (1667–1745)

We next went to the school of languages, where three professors sat in consultation upon improving that of their own country.

The first project was to shorten discourse by cutting polysyllables into one, and leaving out verbs and participles, because in reality all things imaginable are but nouns.

The other project was a scheme for entirely abolishing all words whatsoever; and this was urged as a great advantage in point of health as well as brevity. For it is plain, that every word we speak is in some degree a diminution of our lungs by corrosion, and consequently contributes to the shortening of our lives. An expedient was therefore offered, that since words are only names for *things,* it would be more convenient for all men to carry about them such things as were necessary to express the particular business they are to discourse on. And this invention would certainly have taken place, to the great ease as well as health of the subject, if the women, in conjunction with the vulgar and illiterate, had not threatened to raise a rebellion, unless they might be allowed the liberty to speak with their tongues, after the manner of their ancestors; such constant irreconcilable enemies to science are the common people. However, many of the most learned and wise adhere to the new scheme of expressing themselves by things, which hath only this inconvenience attending it, that if a man's business be very great, and of various kinds, he must be obliged in proportion to carry a greater bundle of things upon his back, unless he can afford one or two strong servants to attend him. I have often beheld two of those sages almost sinking under the weight of their packs, like pedlars among us; who, when they met in the streets, would lay down their loads, open their sacks, and hold conversation for an hour together; then put up their implements, help each other to resume their burthens, and take their leave.

But for short conversations a man may carry implements in his pockets and under his arms, enough to supply him, and in his house he cannot be at a loss. Therefore the room where company meet who practice this art, is full of all things ready at hand, requisite to furnish matter for this kind of artificial converse.

Another great advantage proposed by this invention was that it would serve as an universal language to be understood in all civilised nations, whose goods and utensils are generally of the same kind, or nearly resembling, so that their uses might easily be comprehended. And thus ambassadors would be qualified to treat with foreign princes or ministers of state, to whose tongues they were utter strangers.

POISONED PARADISE: THE UNDERSIDE OF POOH

Myron Masterson [Frederick C. Crews° (1933–)]

Before going further I would like to thank all the people who have made this article possible: Karl Marx, St. John of the Cross, Friedrich Nietzsche, Sacco and Vanzetti, Sigmund Freud, and C. G. Jung. Some finicky "experts" have said that there exist differences of opinion among these thinkers. The point, however, is that each of them has helped to shape my literary and moral consciousness; and that, frankly, is enough for me. If the reader is surprised by the eclecticism with which I draw inspiration from a free-wheeling, broad-minded range of sources, that is his problem and not mine.

Perhaps one more private note would not be out of place in this otherwise impersonal analysis. I first discovered the real meaning of *Winnie-the-Pooh* when I was reading selections from *When We Were Very Young* to my twelve children. Suddenly my youngest son, Charlie, stopped me and asked to hear these lines from "The Mirror" again:

> *And there I saw a white swan make*
> *Another white swan in the lake.*

"God, how did they let that one get through?" lisped Trudy. And little Steven said, "That's nothing. Read that real wild couplet from 'Vespers.'" With mingled misgivings and interest I allowed Billy and Jane to fumble their tiny fingers through the pages until they came upon these lines, which were recited in gleeful unison:

> God bless Mummy. *I know that's right.*
> *Wasn't it fun in the bath tonight?*

Wisdom from the mouths of babes! A rapid check of the other poems in the volume, and then a similar run-through of *Now We Are Six*, convinced me that all of Milne's verse was more or less equally salacious. With the zeal of Dick Tracy I turned to the *Pooh* books to extend my discovery. The result, printed below for the first time, has shocked and

---

°Crews's book is a series of commentaries on *Winnie-the-Pooh* written from the perspective of various schools of modern criticism; each article is "written" by a different fictitious critic: thus, Myron Masterson, the Freudian critic. The footnotes are, of course, Masterson's.

From the book *The Pooh Perplex* by Frederick C. Crews. Copyright © 1963 by Frederick C. Crews. Published by E. P. Dutton, Inc. and used with their permission.

enraged Philistine audiences from Tokyo to Wauwatosa, Wisconsin, and I am thinking of working it up into a monograph.

To clear the air a bit, let us reach an understanding about the alleged "purity" of children's literature in general. There was a period when I felt it necessary to cancel one title after another from the "approved" list in our family bedtime reading. I don't regard myself as an archconservative, but the atmosphere of polymorphous perverse play in *Little Women* was too much for me; while the uterine fantasies in *Alice in Wonderland* have been known to scholarship for years. One volume after another had to be transferred from the toddlers' shelf to my own locked bookcase—*Uncle Wiggly*(!), *The Arabian Nights, The Tale of Mrs. Tittlemouse*—until one day I realized that soon there would be nothing left! I was forced to reconsider the entire question of Repugnancy in Literature. After a good deal of soul-searching I came up with this answer: All children's books, like all other books, are knit together by archetypal patterns emanating from the collective unconscious of the race. Children, being essentially people, are likewise shot through with archetypes; hence the appeal of children's literature to them. The difference between *Peter Rabbit* and *Peyton Place* is not that one is pure and the other impure, but that the archetypes are disguised in one case and fairly obvious in the other. Since the communication of archetypes occurs largely in the unconscious, the average child never knows, as it were, what is hitting him. And thus we can go back to the nursery with a clear conscience and an armload of restored classics. The special insight shown by my own children—Susie, Henry, Jane, and the rest—should be attributed to the fact that they have attended many of my public lectures.

Ignoring, then, the superficial level of *Winnie-the-Pooh*, let us dive at once, like Melville's Catskill eagle, into the profundities and subprofundities of the matter. It is not hard to dismiss the generally accepted impression of this book as a cheery, chins-up collection of anecdotes designed to educate Christopher Robin in the gentle virtues of English social life. Milne's chief spokesman, Eeyore, is a veritable Thersites, a malcontent who would have put Marston to shame. No pretense of "helpfulness" or "conviviality" escapes his wickedly incisive rebuttal. Nor, when we look around at the other characters, do we find a much rosier picture. The "lovable" Pooh is tragically fixated at the narcissistic stage of development.° Rabbit and Owl are aging bachelors whose respective megalomania and fussiness are tempered only by their mutual friendship, of which the less said, the better. Kanga is the archetypal mawkish "Mom"-figure we see exemplified everywhere in America. And Piglet, Tigger, and Roo are such advanced cases that their problems must be analyzed separately below. As for Christopher Robin, his interest in

---

° "'Oh, Bear!' said Christopher Robin. 'How I do love you!' 'So do I,' said Pooh."

these toy animals is undoubtedly "normal," if by normality we understand a neurotic effort to transfer onto one's furry dolls all the grievances and secret fantasies that characterize the onset of the latency period. "Aye, madam, it is common," as Hamlet remarked to his mother—but it isn't pretty!

The fact, indeed, that Christopher Robin has recently suffered the destruction and repression of his Oedipus Complex provides a key to the whole tone, as well as to many of the incidents, in *Winnie-the-Pooh*. The phase Christopher is entering is that of maximum repression, when toys, hobbies, games, and schoolwork hopefully will receive the libido that was previously lavished upon thoughts of "Mummy." Even in the most successful cases, however, the repression is incomplete; we can always see, if we try, a survival of the old incestuous wishes and a rather suspiciously overeager attempt to desexualize oneself and one's imaginary companions. Not without significance does Milne, who must be only too happy to see his little boy finally turning his conscious thoughts elsewhere, dedicate the book "To Her"—the mother who never appears *in propria persona,* but who lurks behind every page as the not-quite-relinquished goal, the secretly intended object of all Christopher Robin's "portentous little activity" (to quote *The Turn of the Screw*).° The animals in *Winnie-the-Pooh* are lacking in genitalia, they seem to have no other activity in life beyond calling on one another and eating snacks —but the experienced critic need not be fooled. The real subject of the book is Christopher Robin's loss of his mother, which is alternately symbolized, accepted, protested against, denied, and homoerotically compensated for in the various "nursery" stories of the plot.

From the portrait of Christopher Robin himself, of course, we should expect the least enlightenment, since it is upon his toy animals that he attempts to project his forbidden fantasies. It is clear to the reader that Christopher knows what is off limits once one has entered the latency period in earnest.° More revealing is the almost total absence of parents for the other characters in the story. Whenever Pooh and Piglet imagine that they are in danger they wish to be soothed, not by their own fathers and mothers, but by Christopher Robin; and the same holds true for the

---

°After I gave this lecture at Majorca last year, Robert Graves told me that in his opinion "Her" meant the White Goddess, the Belle Dame Sans Merci of whom Graves has written so very, very often. This is entirely possible, and the reader may entertain both Graves's idea and mine at once, only remembering that mine came first.

°See, e.g., the way he shies away from the subject of phallic "Poles," of which he professes to be ignorant because "people don't like talking about them." Pooh, on the contrary, wants to go at once in search of the East Pole, "but Christopher Robin had thought of something else to do with Kanga." This last clause may imply a return of the repressed; note the vague intentions regarding the mother-surrogate Kanga.

other animals. Surely this cannot be explained by saying that these dolls weren't *anyone's* children. *Winnie-the-Pooh* is virtually haunted by ancestral figures: Piglet's grandfather Trespassers William, Owl's revered Uncle Robert, Pooh's mysterious forebear Mr. Sanders, and so on. The amazing fact is that there is no shortage of distant and dead relations but a severe want of immediate ones on the scene. And the point of it all is indisputable: Christopher Robin, still smarting under the paternal castration threat and the enforced renunciation of the mother, has decreed a ban on mothers and fathers in general. He has imagined for himself a blissful teddy-bearland in which no adult is permitted to intrude. He himself will be the sole father figure, and will "show up" his own severe parents by exercising only a gentle brotherly supervision of his charges.

Here, then, we have the rationale of the ideal world that Christopher Robin has hallucinated—a pastoral paradise, a garden of fun in which the danger of incest and punishment is nil. But like all such gardens, as Hawthorne was I believe the first to notice, something is likely to go awry sooner or later. In this case it is the entrance of Kanga that transforms *Winnie-the-Pooh*, with one brutal stroke, from the genre of bucolic idyll to that of depth-psychological Gothic tale of terror. The true meaning of Kanga's arrival—the installation of the emasculatng Female as overseer of the doomed frolickers—is not lost on Rabbit, who does everything in his power to exclude her. All in vain! From the very moment of Kanga's appearance the pastoral playground is overshadowed by doubt and guilt, for the all-too-loving *anima*-Woman has pitched her temple here!

We should pay special attention to the fact that Baby Roo forms part of this invasion, for it is *as Roo's mother* that Kanga threatens the common happiness. All Christopher Robin's animals had, by his fiat, entered a kind of latency period of their own, never bothering themselves over the fundamental questions that small children want to ask their parents. Now Enter Kanga:

> Nobody seemed to know where they came from, but there they were in the Forest: Kanga and Baby Roo. When Pooh asked Christopher Robin, "How did they come here?" Christopher Robin said, "In the Usual Way, if you know what I mean, Pooh," and Pooh, who didn't, said, "Oh!" Then he nodded his head twice and said, "In the Usual Way. Ah!"

No one, I think, will deny that these lines deal with the topic, "Where do babies come from?" No one can fail to draw the inference that Christopher Robin feels basically evasive on this subject; and no one will forget that this is entirely in keeping with my understanding of Kanga's role. The verification of my inspired guesswork, I confess, strengthens my resolution never to read the criticism of others but merely to rely on placing my unconscious in sympathetic rapport with that of the writer.

Kanga's corrosive effect on Christopher Robin's ideal society, like Margaret Fuller's on Brook Farm, stems from her desire to bring every male under her sway. I need hardly dwell on her treatment of Roo ("Later, Roo dear," "We'll see, Roo dear"); it is enough to make us all breathe a sigh of relief at having successfully crossed the border of puberty. More interesting thematically is her capture of Piglet. Piglet is, we may say, the very archetype of the sickly, nervous little boy who is terrified by father and mother alike.° His fear of emasculation and his horror of intercourse converge in his abject quaking before the pit for Heffalumps, the "Cunning Trap" as he slyly calls it. He and King Lear agree entirely about this "sulphurous pit." And his misgivings turn out to have been all too justified. Piglet becomes Kanga's very first victim outside her immediate family. Instead of helping in the plan to blackmail Kanga into leaving, he finds himself stuffed into her womblike pouch, vigorously bathed and rubbed, and nearly made to swallow Roo's fulsome baby medicine. Ugh! It is a section of the book that I can scarcely stand to reread! Piglet's symbolic spaying is complete when Kanga, continuing the pretense that she is serving Roo, explains that the medicine is "to make you grow big and strong, dear. You don't want to grow up small and weak like Piglet, do you? Well, then!" From this moment onward Piglet, who certainly never showed much virility before, is fit only to try out for countertenor in a choir.°

Kanga's role is raised to positively allegorical dimensions when she encounters Tigger in *The House at Pooh Corner*. Tigger is the one "intruder" in that volume, as Kanga and Roo were in the previous one, and this fact alone shows us how gutless the Pooh-world has become in the interim under Kanga's influence. For Tigger, the embodiment of pure Dionysiac energy, of sheer animal potency, appears strange and unwelcome to this melancholy band of castrati.° Alas, poor Tigger! Nothing in the Forest is fit for him to eat but Roo's extract of malt, which

---

° Don't get me wrong; Piglet's actual father doesn't appear in the flesh. He comes in his essential traumatic form as angry castrator. See Piglet's nightmare in which he is chased by the grossly phallic Heffalump, and in which he hopes desperately for protection from his grandfather—a typical childish recourse in such cases, by the way.

° Note also the irony that Piglet is trapped and degraded by Kanga as a result of his expectation that *he* would trap *her*. How frighteningly womanly that is!

° Bear in mind that Tigger arrives *without a family,* indeed without any real certainty that there exist others of his species. Like modern America, the Pooh-world is one in which a Whole Man must find himself alone, resented, and misunderstood.

must be administered by Kanga. And could we reasonably expect this matriarch to stand by idly and watch her household being overrun with sheer maleness? She sinks her hooks into Tigger at once:

> "Well, look in my cupboard, Tigger dear, and see what you'd like." Because she knew at once that, however big Tigger seemed to be, he wanted as much kindness as Roo.

As much kindness as Roo, forsooth! This is the beginning of the end. Sinclair Lewis, Wright Morris, and Evan S. Connell, Jr., all working together, could never nauseate us half so successfully as does the picture of Kanga waving good-bye to Roo and Tigger as they take their watercress and extract-of-malt sandwiches off for a sexless *déjeuner sur l'herbe*.

It is when things have reached this sorry pass that the inevitable homoerotic alternative to compulsory innocence suddenly offers itself to Kanga's victims. Already in *Winnie-the-Pooh* Piglet had reached a point comparable to Huckleberry Finn's satanic resolution to prefer hellfire to the female-dominated world he has thus far inhabited.° Now, in the excitement over getting Tigger and Roo down from a heavily symbolic tree, Piglet flips:

> But Piglet wasn't listening, he was so agog at the thought of seeing Christopher Robin's blue braces again. He had only seen them once more, when he was much younger, and, being a little over-excited by them, had had to go to bed half an hour earlier than usual . . .

Christopher Robin is flattered and attracted by this fetishistic response to his little striptease, but he is naturally reluctant to enter into serious relations with a pig. Doubtless he has designs on one of the tiny scholars with whom he is now learning spelling and mathematics. Piglet, therefore, is thrown into the willing arms of Pooh, who at the end of the book welcomes him into his house as permanent roommate. Nor should we omit Tigger and Roo from this account. What, after all, did Roo have in mind ascending that tree on Tigger's back, squeaking "Oo, Tigger—oo, Tigger—oo, Tigger"? What is the meaning of Tigger's compulsion to "bounce" upon all his male friends? Roo, at least, gets the point even if innocent readers have not done so: "Try bouncing *me,* Tigger," he passionately pleads.

° "At first he thought that the whole world had blown up; and then he thought that perhaps only the Forest part of it had; and then he thought that perhaps only *he* had, and he was now alone in the moon or somewhere, and would never see Christopher Robin or Pooh or Eeyore again. And then he thought, 'Well, even if I'm in the moon, I needn't be face downwards all the time . . .' "

Well then! This, within the limits of my volatile, intuitive temperament, is a sober and accurate account of *Winnie-the-Pooh*'s meaning. Were I to read other critics I would be sure to find that my interpretation has contradicted every threadbare cliché on the subject. I am sincerely sorry if this article must spread consternation in the ranks of four-eyed old professors and mooning Moms. But the truth, after all, must be told by someone; someone must bear the burden of demonstrating that English literature, since Shakespeare's day, has demoted itself continually from maturity down through pimply post-pubescence to the nervous sublimations of the latency period, and now stands on the brink of re-entry through the Oedipus and castration complexes. It is a fascinating, rewarding process to watch—particularly for myself, a simple, milk-fed boy of the Mesas, just glad to be a vigorous American critic in the middle of the twentieth century!

*   *   *

Affirmations and Signs

In the work of Thomas Carlyle and Norman O. Brown, we encounter writers who specifically and adamantly reject "univocation," insisting instead upon "symbolic consciousness," upon nonliteral senses of language, and upon the special philosophic consequences of these views. There is more involved than literary criticism. Symbolism is not merely for literary purposes; it is a basis for a new way of knowing, for acquisition of new insights into the nature of man's mind and into his relationships to the world outside his mind.

Thomas Carlyle was one of the most egotistical, opinionated, dogmatic, and brilliant of Victorian writers. His interests in symbolism arise (as they did for Coleridge) from the way in which he sees this mode of perception as offering a crucial salvation for the spirit in a world more and more given to "mechanism," to materialism, literalism, science, rationalism, and analytic modes of thought. Carlyle argues that without symbolism, without recognizing the "vesture," the dress of things, there can be no spirit; and where there is no spirit, there is no religion, only analytic science, converting men's feelings to nervous pulses, men's religion to anthropology, and men's God to a historical event.

Yet to say as much, however passionately, in the language of rational discourse, is to become as analytic, as devoid of feeling, as the anti-symbolic doctrine itself. Carlyle had the poet's healthy distrust of philosophic abstractions. In *Sartor Resartus,* therefore, Carlyle adopted a number of devices by which a more imaginative perception of the argument being made is invited. One such device is the metaphorical density of the style in which religious and social institutions are described as the garments wherein the essential spiritual nature of man is "dressed." Because institutions and beliefs are only "dress," they can be seen also as subject to changes in fashion, liable to becoming out of date, worn, or insufficient to their original purposes. Yet the importance and validity of that purpose may remain, since the fact that one's clothes are worn denies neither the importance of clothes in general, nor the worth of the wearer.

When this happens (as Carlyle saw happening to Christianity), the poet must create a new style, a new mythology, refurbishing the old dress. The garment must be retailored: *Sartor Resartus*—"the tailor retailored."

From SARTOR RESARTUS

Thomas Carlyle (1795–1881)

CHURCH-CLOTHES

Church-Clothes defined; the Forms under which the Religious Principle is temporarily embodied. Outward Religion originates by Society: Society becomes possible by Religion. The condition of Church-Clothes in our time.

Not less questionable is his° Chapter on *Church-Clothes*, which has the farther distinction of being the shortest in the Volume. We here translate it entire:

'By Church-Clothes, it need not be premised that I mean infinitely more than Cassocks and Surplices; and do not at all mean the mere haberdasher Sunday Clothes that men go to Church in. Far from it! Church-Clothes, are, in our vocabulary, the Forms, the *Vestures*, under which men have at various periods embodied and represented for themselves the Religious Principle; that is to say, invested the Divine Idea of the World with a sensible and practically active Body, so that it might dwell among them as a living and life-giving WORD.°

°*his:* the basic "fiction" of this work is this: that we are reading a rather clumsy edition of the obscure philosophic writings of a strange German philosopher named Diogenes Teufelsdröckh. Thus, the "we" refers to the hard-pressed editor, trying to make sense of the German work, and the "he" (or "I" in passages "quoted" from Teufelsdröckh) represents the philosopher himself.

°*invested . . . WORD:* In Carlyle's view the "Religious Principle" or "Divine Idea" remains constant underneath the changing Forms of Churches and Doctrines.

'These are unspeakably the most important of all the vestures and garnitures of Human Existence. They are first spun and woven, I may say, by that wonder of wonders, SOCIETY; for it is still only when "two or three are gathered together,"° that Religion, spiritually existent, and indeed indestructible, however latent, in each, first outwardly manifests itself (as with "cloven tongues of fire"),° and seeks to be embodied in a visible Communion and Church Militant. Mystical, more than magical, is that Communing of Soul with Soul, both looking heavenward: here properly Soul first speaks with Soul; for only in looking heavenward, take it in what sense you may, not in looking earthward, does what we call Union, mutual Love, Society, begin to be possible. How true is that of Novalis°: "It is certain, my Belief gains quite *infinitely* the moment I can convince another mind thereof." Gaze thou in the face of thy Brother, in those eyes where plays the lambent fire of Kindness, or in those where rages the lurid conflagration of Anger; feel how thy own so quiet Soul is straightway involuntarily kindled with the like, and ye blaze and reverberate on each other, till it is all one limitless confluent flame (of embracing Love, or of deadly-grappling Hate); and then say what miraculous virtue goes out of man into man. But if so, through all the thick-plied hulls of our Earthly Life; how much more when it is of the Divine Life we speak, and inmost ME is, as it were, brought into contact with inmost ME!

'Thus was it that I said, the Church-Clothes are first spun and woven by Society; outward Religion originates by Society, Society becomes possible by Religion. Nay, perhaps, every conceivable Society, past and present, may well be figured as properly and wholly a Church, in one or other of these three predicaments: an audibly preaching and prophesying Church, which is the best; second, a Church that struggles to preach and prophesy, but cannot as yet, till its Pentecost come; and third and worst, a Church gone dumb with old age, or which only mumbles delirium prior to dissolution. Whoso fancies that by Church is here meant Chapterhouses and Cathedrals, or by preaching and prophesying, mere speech and chanting, let him,' says the oracular Professor, 'read on, light of heart (*getrosten Muthes*).°

'But with regard to your Church proper, and the Church-Clothes specially recognised as Church-Clothes, I remark, fearlessly enough, that without such Vestures and sacred Tissues Society has not existed, and will not exist. For if Government is, so to speak, the outward SKIN of the Body Politic, holding the whole together and protecting it; and all your Craft-Guilds, and Associations for Industry, of hand or of head, are

---

°*two . . . together:* Matthew, xviii, 20.   °*cloven . . . fire:* Acts, ii, 3.
°*Novalis:* pseudonym of Friedrich von Hardenberg, German mystic and poet
°*getrosten Muthes:* Carlyle gives Teufelsdröckh's "original" German phrase

the Fleshly Clothes, the muscular and osseous Tissues (Lying *under* such SKIN), whereby Society stands and works;—then is Religion the inmost Pericardial and Nervous Tissue, which ministers Life and warm Circulation to the whole. Without which Pericardial Tissue the Bones and Muscles (of Industry) were inert, or animated only by a Galvanic vitality; the SKIN would become a shrivelled pelt, or fast-rotting raw-hide; and Society itself a dead carcass,—deserving to be buried. Men were no longer Social, but Gregarious; which latter state also could not continue, but must gradually issue in universal selfish discord, hatred, savage isolation, and dispersion;—whereby, as we might continue to say, the very dust and dead body of Society would have evaporated and become abolished. Such, and so all-important, all-sustaining, are the Church-Clothes to civilised or even to rational men.

'Meanwhile, in our era of the World, those same Church-Clothes have gone sorrowfully out-at-elbows: nay, far worse, many of them have become mere hollow Shapes, or Masks, under which no living Figure or Spirit any longer dwells; but only spiders and unclean beetles, in horrid accumulation, drive their trade; and the mask still glares on you with its glass-eyes, in ghastly affectation of Life,—some generation-and-half after Religion has quite withdrawn from it, and in unnoticed nooks is weaving for herself new Vestures, wherewith to reappear, and bless us, or our sons or grandsons. As a Priest, or Interpreter of the Holy, is the noblest and highest of all men, so is a Sham-priest (*Schein-priester*) the falsest and basest; neither is it doubtful that his Canonicals, were they Popes' Tiaras, will one day be torn from him, to make bandages for the wounds of mankind; or even to burn into tinder, for general scientific or culinary purposes.

'All which, as out of place here, falls to be handled in my Second Volume, *On the Palingenesia, or Newbirth of Society*, which volume, as treating practically of the Wear, Destruction, and Retexture of Spiritual Tissues, or Garments, forms, properly speaking, the Transcendental or ultimate Portion of this my work *on Clothes*, and is already in a state of forwardness.'

And herewith, no farther exposition, note, or commentary being added, does Teufelsdröckh, and must his Editor now, terminate the singular chapter on Church-Clothes!

SYMBOLS

The benignant efficacies of Silence and Secrecy. Symbols; revelations of the Infinite in the Finite: Man everywhere encompassed by them; lives and works by them. Theory of Motive-millwrights, a false account of human nature. Symbols of an extrinsic value; as Banners, Standards: Of intrinsic value; as Works of Art, Lives and Deaths of Heroic men. Religious Symbols; Christianity. Symbols hallowed by Time; but finally defaced and desecrated. Many superannuated Symbols in our time, needing removal.

Probably it will elucidate the drift of these foregoing obscure utterances, if we° here insert somewhat of our Professor's speculations on *Symbols.* To state his whole doctrine, indeed, were beyond our compass: nowhere is he more mysterious, impalpable, than in this of 'Fantasy being the organ of the Godlike';° and how 'Man thereby, though based, to all seeming, on the small Visible, does nevertheless extend down into the infinite deeps of the Invisible, of which Invisible, indeed, his Life is properly the bodying forth.' Let us, omitting these high transcendental aspects of the matter, study to glean (whether from the Paper-bags° or the Printed Volume) what little seems logical and practical, and cunningly arrange it into such degree of coherence as it will assume. By way of proem, take the following not injudicious remarks:

'The benignant efficacies of Concealment', cries our Professor, 'who shall speak or sing? SILENCE and SECRECY! Altars might still be raised to them (were this an altar-building time) for universal worship. Silence is the element in which great things fashion themselves together; that at length they may emerge, full-formed and majestic, into the daylight of Life, which they are thenceforth to rule. Not William the Silent° only, but all the considerable men I have known, and the most undiplomatic and unstrategic of these, forbore to babble of what they were creating and projecting. Nay, in thy own mean perplexities, do thou thyself but *hold thy tongue for one day:* on the morrow, how much clearer are thy purposes and duties; what wreck and rubbish have those mute workmen within thee swept away, when intrusive noises were shut out! Speech is too often not, as the Frenchman defined it, the art of concealing Thought;° but of quite stifling and suspending Thought, so that there is none to conceal. Speech too is great, but not the greatest. As the Swiss Inscription says: *Sprechen ist silbern, Schweigen ist golden* (Speech is silvern, Silence is golden); or as I might rather express it: Speech is of Time, Silence is of Eternity.

'Bees will not work except in darkness; Thought will not work except in Silence: neither will Virtue work except in Secrecy. Let not thy left hand know what thy right hand doeth!° Neither shalt thou prate even to thy own heart of "those secrets known to all.°" Is not Shame *(Schaam)*

°*we:* Carlyle shifts here to the editor's voice. °*Fantasy . . . the Godlike:* quoted from Schlegel °*Paper-bags:* Some of Teufelsdröckh's opinions came to the editor in scraps contained in paper bags. °*William the Silent:* Prince of Orange (1533–1584), founder of the Dutch Republic °*Speech . . . Thought:* attributed to Voltaire and Talleyrand °*Let . . . doeth:* quoted from Matthew, vi, 3 °*"those . . . all":* Goethe, *Wilhelm Meister*

the soil of all Virtue, of all good manners and good morals? Like other plants, Virtue will not grow unless its root be hidden, buried from the eye of the sun. Let the sun shine on it, nay do but look at it privily thyself, the root withers, and no flowers will glad thee. O my Friends, when we view the fair clustering flowers that overwreathe, for example, the Marriage-bower, and encircle man's life with the fragrance and hues of Heaven, what hand will not smite the foul plunderer that grubs them up by the roots, and with grinning, grunting satisfaction, shows us the dung they flourish in! Men speak much of the Printing-Press with its Newspapers: *du Himmel!* what are these to Clothes and the Tailor's Goose?°

'Of kin to the so incalculable influences of Concealment, and connected with still greater things, is the wondrous agency of *Symbols.* In a Symbol there is concealment and yet revelation: here therefore, by Silence and by Speech acting together, comes a double significance. And if both the Speech be itself high, and the Silence fit and noble, how expressive will their union be! Thus in many a painted Device, or simple Seal-emblem, the commonest Truth stands out to us proclaimed with quite new emphasis.

'For it is here that Fantasy° with her mystic wonderland plays into the small prose domain of Sense, and becomes incorporated therewith. In the Symbol proper, what we can call a Symbol, there is ever, more or less distinctly and directly, some embodiment and revelation of the Infinite; the Infinite is made to blend itself with the Finite, to stand visible, and as it were, attainable there. By Symbols, accordingly, is man guided and commanded, made happy, made wretched. He everywhere finds himself encompassed with Symbols, recognised as such or not recognised: the Universe is but one vast Symbol of God; nay if thou wilt have it, what is man himself but a Symbol of God; is not all that he does symbolical; a revelation to Sense of the mystic god-given force that is in him; a "Gospel of Freedom," which he, the "Messias° of Nature," preaches, as he can, by act and word? Not a Hut he builds but is the visible embodiment of a Thought; but bears visible record of invisible things; but is, in the transcendental sense, symbolical as well as real.'

'Man,' says the Professor elsewhere, in quite antipodal contrast with these high-soaring delineations, which we have here cut-short on the verge of the inane, 'Man is by birth somewhat of an owl. Perhaps, too, of all the owleries that ever possessed him, the most owlish, if we consider it, is that of your actually existing Motive-Millwrights.° Fantastic

---

°*Tailor's Goose:* tailor's iron   °*Fantasy:* Carlyle means by Fantasy the higher imaginative powers of the mind.
°*Messias:* Greek form of Hebrew Messiah, or Christ   °*Motive-Millwrights:* utilitarian philosophers who thought that all Will or Motives were created from the desire to gain pleasure and avoid pain

tricks enough man has played, in his time; has fancied himself to be most things, down even to an animated heap of Glass:° but to fancy himself a dead Iron-Balance for weighing Pains and Pleasures on, was reserved for this latter era. There stands he, his Universe one huge Manger, filled with hay and thistles to be weighed against each other; and looks long-eared enough.° Alas, poor devil! spectres are appointed to haunt him: one age he is hagridden, bewitched; the next, priest-ridden, befooled; in all ages, bedevilled. And now the Genius of Mechanism smothers him worse than any Nightmare did; till the Soul is nigh choked out of him, and only a kind of Digestive, Mechanic life remains. In Earth and in Heaven he can see nothing but Mechanism; has fear for nothing else, hope in nothing else: the world would indeed grind him to pieces; but cannot he fathom the Doctrine of Motives, and cunningly compute these, and mechanise them to grind the other way?

'Were he not, as has been said, purblinded by enchantment, you had but to bid him open his eyes and look. In which country, in which time, was it hitherto that man's history, or the history of any man, went-on by calculated or calculable "Motives"? What make ye of your Christianities and Chivalries, and Reformations, and Marseillese Hymns, and Reigns of Terror? Nay, has not perhaps the Motive-grinder himself been *in Love?* Did he never stand so much as a contested Election? Leave him to Time, and the medicating virtue of Nature.'

'Yes, Friends,' elsewhere observes the Professor, 'not our Logical, Mensurative faculty, but our Imaginative one is King over us; I might say, Priest and Prophet to lead us heavenward; or Magician and Wizard to lead us hellward. Nay, even for the basest Sensualist, what is Sense but the implement of Fantasy; the vessel it drinks out of? Ever in the dullest existence there is a sheen either of Inspiration or of Madness (thou partly hast it in thy choice, which of the two), that gleams-in from the circumambient Eternity, and colours with its own hues our little islet of Time. The Understanding is indeed thy window, too clear thou canst not make it; but Fantasy is thy eye, with its colour-giving retina, healthy or diseased. Have not I myself known five-hundred living soldiers sabred into crows'-meat for a piece of glazed cotton, which they called their Flag; which, had you sold it at any market-cross, would not have brought above three groschen? Did not the whole Hungarian Nation rise, like some tumultuous moon-stirred Atlantic, when Kaiser Joseph pocketed their Iron Crown; an implement, as was sagaciously observed, in size and commercial value little differing from a horseshoe? It is in and through Symbols that man, consciously or unconsciously, lives, works, and has his being: those ages, moreover, are accounted the noblest which

---

°*down . . . Glass:* Burton's *Anatomy of Melancholy* °*long-eared enough:* as in the fable in which the ass starved midway between two bales of hay

can the best recognise symbolical worth, and prize it the highest. For is not a Symbol ever, to him who has eyes for it, some dimmer or clearer revelation of the God-like?

'Of Symbols, however, I remark farther, that they have both an extrinsic and intrinsic value; oftenest the former only. What, for instance, was in that clouted Shoe, which the Peasants bore aloft with them as ensign in their *Bauernkrieg* (Peasants' War)?° Or in the Wallet-and-staff round which the Netherland *Gueux*, glorying in that nickname of Beggars, heroically rallied and prevailed, though against King Philip himself?° Intrinsic significance these had none; only extrinsic; as the accidental Standards of multitudes more or less sacredly uniting together; in which union itself, as above noted, there is ever something mystical and borrowing of the Godlike. Under a like category, too, stand, or stood, the stupidest heraldic Coats-of-arms; military Banners everywhere; and generally all national or other sectarian Costumes and Customs: they have no intrinsic, necessary divineness, or even worth; but have acquired an extrinsic one. Nevertheless through all these there glimmers something of a Divine Idea; as through military Banners themselves, the Divine Idea of Duty, of heroic Daring; in some instances of Freedom, of Right. Nay the highest ensign that men ever met and embraced under, the Cross itself, had no meaning save an accidental extrinsic one.

'Another matter it is, however, when your Symbol has intrinsic meaning, and is of itself *fit* that men should unite round it. Let but the Godlike manifest itself to Sense; let but Eternity look, more or less visibly, through the Time-Figure *(Zeitbild)!* Then is it fit that men unite there; and worship together before such Symbol; and so from day to day, and from age to age, superadd to it new divineness.

'Of this latter sort are all true Works of Art: in them (if thou know a Work of Art from a Daub of Artifice) wilt thou discern Eternity looking through Time; the Godlike rendered visible. Here too may an extrinsic value gradually superadd itself; thus certain *Iliads*, and the like, have, in three-thousand years, attained quite new significance. But nobler than all in this kind are the Lives of heroic god-inspired Men; for what other Work of Art is so divine? In Death too, in the Death of the Just, as the last perfection of a Work of Art, may we not discern symbolic meaning? In that divinely transfigured Sleep, as of Victory, resting over the beloved face which now knows thee no more, read (if thou canst for tears) the confluence of Time with Eternity, and some gleam of the latter peering through.

'Highest of all Symbols are those wherein the Artist or Poet has risen into Prophet, and all men can recognise a present God, and

---

°*(Peasants' War):* in 1524-1525, one aspect of the Reformation   °*Or . . . himself:* in 1566

worship the same: I mean religious Symbols. Various enough have been such religious Symbols, what we call *Religions;* as men stood in this stage of culture or the other, and could worse or better body-forth the Godlike: some Symbols with a transient intrinsic worth; many with only an extrinsic. If thou ask to what height man has carried it in this manner, look on our divinist Symbol: on Jesus of Nazareth, and his Life, and his Biography, and what followed therefrom. Higher has the human Thought not yet reached: this is Christianity and Christendom; a Symbol of quite perennial, infinite character; whose significance will ever demand to be anew inquired into, and anew made manifest.

'But, on the whole, as Time adds much to the sacredness of Symbols, so likewise in his progress he at length defaces, or even desecrates them; and Symbols, like all terrestrial Garments, wax old. Homer's Epos has not ceased to be true; yet it is no longer *our* Epos, but shines in the distance, if clearer and clearer, yet also smaller and smaller, like a receding Star. It needs a scientific telescope, it needs to be reinterpreted and artificially brought near us, before we can so much as know that it *was* a Sun. So likewise a day comes when the Runic Thor, with his Eddas,° must withdraw into dimness; and many an African Mumbo-Jumbo and Indian Pawaw be utterly abolished. For all things, even Celestial Luminaries, much more atmospheric meteors, have their rise, their culmination, their decline.'

'Small is this which thou tellest me, that the Royal Sceptre is but a piece of gilt-wood; that the Pyx° has become a most foolish box, and truly, as Ancient Pistol° thought, "of little price." A right Conjuror might I name thee, couldst thou conjure back into these wooden tools the divine virtue they once held.'

'Of this thing, however, be certain: wouldst thou plant for Eternity, then plant into the deep infinite faculties of man, his Fantasy and Heart; wouldst thou plant for Year and Day, then plant into his shallow superficial faculties, his Self-love and Arithmetical Understanding, what will grow there. A Hierarch, therefore, and Pontiff of the World will we call him, the Poet and inspired Maker; who, Prometheus-like, can shape new Symbols, and bring new Fire from Heaven to fix it there. Such too will not always be wanting; neither perhaps now are. Meanwhile, as the average of matters goes, we account him Legislator and wise who can so much as tell when a Symbol has grown old, and gently remove it.

'When, as the last English Coronation was preparing,' concludes this wonderful Professor, 'I read in their Newspapers that the "Champion of England°," he who has to offer battle to the Universe for his

---

°*Eddas:* Norse myths and hymns   °*Pyx:* the case in which the Eucharist is kept
°*Ancient Pistol: Henry V,* III, vi, 47   °*"Champion of England":* a part of the ceremony of Coronation

new King, had brought it so far that he could now "mount his horse with little assistance," I said to myself: Here also we have a Symbol well-nigh superannuated. Alas, move whithersoever you may, are not the tatters and rags of superannuated worn-out Symbols (in this Rag-fair of a World) dropping off everywhere, to hoodwink, to halter, to tether you; nay, if you shake them not aside, threatening to accumulate, and perhaps produce suffocation?'

*   *   *

No one takes the doctrine of symbolism—its importance to the spirit, its opposition to literal science, its ability to liberate the human psyche —further than Norman O. Brown, For Brown, "univocation," the narrowness of Protestant literalism, man's childish dependence upon denotation, and on scientific definitions of "reality," all constrain meaning and consciousness and, therefore, the dimensions of experience itself. Such limits, Brown argues, can be replaced with full "symbolic consciousness" which, if accepted, would mean the "resurrection" of man into a richer, "polysemiotic" sense of experience, in which flesh and spirit, the self and the other, the word and meaning would come together, unified in higher consciousness.

Such an argument, especially as here stated, is easy to dismiss. But one must recognize the superb understanding Brown has of Western intellectual history, both classical and modern, his wide reading and broad grasp of both traditional and modern views of the relations between art, myth, philosophy, and psychology: Augustine, the medieval Christian writers, Romanticism, Blake, Yeats, Freud, and post-Freudians. The depth of Brown's intelligence, the range and force of his creativity may be seen in his best known work—*Life Against Death,* which carries forward in many stimulating ways the implications of Freud's view of history and the historical process.

In *Love's Body,* Brown abandons the usual discursive prose style, in which evidence is supplied in detail, in favor of an aphoristic, abbreviated manner, in which short statements or assertions are grouped under chapter headings, with brief documentation and sources (here omitted) given in footnotes to each paragraph. Like Carlyle he seems anxious to involve the imagination of the reader as well as, or in addition to, his understanding. To write symbolically about symbolism is to say and do at the same time, to show and tell. If the argument for symbolic understanding and for "modern mythology" has a final statement (at least for the moment), it is in these passages from Brown's chapter on "Resurrection."

From RESURRECTION

Norman O. Brown (1913–   )

The return to symbolism would be the end of the Protestant era, the end of Protestant literalism. Symbolism in its pre-Protestant form consisted of typological, figural, allegorical interpretations, of both scripture and liturgy. But the great Protestant Reformers were very explicit in their condemnation of the typological method: "The literal sense of Scripture alone is the whole essence of faith and of Christian theology." *Sola fide, sola litera:* faith is faith in the letter.

Protestant literalism: the crux is the reduction of meaning to a single meaning—univocation. Luther's word is *Eindeutigkeit:* the "single, simple, solid and stable meaning" of scripture; *unum simplicem solidum et constantem sensum.* Compare Calvin of Galatians IV, 22-26: "But as the apostle declares that these things are allegorized, Origen, and many others along with him, have seized the occasion of torturing Scripture in every possible manner away from the true sense. Scripture they say is fertile, and thus produces a variety of meanings. I acknowledge that Scripture is a most rich and inexhaustible fountain of wisdom: but I deny that its fertility consists in the various meanings which any man at his pleasure may assign. Let us know that the true meaning of Scripture is the natural and obvious meaning, and let us embrace and abide by it resolutely."°

Augustine had said: "What more liberal and more fruitful provision could God have made in regard to Sacred Scriptures than that the same words might be understood in several senses, all of which are sanctioned by the concurring testimony of other passages equally divine?" The Medieval schema of a fourfold meaning in everything°—the quadriga, the four-horsed chariot—however mechanical in practice, is at least a commandment not to rest in one simple solid and constant meaning. As in Blake also:

> Now I a fourfold vision see,
> And a fourfold vision is given to me;
> 'Tis fourfold in my supreme delight

°*But . . . resolutely:* Notice the similarity of this complaint of Calvin's to complaints against "interpretation" of symbolic works of literature.

°*The . . . everything:* Medieval literary theory, based upon interpretation of Scripture, contained a system of four levels of meaning.

And threefold in soft Beulah's night
And twofold Always. May God us keep
From Single Vision and Newton's Sleep!

So also the psychoanalytic principle of over-determination: "Psychical acts and structures are invariably over-determined." The principle of over-determination declares that there cannot be just one "true" interpretation of a symptom or symbol: it forbids literal-mindedness.

Protestant literalism is modern scholarship.° Parallel to the emphasis on the one true meaning of scripture there was an increase in Luther's interest in grammar and textual criticism; to establish the text, *die feste Schrift,*° a mighty fortress; the authoritative text. . . .

The crux in the reduction of meaning to a single meaning—both in scriptural and in literary exegesis—the crux in univocation, is the reduction of meaning to conscious meaning: *intentio auctoris,* the author's intention. But the unconscious is the true psychic reality; and the unconscious is the Holy Spirit. The opposite of the letter is the spirit. "The *sensus plenior* is that additional, deeper meaning, intended by God but not clearly intended by the human author."

The spirit inspires (the god is Dionysus). The orthodox Protestant faith is Protestant fundamentalism; if meaning is restricted to the conscious intention of the author, then divine inspiration means that the holy spirit is literally the author; the holy scripture is literally inspired. The inspiration of scripture is reduced to the infallibility of scripture, literally understood.

The identification of God's word with scripture, the written or printed word; somewhat to the neglect of the word made flesh.° The book is a materialization of the spirit; instead of the living spirit, the worship of a new material idol, the book.

There is also the new hierarchy of scribes, controlling the interpretation, the higher scholarship. Since the one single and solid meaning does not in fact reveal itself, the commentary which does establish it becomes the higher revelation. The apparent deference of the expert to the text is a fake.

°*Protestant . . . scholarship:* modern literary scholarship (in some "Germanic" branches) has emphasized "scientific" pursuits: the establishment of textual authority and close attention to language forms   °*die feste Schrift:* Luther's famous hymn, "a mighty fortress is our God"   °*word made flesh:* i.e., Jesus Christ

There is another kind of Protestantism possible; a Dionysian Christianity; in which the scripture is a dead letter to be made alive by spiritual (symbolical) interpretations; in which meaning is not fixed, but ever new and ever changing; in a continuous revelation; by fresh outpouring of the holy spirit. Meaning is made in a meeting between the holy spirit buried in the Christian and the holy spirit buried underneath the letter of scripture; a breakthrough, from the *Abgrund,* from the unconscious of the reader past the conscious intention of the author to the unconscious meaning; breaking the barrier of the ego and the barrier of the book. *Spiritus per spiritum intellegitur.*° . . .

The conflict between science and religion in the modern world stems not from Medieval obscurantism but from modern literalism; Protestant literalism and Catholic scholasticism; both exterminators of symbolism. William Whiston, *New Theory of the Earth* (1696), dedicated to "Summo Viro Isaaco Newton": "The burden of the treatise was an attack on the allegorical interpretation of the Creation in Genesis and proof that the Mosaic account was literally true in the sense that the new astronomy and the new physics were completely harmonious with it. Its key proposition was: 'The Mosaic Creation is not a Nice and Philosophical account of the Origin of All Things, but an Historical and True Representation of the formation of our single Earth out of a confused Chaos, and of the successive and visible changes thereof each day, till it became the habitation of Mankind.' The 'postulata' which Whiston set down in this work were completely acceptable to his patron. 'I. The obvious or Literal Sense of Scriptures is the True and Real One, where no evident Reason can be given to the contrary. . . .' " . . .

The modern historical consciousness is Protestant literalism. The aim of modern historical science is to establish for historical events a single simple, solid, and constant meaning—what *really* happened: *"Wie es eigentlich gewesen ist."*° Ranke's° phrase, without his respect for the mystery of individuality, was what the American professors brought back from Germany; to become the motor of the Ph.D. factory, mechanical literalism in action.

The fetishism of the document: the historian believes that the document speaks, speaks for itself. It is Luther's principle of *scriptura sui ipsius interpres;*° the integrity of scripture, or the historical document, or the literary text; *"in eine Urkunde nicht fremde Begriffe herein-*

°*Spiritus . . . intellegitur:* the Spirit is understood by means of the spirit   °*"Wie . . . ist":* 'how it actually was"   °*Ranke:* German historian (1795–1886)   °*scriptura . . . interpres:* the writing interprets itself

tragen."° The principle that every document must be interpreted in its own terms was necessarily first established in the case of sacred scripture.

Literalism does not get rid of the magical element in scriptural or historical interpretation. The Holy Spirit, instead of a living spirit in the present, becomes the Holy Ghost, a voice from the past, enshrined in the book. The restriction of meaning to conscious meaning makes historical understanding a personal relation between the personality of the reader and the personality of the author, now dead. Spiritual understanding *(geistiges Verstehen)* becomes a ghostly operation, an operation with ghosts *(Geisteswissenschaft)*. The document starts speaking for itself; •the reader starts hearing voices. The subjective dimension in historical understanding is to animate the dead letter with the living reader's blood, his "experience"; and simultaneously let the ghost of the dead author slide into, become one with, the reader's soul. It is necromancy, or shamanism; magical identification with ancestors; instead of living spirit, to be possessed by the dead. . . .

Instead of a living spirit, possession by the dead. The Protestant substituted for the ritual (magical) repetition of the past (Christ's passion), a purely mental invocation; a historical commemoration. Instead of a dramatic reënactment a reanimation in the mind only—the quest for the historical Jesus. But the Jesus of historical commemoration can only be the ghost of Jesus—*die Historie erreichet nicht Christi Fleisch und Blut,* history reaches not Christ's flesh and blood. The Jesus of commemorative ceremony and historical reconstruction is the passive, not the active, Jesus. The active Jesus can only be actively recreated. The historical reconstruction is a spectral image in a passive viewer.

To say that historical events have a single meaning is to say that historical events are unique (singular); univocation constructs unilinear time. And on the other hand to see symbolism is to see eternal recurrence. The figural interpretation of scripture, which the Reformers suppressed, is inseparable from the idea of prefiguration. And the idea of prefiguration is of certain events corresponding to certain other events, as type to antitype; events anticipating other events; events which are prophetic of other events: events which are the fulfillment of earlier prophecies. At any rate where there is type and antitype, prophecy and fulfillment, there events are not unique and time not unilinear; rather we must say with Tertullian, eternal recurrence is the universal law: nothing happens for the first time. *Universa conditio recidiva est: nihil non iterum est.*

°*"in . . . hereintragen":* "nothing foreign may be brought to a given text"

Nothing happens for the first time. There is nothing in the Old Testament which does not recur in the New Testament. This is the *concordia scripturarum,* the mysterious correspondence between the two scriptures, to be seen by those who have eyes to see. Its effect is to make Old and New contemporaneous; to transform time into eternity; history *sub specie aeternitatis.* Or history as poetry; prose goes straight forward without verses.

Christianity is identified with unilinear time when Christianity no longer lives in expectation of a second coming. But if no second coming, then no first coming either; unless we are born again, we are not born at all. Nothing happens for the first time. . . .

The symbolic interpretation of prophecy makes the interpreter a prophet; *spiritus per spiritum intellegitur.* All the Lord's people to be prophets. Prophets, or poets: sing unto the Lord a new song. The song must be new, or it is no song; the spirit is the creator spirit, making new creations. The spirit is understood by the spirit; by the same spirit, i.e., in the same style. The proper response to poetry is not criticism but poetry.

The redemption of the Old does not abolish but fulfills it; not to destroy but to fulfill. Symbolical consciousness finds the New in the Old, and the Old in the New; *in veteribus novam, in novis veterem.* The symbolical interpretation of the old makes it new: this is the flowering of the rod, Aaron's rod that budded; the bitter waters of Marah made sweet.

Newness is not the gift of a *tabula rasa,* but a resurrection: or miraculous pregnancy. A virgin shall conceive, in old age, as in the case of Sarah, or the Roman Empire. Natural innocence is only an image of the real, the supernatural, the second innocence. After the fall; in old age: *sero te amavi, pulchritudo tam antiqua et tam nova, sero te amavi.* Late I learnt to love thee, beauty as ancient as thou art new; late I learnt to love thee. . . .

The dead letter. The dead metaphor. It is only dead metaphors that are taken literally, that take us in (the black magic). Language is always an old testament, to be made new; rules, to be broken; dead metaphor, to be made alive; literal meaning, to be made symbolical; oldness of letter to be made new by the spirit. The creator spirit stands in the grave, in the midden heap, the dunghill of culture (as in *Finnegan's Wake);* breaking the seal of familiarity; breaking the cake of custom; rolling the stone from the sepulcher; giving the dead metaphor new life.

Symbolical consciousness begins with the perception of the invisible reality of our present situation: we are dead and our life is hid. Real life is life after death, or resurrection. The deadness with which we are dead here now is the real death; of which literal death is only a shadow, a bogey. Literalism, and futurism, are to distract us from the reality of the present.

*　　*　　*

COMING BACK TO AMERICA

James Dickey (1923–　　)

We decended the first night from Europe　　riding the ship's sling
Into the basement.　　Forty floors of home weighed on us.　　We
　　broke through
To a room, and fell to drinking madly with all those boozing, reading
The Gideon Bible in a dazzle of homecoming scripture　　Assyrian
　　armies
The scythes of chariots blazing like the windows of the city　　all cast
Into our eyes in all-night squinting barbaric rays of violent unavoid-
　　able glory.
There were a "milion dollars in ice cubes" outside our metal door;
The dead water clattered down hour after hour as we fought with
　　salesmen
For the little blocks that would make whole our long savage drinks.
I took a swaying shower, and we packed the whole bathroom of towels
　　into
Our dusty luggage, battling paid-for opulence with whatever weapon
Came to hand.　　We slept; I woke up early, knowing that I was
　　suffering
But why not. My breath would not stir, nor the room's.　　I sweated
Ice in the closeness　　my head hurt with the Sleep of a Thousand
　　Lights
That the green baize drapes could not darken.　　I got up, bearing
Everything　　found　　my　　sharp　　Roman　　shoes　　went　　out
　　following signs
That said SWIMMING POOL.　　Flashing bulbs on a red-eyed panel,
　　I passed

Through ceiling after ceiling of sleeping salesmen and whores, and came out
On the roof.   The pool water trembled with the few in their rooms
Still making love.   This was air.   A skinny girl lifeguard worked
At her nails; the dawn shone on her right leg in a healthy, twisted flame.
It made me squint   slick and lacquered with scars, with the wild smoky city
Around it   the great breath to be drawn above sleepers   the hazy
Morning towers.   We sat and talked   she said a five-car wreck
Of taxis in Bensonhurst had knocked her out and taken her kneecap
But nothing else.   I pondered this   the sun shook off a last heavy
Hotel   and she leapt and was in the fragile green pool as though
I were still sleeping it off eleven floors under her: she turned in a water
Ballet by herself   graceful   unredeemable   her tough face exactly
As beautiful and integral as the sun come out of the city.   Vulnerable,
Hurt in my country's murderous speed, she moved   and I would have taken
Her in my arms in water throbbing with the passion of travelling men,
Unkillable, both of us, at forty stories in the morning   and could have
Flown with her   our weightlessness preserved by the magic pool drawn from
Under the streets   out of that pond   passing over the meaningless
Guardrail   feeling the whole air pulse like water sleepless with desperate
Love-making   lifting us out of sleep into the city summer dawn
Of hundreds of feet of gray space spinning with pigeons now under
Us   among new panels of sun in the buildings blasting light silently
Back and forth across streets between them: could have moved with her
In all this   over the floods of glare raised up in sheets   the gauze
Distances where warehouses strove to become   over the ship I had ridden
Home in   riding gently   whitely   beneath.   Ah, lift us, green
City water, as we turn the harbor around with our legs   lazily changing
The plan of the city with motions like thistles   like the majestic swirl
Of soot   the winged seed of pigeons   and so would have held her
As I held my head   a-stammer with light   defending it against the terrible

Morning sun of drinkers   in that pain, exalting in the blind notion
Of cradling her somewhere above ships and buses   in the air like a
water
Ballet   dancing deep among the dawn buildings in a purely private
Embrace of impossibility   a love that could not have been guessed:
Woman   being   idea   temple   dancer   tough   girl   from
Bensonhurst
With a knee rebuilt out of sunlight   ᵎreturned-to amazement
O claspable
Symbol   the unforeseen on home ground   The thing that sustains
us forever
In other places!

*   *   *

QUESTIONS

1. In a German dictionary, look up Teufel and Dröckh. If Diogenes means "born of God," why did Carlyle choose this name for his philosopher?
2. Explain why Carlyle thinks that Society and Government are so importantly related to religion. Notice the broad relations which Carlyle gives to these terms. What does he see as the condition of religions, (that is, the "Church-Clothes") of his time?
3. Carlyle is a good example of an explicit remythologizer, one who offers a historical theory about the way beliefs change. What has this historical theory to do with symbolism? What is most likely to ensure that a symbol will not become worn out with the passage of time?
4. Carlyle's tone is difficult partly because of the devices of editor and philosopher, and partly because he mixes seriousness and humor. Find illustrations of these practices, and discuss the problems they raise. What do you think his purpose is in adopting these forms?
5. Crews is, occasionally, an excellent close reader and psychoanalytic critic. What attitudes toward symbolism and psychoanalysis is he satirizing in this passage?
6. What characteristics of *Winnie-the-Pooh* make it particularly susceptible to this kind of satirical approach? What other children's stories could receive similar attention, and why?
7. Give an example of a "problem" in Biblical interpretation and explain the different accounts given by a literalist and a figurative reading. What is Brown's objection to literalist interpretations of the Bible? What advantages do such readings have? Read the Song of Solomon in this connection.

8. Literalism is the ascendant point of view, although, according to Brown, not the doctrine that will prevail in the future. Where does literalism locate its major strength and support? At what historical period does it begin? Who are the major figures of its rise? Where in modern society does one find the greatest reliance upon the authority of the written word?

9. Brown is very adamant in his views of the figurative-literalist difference. What issues does he see connected to the problem? What aspects of the difficulty does he discuss that have not been noted before? At what points does he seem to be on strongest and weakest ground?

PART VIII

*Projects, General Questions, and
Additional Readings*

Projects, General Questions, and Additional Readings

Theory

1. Look up definitions of the following terms in a dictionary and in a handbook of literary terms (for instance, *A Glossary of Literary Terms*, revised by M.H. Abrams, Rinehart English Pamphlets). Compare the judgments and definitions offered: realism, surrealism, symbol, symbolism, allegory, metaphor, myth, mythology, archetype, sign, literal, figurative. Construct your own definitions of these terms.
2. Write an explanation of symbolism and modern mythology that would appeal to a skeptic, to a scientist, to one who only believes things to be real which he can touch and see. Write a dialogue between the scientist and the poet on these questions. Find a setting in contemporary society where such discussions usually take place.
3. What kind of scientific research is needed to carry forward the work suggested by Susanne Langer? Write a research plan which would advance our sense of these questions.
4. Construct a defense in social and historical terms of the utility of poetry as myth, as a necessary mode of keeping our beliefs alive and meaningful. What social conditions are most hostile to the myth maker? What most beneficial? Write a letter to a congressman explaining the need for support for symbolist poets and modern mythographers.

Remythologizing

1. Apply the methods of remythologizing to other familiar stories. Write modern versions of Satan, Eve, and the Serpent, of Evil Witches in the Dark Forest, The Quest for the Holy Object, The Voyage into the Interior.
2. Write the further adventures of the Great Warrior: Arthur, Launcelot, Siegfried, Muhammad Ali; and of the Great Lover: Don Juan, Romeo, Robert Redford, Mick Jagger.
3. What historical figures seem most popular in the present historical interpretations of the past? What kinds of historical figures seem of most interest to contemporary Americans? What are the various sources of remythologizing for American Historical Figures? Write a conversation between George Washington and George III, between Washington and a contemporary political leader.
4. Watch television and advertising and popular music for indications of the myths which are most prevalent in popular culture. What Bibli-

cal and historical stories and figures are most useful in the interpretation of contemporary culture? Which figures and stories can be made fun of, or used humorously, and which cannot? Which stories seem most useful for selling things?

5. Consider the kinds of stories which occur most in popular literature, television series, and sports. What situations do we like to read about or see exemplified in the newspapers? in popular songs? in magazine fiction? List the archetypes which occur in these sources.

6. Notice the representations of high and low symbolism and verticality in popular culture and in our national life. Analyze the symbols involved in space flight (rockets, space suits, ascents), scuba diving, deep sea fishing, submarines, Captain Nemo, sharks, whales, seagulls, mountain climbing, rock climbing, trees, skyscrapers, towers, fields, meadows.

7. Choose a number of different translations of a classical work, the *Iliad* or the *Odyssey*, for instance, and compare the judgments made of specific characters or situations.

8. The following works of modern fiction refer explicitly to older mythology:

Jean Anouilh,   *Antigone, Euridice, Orphee, Medea*
Dorothy Baker,   *Cassandra at the Wedding*
John Barth,   *Chimera, Giles Goat-Boy*
Saul Bellow,   *Henderson the Rain King*
Brigid Brophy,   *Black Ship to Hell*
Anthony Burgess,   *The Eve of Saint Venus*
Agatha Christie,   *The Labours of Hercules*
Jean Cocteau,   *Antigone, Oedipe-Roi*
Janice Elliot,   *The Singing Head*
William Gass,   *Omensetter's Luck*
Andre Gide,   *Oedipus, Theseus*
Jean Giraudoux,   *Amphitryon 38, Electra*
Nathaniel Hawthorne,   *The Marble Faun*
John Hersey,   *Too Far to Walk*
Hermann Hesse,   *Demian*
James Joyce,   *A Portrait of the Artist as a Young Man, Ulysses*
Bernard Malamud,   *The Natural*
Thomas Mann,   *Joseph and His Brothers, Dr. Faustus*
Herman Melville,   *Billy Budd, Sailor*
Iris Murdoch,   *A Severed Head, Under the Net*
Eugene O'Neill,   *Mourning Becomes Electra*
Bernard Shaw,   *Pygmalion*
John Updike,   *The Centaur*
Tennessee Williams,   *Orpheus Descending*

Sex and Symbol

1. Look for sexual symbols in the clothes your friends wear. Notice particularly the meaning of jewelry, ornaments, and other accessories. What items are female, what male or is that a meaningless distinction these days? How do the styles of today compare symbolically with the styles of 5 and 10 years ago? Find examples of the fashion makers adapting style to political positions.
2. Write an analysis of an explicitly symbolist painter: Dali, Magritte, Rossetti.
3. Study the imagery which surrounds the characters and action of a film by Bergman or Fellini. Notice particularly the clothes worn, the locations and setting in which characters meet. Why is symbolism so evident in modern films?